"雅思9分真题库"系列

雅思9分真题库
——口语密题及解析

启德考培产品中心　编著

電子工業出版社.

Publishing House of Electronics Industry

北京·BEIJING

图书在版编目(CIP)数据

雅思9分真题库. 口语密题及解析 / 启德考培产品中心编著. —北京：电子工业出版社，2023.12
ISBN 978-7-121-46730-1

Ⅰ.①雅… Ⅱ.①启… Ⅲ.①IELTS－听说教学－自学参考资料 Ⅳ.①H310.41

中国国家版本馆CIP数据核字（2023）第223601号

雅思9分真题库——口语密题及解析

启德考培产品中心　编著

责任编辑：王昭松

印　　刷：北京市大天乐投资管理有限公司
装　　订：北京市大天乐投资管理有限公司
出版发行：电子工业出版社
　　　　　北京市海淀区万寿路173信箱　　邮编：100036
开　　本：787×1 092　1/16　**印张：**19.5　**字数：**649千字
版　　次：2023 年 12 月第 1 版
印　　次：2024 年 4 月第 2 次印刷
印　　数：2 500 册　**定价：**78.00 元

凡所购买电子工业出版社图书有缺损问题，请向购买书店调换。若书店售缺，请与本社发行部联系，联系及邮购电话：（010）88254888，88258888。

质量投诉请发邮件至zlts@phei.com.cn，盗版侵权举报请发邮件至dbqq@phei.com.cn。

本书咨询联系方式：（010）88254015，wangzs@phei.com.cn。

《雅思9分真题库——口语密题及解析》
编委会

主　　编：郑庆利

编　　委：（按姓氏笔画排序）

　　　　　石金娥　李小涵　李碧燕　杨瑞平

　　　　　张　萌　苑　文　陶　睿

编写团队：（按姓氏笔画排序）

　　　　　牛　佳　乐　乐　刘　苏　刘梦一

　　　　　张　萌　俞　丹　郭星彤　高璨然

　　　　　曹　彧　Michael Tai（美）

PREFACE 前言

现如今，无论是考生还是教师，都可以在互联网上找到雅思口语考试的评分标准（包括对标准的解释及与标准匹配的范文）、题库及相关的范文、由范文衍生出的高频词汇、高分词组及常用句式等。2023 年，随着人工智能（AI）技术的发展，人们开始尝试使用各类 AI 技术进行范文创作、范文修改，甚至录音。然而，目前的 AI 创作仍有一定的局限性，并且容易涉及抄袭；AI 范文也缺乏深度与广度。如果想借助 AI 技术获得较为理想的答案，使用者需要有较强的逻辑思维能力和较高的语言水平。此外，即便我们可以提前给所有的高频题目和新题准备好答案，我们的大脑也没有那么厉害，可以存储如此庞大的信息。

鉴于以上的现状，我们深入研究雅思口语考试的评分标准和考试题目，并参考考生的考场经验和教师的授课经验，编写了此书。本书回顾了从 2014 年至今的雅思口语题目，涵盖了雅思口语考试的各类话题，并为其中大部分的题目撰写了范文、录制了音频。所有范文和素材均由母语为英语的教师及研发人员撰写。这些表达及素材可以灵活使用，扩展应用到不同的题目，真正帮助考生做到触类旁通。

本书的主要内容和特点如下：

1. 在对雅思口语考试进行基本介绍之后，参照考试的流程，分别对 Part 1、Part 2 和 Part 3 进行讲解。Part 1 作为雅思口语考试的第一部分，由于难度系数不高且只是考试的热身部分，所以在本书中未做过多介绍，只做题目类型、答题技巧和口语题库的展示。

2. 针对 Part 2，基于对题目、答题要求的分析，以及对当下热门话题、事件及人物的总结，我们列出 20 个话题。这 20 个话题及相关的表达和素材将尽可能多的口语题目串联起来，有助于考生在备考过程中扩展应用。此外，为了帮助考生记忆话题相关的表达，书中还提供了大量的场景图片。这些图片有助于考生联想记忆相关的表达，使备考学习变得更加有趣。

3. Part 3 的话题分类、素材撰写和分析弥补了目前市场上这部分参考资料的空白。在话题分类方面，首先提出了大话题的概念。这些话题涉及学习、工作和生活的方方面面，按照话题的出现频率进行介绍。每个大话题下面又细分了数个小话题，每个小话题包含对应的话题解读、题目、答题思路分析、表达与素材、表达与素材解读，以及表达和积累。在答题策略方面，总结了"五大答题要素"及三大题目类型的答题结构。本书提供的不是一些流于表面的、笼统的答题词汇，而是尽可能详尽的短语、句子及素材。

4. Part 2 和 Part 3 都在开篇给出了本章内容的使用指南，方便考生进行后续的学习。

5. 所有的表达及素材的编写以表达精准、方便运用及在考试时容易记起为中心，让考生在缩短备考时间的同时确保备考质量。在真实的考试环境中，Part 2 只有一分钟的准备时间，而 Part 3 没有准备时间，所以快速地从大脑中提取答题结构、素材及表达是非常重要的，因为我们的大脑并没有太多时间进行思考。

6. 书中的表达和素材及其难度适合绝大多数参加雅思考试的考生，我们不追求高难度，但求足够地道、好记。

希望在读完本书之后，各位考生能从中获得启发与帮助！

启德考培产品中心

CONTENTS 目录

SPEAKING

第一章　雅思口语考试内容介绍

　　雅思口语考试是通过考生与考官之间一对一的交流对考生的英语口语水平进行考查。考官将在口语考试全程对考生的表现进行评分。口语考试分为三个部分：Part 1、Part 2、Part 3，总时长为 11 ～ 14 分钟。此外，口语考试将被录音。

CHAPTER **ONE**

雅思口语考试简介

部分	时长	测试方式及内容	考查的能力
1	4～5分钟	**个人简介和问答** 询问一些关于背景信息的问题（名字、工作／学习情况、住的地方等）。 询问一些关于个人信息的问题（休闲活动、习惯等）	考生能否用英语表达自己的想法、经历或者日常生活
2	3～4分钟	**个人陈述** 考生会得到一张答题任务卡、一根铅笔和一张草稿纸用来做笔记。答题任务卡上会给出一个话题和需要在个人陈述中包含的要点，并在最后提示考生解释这个话题的某一方面。考生有一分钟的准备时间（期间考生可以做笔记），然后需就此话题进行1～2分钟的陈述。考官会在2分钟后打断考生，并在最后提出1～2个问题作为结束语	考生能否就一个特定的话题进行较长时间的陈述； 考生是否能恰当地运用英语及连贯地组织自己的观点
3	4～5分钟	**双向讨论** 考官将与考生就 Part 2 中出现的较为抽象的内容进行双向讨论。Part 3 考试没有固定题目，所有题目均基于考生对 Part 2 题目的回答	考生能否表达和论述看法，是否具备分析、讨论以及深入思考问题的能力； 考生能否流利地回答问题并与考官进行对话

雅思口语考试评分标准

考官按照四项标准分别评分，每项分数为 1～9，只要出席了就会得到 1 分。每个口语部分不单独评分。一般来说，Part 1 只给考官留下对考生的初印象，考生无法在这部分得到太高的分数，Part 2 和 Part 3 才是重点得分部分。

// 得分对应口语能力描述 //

Band Score（分数）	描述
3.5 分及以下	该分数段的考生通常交流能力非常有限，仅能做出有限的、基本的回应，可能会频繁出现长时间停顿。仅能使用基本词汇和语法，错误频出。仅能说出背记的短语或个别单词。发音会造成相当大的理解困难
Band Score 4（4 分）	考生在某些领域能较为顺畅地使用英语交流，但是在大多数话题和问题上都存在许多问题。通常不能使用复杂句型且交流过程中出现明显的停顿。大量的语法和单词错误导致交流不顺畅

续表

Band Score（分数）	描述
Band Score 5（5分）	考生能将信息传达给考官，并使考官理解大概意思。然而，考生在语法和发音方面出现许多错误，并且很难使用合适的单词或需要花时间挑选合适的单词
Band Score 6（6分）	考生有足够运用英语的能力而且能使用正确的复杂句型。考生通常不会有理解上的问题，但有许多不合适的表达。考生的回答普遍流利但是会因短暂停顿、自我改正、重复词汇导致偶尔的不顺畅。同时也存在一些语法错误，但这些错误并不严重且没有改变表达的意思
Band Score 7（7分）	考生能够很自如地谈论很多话题，不限于熟悉的话题。考生交谈时很流利，几乎没有任何迟疑的现象。不时会出现一些错误或不合适的句子，在词汇上也有一些问题。但是一个母语为英语的人只要能容忍一些错误，就能与这类考生顺畅交流且没有任何困难。通常来说，一个口语7分的考生能够就一个话题进行较深层次的讨论
Band Score 8（8分）	考生在表达上几乎没有错误而且很自然。错误通常都在讨论不熟悉的话题时出现。虽然可能存在重音和节奏方面与母语为英语的人士的差异，但并不影响意思的表达且能被理解。考生的词汇量非常大，尽管有时可能记不起一些词汇，但完全不影响整体表达
Band Score 9（9分）	9分意味着考生交谈非常流利且能展示多项母语为英语的人士的话术技巧。在交谈过程中出现的错误与母语为英语的人士出现的错误雷同

■ // 四项评分标准详解 //

在了解了每个分数段所代表的口语能力之后，我们来介绍四项评分标准所包含的内容。

★语言的流利度和连贯性（Fluency and Coherence，简称 FC）。

★词汇变化（Lexical Resource，简称 LR）。

★句式丰富性和语法准确性（Grammatical Range and Accuracy，简称 GRA）。

★发音（Pronunciation，简称 P）。

对于大部分的考生而言，最需要了解的是 4 ~ 7 分这个分数段的评分标准。

语言的流利度和连贯性

7分	1. 表达详尽，并无明显困难或不连贯 2. 有时出现与语言相关的犹豫或出现重复及/或自我纠正 3. 在一定程度上能灵活地使用一系列连接词
6分	1. 表现出充分交流的意愿，但有时由于偶尔的重复、自我纠正或犹豫而缺乏连贯性 2. 能使用一系列连接词，但无法保持连贯和恰当
5分	1. 通常能保持语速，但需通过重复、自我纠正及/或降低语速来维持表达 2. 过度使用某些连接词 3. 能用简单的语言进行流利地表达，但在进行更为复杂的交流时则表达不畅
4分	1. 作答时有明显停顿，且语速有时缓慢，出现频繁重复及自我纠正 2. 能连接简单句子，但重复使用简单的连接词，有时缺乏连贯性

词汇变化

7分	1. 能灵活地使用词汇讨论各种话题 2. 能使用一些非常见的词汇及习语，对词汇搭配有所认识，但有时词语选择不甚恰当 3. 能有效地进行改述
6分	1. 有足以详尽讨论各种话题的词汇量，虽然有时使用不当但意思表达清晰 2. 基本上能成功地进行改述
5分	1. 能谈论熟悉或不熟悉的话题，但使用词汇的灵活性有限 2. 能尝试进行改述，但有时成功、有时失败
4分	1. 能谈论所熟悉的话题，但对不熟悉的话题仅能表达基本意思，且经常用词不当 2. 很少尝试改述

句式丰富性和语法准确性

7分	1. 能较灵活地使用一系列复杂的语法结构 2. 虽然反复出现一些语法错误，但语句通常正确无误
6分	1. 能结合使用简单与复杂的句型，但灵活度有限 2. 使用复杂结构时经常出现错误，尽管这些错误极少造成理解困难
5分	1. 能使用基本的句型，且具有合理的准确性 2. 能使用有限的复杂句式结构，但通常会出错且会造成某些理解困难
4分	1. 能使用基本句型并正确使用一些简单句型，但极少使用从句 2. 常出现错误，且会造成误解

发音

7分	展现出 6 分水平中所有积极表现，但也展现出 8 分水平中的部分积极表现
6分	1. 能够运用多种发音，但掌握程度不一 2. 展现出能够运用多种发音的能力，但不能持续表现这一能力 3. 在表达过程中基本能被理解，但部分单词或音节发音不准，导致有时清晰度下降
5分	展现出 4 分水平中所有积极表现，但也展现出 6 分水平中的部分积极表现
4分	1. 使用有限的发音 2. 尝试表现多种发音特点，但频繁出现偏差 3. 经常出现发音错误，给听者理解造成一些困难

// 评分标准之词汇变化案例分析 //

　　对于流利度、连贯性以及发音的评分标准的描述是比较容易理解的，如一个单词发音不准或者句子说得断断续续，肯定会影响评分。另外，如果考生不能很准确地回答问题或者答非所问，那也会扣分。至于语法的评分标准，也比较好理解，使用正确且有变化的句子肯定是能得到高分的。词汇部分的评分标准是最值一提的。很多考生都会问，什么样的词汇才会获得高分？是不是用了"高级"词汇就能得到 7 分及以上的分数？

我们先来看一下雅思官方给出的一个 7 分回答中考生所用的词汇吧。

Part 2[①]	Part 3[②]
the one thing special about	flowing in the middle
arch	somehow
shaped as	build a lot of facilities
elegant	convenient
courtyard	shopping malls
right above	career opportunities
roof	decorations
sunny weather	core
sunshine	Paris
highest floor	months ago
transparent roof	curtain
no matter what	remote
view	lazier
definitely	partly
gorgeous	whole society
have so many good memories there	take care of
design	build shelters
sculpture	find them jobs
carved	sacrifice
delicate	provide more
meeting hall	build a new bridge
	one of the solutions

不难发现，这些词汇及短语其实都比较常见，并没有多少高深和酷炫。评分标准中所谓的地道的词汇和习语，其实并不是要求考生使用多么华丽的语言，而是要求准确、多变且符合英语的规则。针对词汇的多样性和准确性，回答问题时我们需要记住以下两点：

★ 有些词汇看似简单但未必代表得分不高，最重要的是搭配和地道。

★ 词汇变化只是四项评分标准之一，雅思的口语评分是四项分数的平均值，考生不能为了追求某一项的高分而丢了其他项的分数。有的考生会尝试使用一些"高级"的词汇，但这有时会对流利度、发音产生影响，因为考生可能会因此出现犹豫、读错，导致考官无法完全理解考生所说的单词，甚至由于错误地或者不恰当地使用"高级"词汇，使词汇部分的评分受到不利影响。

基于这些原因，考生最好使用那些看起来不是特别令人印象深刻，但足够准确且地道的词汇和短语。当然，如果考生能够轻松驾驭"高级"词汇，且能够自然、流利、正确地使用它们，那肯定是最好的了。

---

① 来源 https://www.chinaielts.org/guide/band_descriptors_speaking/part/53658.shtml

② 来源 https://www.chinaielts.org/guide/band_descriptors_speaking/part/53662.shtml

■■ // 总成绩计算方法 //

雅思口语考试的总成绩计算方法是四项评分相加再求平均数，计算公式如下：

$$(FC+LR+GRA+P)/4$$

根据这个计算方法，想要在口语考试中获得一个不错的成绩，考生需要让自己在这四个方面的表现都达到较高的水平。在日常备考中，除了熟悉考试的话题、掌握话题的相关表达、储备丰富且好用的句式，还需要不断督促自己开口练习。考生可以与一起备考的同学进行口语模拟训练，也可以通过录音来记录自己的口语练习情况。

第二章 Part 1 口语考试介绍

Part 1 是雅思口语考试的第一部分，考生与考官会进行一些关于日常生活的简短对话，通常会涉及 2～3 个话题，话题之间没有联系。话题的内容可以是：

★ 家乡、城市、国家，或者你居住的房子和街道；

★ 工作或者学习；

★ 日常要做的或者喜欢做的事情、你的休闲娱乐活动；

★ 童年经历，如学习经历、记忆深刻的小伙伴、童年爱好等；

★ 拥有的物品，如服饰、手机、电脑、自行车、私家车等；

★ 在日常生活中遇到的人、事、物等。

总而言之，Part 1 的话题繁多，但都是大家熟悉的，在口语考试中起到了热身的作用。在本章中，我们将罗列一些 Part 1 常考的话题及题目，大家可以利用这些话题为考试做热身。

CHAPTER TWO

Part 1 的提问方式

在准备雅思口语考试 Part 1 的过程中，除了需要储备一定的话题词汇，更重要的是了解如何有效地组织答案，因为在一问一答的过程中，考生并没有很多的时间来思考。接下来，我们先来了解 Part 1 有哪些提问方式。

1. 是非喜恶类的问题

Do you like/dislike…

Do you often…

How often…

举例：

Do you like your hometown?

Do you like to read?

Do you like to play sports?

Do you often do housework?

2. 偏爱与最爱类的问题

Do you prefer A or B?

What is your (least) favourite... / What do you ... most?

举例：

What's your favourite kind of music?

Which do you prefer, handwriting or typing?

3. 描述型问题

除此之外，更多的题目需要考生对一个人物、事物或者事件进行描述。

举例：

Can you describe the place where you live?

Please describe your hometown a little.

Tell me something about your high school.

Please describe a story or article that you read.

4. Wh- 型问题

最后，还有一类问题是以特殊疑问词为开头的问题，常见的有 what，what kind，who，where，why，which。

举例：

What do you do to improve your learning efficiency?

What kind of sports do you do?

When do you usually listen to music?

Why do some people find it difficult to focus in the morning?

Which room does your family spend most of the time in?

Part 1 的答题技巧

根据不同的提问方式，回答问题的策略会略有不同。

（1）回答是非喜恶类的问题时，需要表明立场，比如回答 Do you like reading 时，首先应该回答喜不喜欢 reading，然后再增添一些理由。

（2）回答偏爱与最爱类的问题时，需要做出选择，说出自己较为喜爱或者最喜爱的东西，比如回答 What's your favourite kind of music 时，首先表达自己最爱 hip-hop，然后说明喜爱这种音乐的原因。

（3）回答描述型或者 Wh- 型的问题时，不需要明确立场和做出选择，直接根据题目的要求进行回答即可。

一般来说，Part 1 的答案不需要很长，有 2 ～ 3 句话就可以了。下面通过一个例子来展示理想的回答应该是怎样的。

> 题目：Do you prefer public transportation or private transportation?
>
> 差强人意的回答：I prefer public transportation.
>
> 较为理想的回答：I tend to choose public transportation **because** it is more affordable. I'm only a student now, so I don't have money to buy a car.

在这个例子中，不难发现，回答 Part 1 的题目时要学会拓展答案，不能惜字如金。考生需要添加一些内容来让自己的回答更加饱满。以下是最常见也是最简单的几种方法：

· **添加例子**（For example.../For instance.../like.../such as...）

· **说明原因**（because.../as.../since.../I think this is because.../The reason for this is...）

· **说明结果**（so.../That's why.../As a result...）

· **对比与转折**（but.../however.../despite...）

· **罗列观点**（What's more.../Moreover...）

以上这些方法都可以非常有效地帮助考生拓展答案。在实际考试中，考生可以选择任何一种方法或将两种方法结合，不必拘泥于一种形式。

Part 1 的常见话题及题目

本节罗列了一些常见的 Part 1 口语题目，考生可以选取一些题目进行练习。练习时可以与朋友进行对话，模拟考试现场，也可以用录音软件记录自己的回答。切记，回答不要超时。

1. Work（工作）

What work do you do?

Why did you choose to do that type of work (or that job)?

Do you like your job?

Is it very interesting?

(Possibly) Do you miss being a student?

2. Your Studies/ Study Efficiency（学习与学习效率）

What subject(s) are you studying? / What is your major?

Why did you choose to study that subject(major)?

Is it very interesting?

Do you prefer to study in the mornings or in the afternoons?

Why do some people find it difficult to focus in the morning?

What do you do to improve your learning efficiency?

3. Name（姓名）

Do you like your name?

Who gave you your name?

Does your name have any special meaning?

What kinds of names are popular in China?

Are there many Chinese people who have the same name with you?

Is there any tradition about naming babies in your country?

Would you like to change your name?

4. Hometown（家乡）

What's the name of your hometown?

Is it a big city or a small place?

How long have you been living there?

Do you like your hometown?

What do you like (most) about your hometown?

Is there anything you dislike about it?

Do you think you will continue living there for a long time?

5. Accommodation（住所）

Do you live in a house or a flat?

Do you prefer living in a house or a flat?

Do you plan to live there for a long time?

Can you describe the place where you live?

Which room does your family spend most of the time in?

Are the transport facilities to your home very good?

Please describe the room you live in.

What part of your home do you like best?

Are you willing to live in the countryside in the future?

6. Transportation（交通）

What is the most popular means of transportation in your hometown?

Can you compare the advantages of planes and trains?

How often do you take buses?

Is driving to work very popular in your country?

Would you ride bikes to work in the future?

Do you prefer public transportation or private transportation?

Do you think people will drive more in the future?

What will become the most popular means of transportation in China?

7. Headphones（耳机）

Do you use headphones?

What type of headphones do you use?

When would you use headphones?

In what conditions would you not use headphones?

8. Shoes（鞋子）

Do you like buying shoes? How often?

Have you ever bought shoes online?

How much money do you usually spend on shoes?

Which do you prefer, fashionable shoes or comfortable shoes?

9. Pets and Animals（宠物与动物）

What's your favourite animal? Why?

Where do you prefer to keep your pet, indoors or outdoors?

Have you ever had a pet before?

What is the most popular animal in China?

10. Science（科学）

Do you like science?

When did you start to learn about science?

Which science subject is interesting to you?

What kinds of interesting things have you done with science?

11. Public Gardens and Parks（公共绿地与公园）

Would you like to play in a public garden or park?

What do you like to do when visiting a park?

How are the parks today different from those you visited as a kid?

Would you prefer to play in a personal garden or public garden?

12. Handwriting（手写）

Do you like handwriting?

Do you think handwriting is important?

Which do you prefer, handwriting or typing?

What are the differences between handwriting and typing?

13. Apps（手机软件）

What apps have you recently used?

What kinds of apps are you usually interested in?

What was the first app you used?

What kinds of apps would you like to use in the future?

14. Colours（颜色）

What's your favourite colour?

What's the colour you dislike? Why?

What colour do your friends like most?

What colour makes you uncomfortable in your room?

15. Getting Lost（迷路）

Have you ever lost your way?

How can you find your way when you are lost?

Can you read a map when you get lost?

Have you ever helped someone who got lost?

16. Weather（天气）

What kind of weather do you like most?

What's the weather like in your hometown?

Do you like the weather in your hometown?

Do you prefer dry or wet weather?

17. Concentration（集中注意力）

Is it difficult for you to stay focused on something?

What do you do to help you concentrate?

What may distract you when you're trying to stay focused?

When do you need to be focused?

18. Environmental Protection（环境保护）

Would you like to work in a company related to environmental protection?

How can we protect the environment?

Do you think you've done enough to protect the environment?

Is there education about environmental protection at school?

19. Advertisements（广告）

What kind of advertisements do you watch?

Where can you see advertisements?

Have you ever bought something because of its advertisement?

Do you watch advertisements from the beginning to the end?

20. Flowers（花）

What kinds of flowers do you know?

Are there any flowers that have special meanings in China?

Have you planted any flowers?

Have you sent flowers to others?

21. Barbecue（烧烤）

Do Chinese people like barbecue?

What kind of food do you like to eat for barbecue?

22. Special Costumes（特别的服装）

Do you like to wear special costumes?

Did you try any special costumes when you were young?

When was your last time to wear special costumes?

Do you ever buy special costumes?

23. Relax（放松）

What would you do to relax?

Do you think doing sports is a good way to relax?

Do you think vacation is a good time to relax?

Do you think students need more relaxing time?

24. Primary School（小学）

How old were you when you started school?

What did you enjoy doing the most back in primary school?

How did you get to school each day?

Have you ever returned to visit your old school?

25. Wallet（钱包）

Do you use a wallet?

Have you ever lost your wallet?

Have you ever sent a wallet to someone as a gift?

Do most of your friends use wallet?

26. Sky and Stars（天空与星星）

Do you like to look at the sky? Why?

Can you see the moon and stars at night where you live?

Do you prefer the sky in the morning or the sky at night?

Is there a good place to look at the sky where you live?

Do you like to see the stars at night?

Do you want to live on other planets?

27. Wild Animals（野生动物）

Do you like to watch TV programs about wild animals?

Did you learn something about wild animals at school?

Where can you see wild animals?

In which country do you think you can see many wild animals?

28. Car Trip（开车旅行）

Where is the farthest place you have travelled to by car?

Do you like to sit in the front or back when travelling by car?

Do you like to travel by car?

When do you travel by car?

29. Holidays（假期）

Where did you go for your last holiday?

Do you like holidays? Why?

Which public holiday do you like best?

What do you do on holidays?

30. Festivals（节日）

How do you celebrate festivals in your country?

What special food and activities do you have for these festivals?

How do you celebrate Spring Festival?

What is your favourite festival?

SPEAKING

第三章 Part 2 口语题库及素材库

　　雅思口语考试 Part 2 的题目有一定的难度，考生有一分钟的准备时间，可以用两分钟的时间去回答。如果没有充足的准备，一旦遇到不熟悉的话题，考生就很容易在回答时出现问题。如果在日常的学习中为所有题目都准备素材，需要考生有强大的记忆力，而且花费的时间也很长。在题目量大与准备时间不够的双重压力下，考生需要掌握一些高效备考策略。本章提供了 Part 2 最常见的口语话题以及与其匹配的素材库。该素材库包括 20 个话题，每个话题下分以下几个步骤进行讲解：话题简介、话题相关口语题集、话题相关素材、口语练习、拓展练习、翻译练习参考答案及拓展练习范文。

　　Part 2 口语题目及素材库有以下特点：

★ 话题覆盖度高，可覆盖常考话题。

★ 以高频话题词汇和表达为核心，将一系列的题目串联起来，使话题词汇和表达的使用效率最大化。

★ 提供大量的口语翻译练习，帮助考生记忆和应用所学的表达及句式。

★ 提供图片和场景帮助记忆，让枯燥的词汇和表达生动具体。

★ 提供地道且接地气的范文，易于考生接受和模仿。

CHAPTER **THREE**

Part 2 口语题库及素材库使用指南

在正式进入 Part 2 口语题库及素材库的学习之前，首先介绍本部分内容的使用指南。

在每个话题下，编者将分以下 5 个步骤进行详细讲解。

STEP 1 话题简介：介绍选择这个话题的原因及话题的普适性。本书挑选的话题都极具代表性，一个话题可以覆盖大量的口语题目。

STEP 2 罗列与话题有关的口语题目：提供与该话题相关的高频题目。

STEP 3 罗列与话题有关的各类素材：包括有用的表达和可以广泛使用的素材、帮助记忆场景的图片及辅助的翻译练习。

STEP 4 口语练习：通过口语题目展示、题目分析、回答范文、范文解析及表达积累来展示如何通过使用所学的表达和素材完成口语回答。

STEP 5 拓展练习：这部分的题目与口语练习相似，旨在帮助考生进行限时的口语训练；拓展练习的题目配有范文，以方便考生学习。

在 20 个话题之后，编者还准备了按照人物、地点、事物、事件分类的补充题目及范文，这些题目和范文是对之前所学内容的补充与拓展。此外，关于最新口语题库及范文，如需了解更多，考生可登录"*启德 i 备考*"*小程序*。

另外，本书还为每个话题的范文录制了音频，考生可以扫描范文旁的二维码进行学习。

话题 1 SWIMMING（游泳）

如今热爱健身运动的人越来越多，无论是室内运动还是户外运动都十分受欢迎。在各类运动中，游泳是大家熟悉且乐于尝试的一项运动。游泳可以使我们全身的肌肉得到锻炼，对膝盖等部位的伤害较低。除了对身体健康有益，游泳还使人心情愉悦，是一项非常棒的消除压力的运动。掌握与游泳有关的表达和素材之后，考生就可以用这些表达和素材来回答一系列与运动、健康、良好生活习惯等有关的问题。

首先，"游泳"这个话题的表达和素材可以运用在以下的口语话题当中：

Describe a competition you want to take part in.

Describe a difficult challenge you met.

Describe a goal you set that you tried your best to achieve.

Describe a good decision someone made.

Describe a good decision you made recently.

Describe a healthy lifestyle you know.

Describe a natural talent (sports, music, etc.) you have that you want to improve.

Describe a new skill you learned that you think is important.

Describe a plan in your life (that is not related to work or study).

Describe a practical skill you learned.

Describe a skill that took you a long time to learn.

Describe a skill that you think you can teach other people.

Describe a sport that you have watched before and want to try.

Describe a sport you want to try for the first time.

Describe a success your friend had achieved.

Describe a time when you encouraged someone to do something that he/she didn't want to do.

Describe a time when you gave advice to others.

Describe a time when you suffered from an illness or a disease.

Describe a water sport you would like to try in the future.

Describe an achievement that you are proud of.

Describe an activity you do to stay healthy.

Describe an ambition that you have had for a long time.

Describe an article on health you read on magazine or the Internet.

Describe an experience when you taught a friend or a relative something.

Describe an important skill which cannot be learned at school.

Describe something you do to help you study or work.

Describe something you do to keep you concentrated.

Describe something you learned in a place or from someone.

　　游泳可以应用于相当多的题目，为了方便掌握这些题目的回答以及积累相关的表达与素材，编者按照以下三个方面进行讲解：游泳的基本动作、游泳与健康生活、游泳与技能。

■ // 游泳的基本动作 //

　　很多运动都有其特殊的场地要求与动作姿势，游泳也是一样。只要题目涉及运动、技能，考生都不可避免地需要描述其动作，因此掌握与游泳动作和学习游泳相关的表达是非常重要的。请看以下图片及与图片匹配的表达，这些表达都与游泳的基本动作及学习游泳有关。

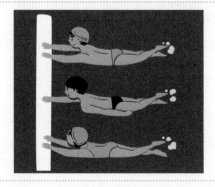

· 公共游泳池
　　public swimming pool
· 训练某人
　　train somebody
· 移动手臂、躯体和双腿
　　move arms, body, and legs
· 改进姿势
　　improve (one's) posture
· 正确地呼吸
　　breathe properly

在掌握了这些与游泳的基本动作和学习游泳有关的表达之后，我们来完成一个句子翻译练习。

原文：我把他带到一个公共游泳池，训练了他一段时间，教他如何移动他的手臂、身体和腿。

翻译：_____

_____

■ // 游泳与健康生活 //

游泳是一项非常有效的健身运动。在回答与游泳相关的问题时，考生需要掌握"游泳是一项健康的运动"的表达和素材。请看以下图片及与图片匹配的表达，这些表达都与游泳的益处有关。

对身体的益处（Physical Benefits）

- 增强力量和耐力
  build strength and endurance
- 锻炼肌肉
  work the muscles (of)/build muscle
- 保持苗条
  keep fit
- 保持体型
  stay in shape/get in shape
- 对心血管好的锻炼
  a good cardiovascular workout

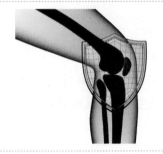

- 受伤的可能性很小
  be less likely to get injuries
- 低强度的运动
  a low-impact sport

对心理的益处（Mental Benefits）

- 令人放松的运动
  a very relaxing activity
- 缓解压力
  relieve stress
- 理清思绪（摒除杂念）
  clear one's mind
- 精神振作的
  refreshed
- 精力充沛的
  invigorated
- 能量提升
  an energy boost
- 有助于注意力集中
  improve concentration/concentrate/focus

在掌握了这些与身心健康有关的表达之后，我们来完成一些句子翻译练习。

1. 原文：游泳可以帮助我保持更好的体型。

翻译：_____

_____

2. 原文：游泳的时间越长，我的心血管就会得到更好的锻炼，而游泳的速度越快，我的力量和耐力就会越强。

翻译：_____

_____

3. 原文：游泳是一种更好的运动，因为它是一种低强度的运动，这意味着我不太可能受伤。

翻译：_____

_____

4. 原文：游泳帮助我放松，缓解压力，并使我的头脑清醒。

翻译：_____

_____

// 游泳与技能 //

游泳不仅是一项非常健康的运动，还是一种非常有用的生活及生存技能。在回答与游泳相关的问题时，考生需要掌握一些与游泳技能相关的表达和素材，请看以下图片及与图片匹配的表达。

· （在深水中）知道如何游泳可以防止自己溺水
  (in deep water) knowing how to swim will stop you from drowning

· 防止（其他人）溺水
  stop somebody from drowning
· 营救溺水的人
  rescue people who are drowning

在掌握了这些与技能有关的表达之后，我们来完成一些句子翻译练习。

1. 原文：如果你发现自己在深水中，知道如何游泳可以防止你溺水。

翻译：_____

_____

2. 原文：会游泳还能让你营救溺水的人。

翻译：_____

_____

■ // 口语练习 //

在掌握了与游泳有关的表达和素材之后，接下来就需要将这些内容综合起来，试着用它们来回答口语题目。

◎ 口语例题

Describe a good decision you made recently.

You should say:

    what it was

    when you made it

    what the result was

and explain how you felt about it.

◎ 题目分析

题目要求你描述最近做的一个很好的决定，这个决定可以是去一个地方旅游、学习一门语言、改掉一个习惯、找一份新工作或者学会一项技能。你可以用各种话题来回答这个问题，如果要用游泳这个话题来回答，应该怎样组织语言呢？你可以使用前面所学的两类素材（游泳的基本动作，游泳与健康生活），将它们按照一定的顺序组合在一起。

◎ 回答问题

你已经了解了题目的要求，也掌握了一定数量的英文单词和相关表达，接下来就请用两分钟的时间来回答这道题吧。

◎ 回答范文

I'm going to describe a good decision I made recently, which is to become a better swimmer. To be specific, I plan to swim for longer periods of time and to also swim faster.

I made this decision partly because it will help me get in better shape. Swimming for longer will give me a better cardiovascular workout, while swimming faster will help me build more strength and endurance. I thought about going running more often instead, but I think that swimming is a better exercise because it's a low-impact sport, which means I'm less likely to get injuries. I also want to see what I'm truly capable of. I think it's important to set goals in life and always try to push yourself.

Anyway, the first thing I need to do is to swim more efficiently and make fewer mistakes when I'm swimming. For example, I could try to improve my posture and breathe properly. This might take a while because I'm used to swimming for fun. Normally, I do it to relax, relieve stress, and clear my mind. But if I really want to become a better swimmer, I'll need to focus and concentrate more. It will probably take some time, but as long as I remain disciplined, I should be able to improve.

If I'm able to do this, I think I would feel fantastic. I've always thought that I have the potential to become a good swimmer, so it would give me a great sense of accomplishment. And of course, I would also feel great about my health and body.

◎ 范文解析

这篇文章选择以"游泳"为主题，即"最近做的一个很好的决定是成为一名更好的游泳者"。作者首先从游泳对身体健康有益入手，介绍了游泳的几大好处，如"游泳对心血管有好处"（a better cardiovascular workout）、"游泳可以增强力量及耐力"（build more strength and endurance）及"游泳强度较低，不容易受伤"（a low-impact sport, less likely to get injuries）。游泳除了对身体好，对缓解精神压力、理清思绪（relax, relieve stress, and clear my mind）也有很大作用。基于这两点，作者觉得学好游泳并努力游得更好是非常有用的。

◎ 表达积累

我们从范文中为考生总结了一些有用的表达，这些表达不仅可以用于描述游泳这项运动，还可以拓展运用到其他运动中，对于与体育运动、健康、技能等有关的题目都是适用的。

help me get in better shape	帮助我保持更好的身材
give me a better cardiovascular workout	给我更好的心血管（方面）的锻炼
help me build more strength and endurance	帮助我增强力量和耐力
a low-impact sport	一种低强度的运动
I'm less likely to get injuries	我不太可能受伤
improve my posture and breathe properly	改善我的姿势及（使我）正确地呼吸
relax, relieve stress, and clear my mind	放松、缓解压力、理清思绪
focus and concentrate	专注和集中
give me a great sense of accomplishment	给我很大的成就感

注意：

如果将这些表达拆成一个个单词，其实每个单词都不难，但组合在一起就不一样了。语言的魅力在于用看似简单但地道的表达来精确阐述想要表达的内容。在学习语言的过程中，除了要记忆单词，更要积累表达。以短语、句式及素材的方式进行积累可以避免在表述时不知道怎么搭配动词和名词、动词和副词、名词和形容词以及各种介词的问题。

■ // 拓展练习 //

根据所掌握的英语词汇及表达，模拟范文，回答以下题目。

Describe a natural talent (sports, music, etc.) you have that you want to improve in.

You should say:

    what it is

    when you discovered it

    how you want to improve it

and how you feel about it.

■ // 翻译练习参考答案及拓展练习范文 //

◎ 游泳的基本动作的翻译练习参考答案

I took him to a public swimming pool and trained him for a while, teaching him how to move his arms, body, and legs.

◎ 游泳与健康生活的翻译练习参考答案

1. Swimming will help me get in better shape.

2. Swimming for longer will give me a better cardiovascular workout, while swimming faster will help me build more strength and endurance.

3. Swimming is a better exercise because it's a low-impact sport, which means I'm less likely to get injuries.

4. Swimming helps me relax, relieve stress, and clear my mind.

◎ 游泳与技能的翻译练习参考答案

1. If you ever find yourself in deep water, knowing how to swim will stop you from drowning.

2. Being able to swim also allows you to rescue people who are drowning.

◎ 拓展练习范文

I'm going to describe something I'm good at that I want to improve in, which is swimming.

I was first introduced to swimming when my friend suggested it to me as a healthy exercise. At the time, I was looking for a way to stay in shape. I had never gone swimming before, so he took me to a public swimming pool and even trained me for a while, teaching me how to move my arms, body, and legs. I quickly became a good swimmer with his help and encouragement, which I'm thankful for. Anyway, even though I'm pretty good at it, I want to be able to swim for a longer time before I get tired. That would give me a better cardiovascular workout. Also, I'd like to be able to swim faster, since that would help me build more strength and endurance. To do all that, I would probably need to swim more efficiently and make fewer mistakes when swimming. For example, I could try to improve my posture and breathe properly.

As for how I feel about it, I think it will be a challenge for sure. Normally, swimming helps me relax, relieve stress, and clear my mind. But to actually improve, I'll need to focus and concentrate more. It will probably take some time, but as long as I remain disciplined, I should be able to improve. My friend thinks I have a lot of potential, so I want to see what I'm capable of. I think it's important to set goals in life and always try to push yourself, because it really gives you a sense of accomplishment.

话题 2 BADMINTON（羽毛球）

除了游泳、跑步，乒乓球、羽毛球等室内活动也很受欢迎。这类运动对场地的要求不是特别高，费用相对便宜，且这些活动大部分时候都是在室内进行的，所以不受天气的影响。此外，由于这些运动需要至少两人参加，所以非常有利于增进友谊、认识新朋友。至于它们带来的好处，那当然是强身健体、愉悦身心了。

首先，我们来看看有哪些话题与"羽毛球"有关：

Describe a competition you want to take part in.

Describe a game that you played in your childhood.

Describe a happy experience you had before.

Describe a healthy lifestyle you know.

Describe a sport that you have watched before and want to try.

Describe a sport you want to try for the first time.

Describe an activity you do to stay healthy.

Describe an experience when you played an indoor game with others.

Describe an experience when you taught a friend or a relative something.

Describe something you learned in a place or from someone.

不难发现，无论是题目里提到的比赛、某个经历还是看过或参加过的体育运动，考生都可以用"羽毛球"这个话题来回答。接下来我们将学习一些与羽毛球有关的词汇及表达。

// 打羽毛球的动作 //

既然是介绍一种运动，那必然会涉及其基本动作，这类描述在相关题目中都不可缺少。

基本动作
· 来回将球打过网
    hit the ball back and forth across the net
腿部动作
· 四处移动、跳跃
    move around, jump around
· 快速地从球场的一边跑到另一边
    run quickly from one side of the court to the other
· 蹲下或跳跃
    crouch or jump
手部动作
· 一直使用你的手臂
    use your arms all the time
· 挥动手臂和手腕
    swing your arm and wrist
· 扣球和打远球
    spike the ball or hit it far

在掌握了这些与动作有关的表达之后，我们来完成句子翻译练习。在翻译时可以思考一下，有哪些表达是在学习"游泳"这个话题时已经学习过了的。

1. 原文：你所要做的就是来回把球打过网。所以，与其他运动相比，这项运动对体力的要求不高。

翻译：_____

_____

2. 原文：羽毛球让你的心血管得到良好的锻炼，因为你基本上在四处移动、跳跃并一直使用你的手臂。

翻译：_____

_____

■ // **打羽毛球的好处** //

既然打羽毛球是一项很受欢迎的室内运动，那必然会带来各种益处。

· 很棒的锻炼
    fantastic workout
· 让你的心血管得到良好的锻炼
    give you a good cardiovascular workout
· 不错的增强感情的经历
    a nice bonding experience
· 缓解压力的好方法
    a good stress-relief

在掌握了这些与"打羽毛的好处"有关的表达之后，我们来完成句子翻译练习。

原文：当你玩双打时，需要大量的团队合作。因此，打羽毛球可以成为一种不错的增进感情的经历。

翻译：_____

_____

// 口语练习 //

在掌握了与羽毛球有关的表达和素材之后，接下来就需要将这些内容综合起来，试着用它们来回答口语题目。

◎ 口语例题

> Describe an experience when you played an indoor game with others.
> You should say:
>   what you played
>   who you played it with
>   why you played it
> and explain how you felt about it.

◎ 题目分析

题目要求描述你与他人一起玩的一项室内活动，打羽毛球就是一个非常不错的选择。你可以描述在某天（也许是雨天或者外面气温过高时）和一群朋友去体育馆打羽毛球，然后介绍打羽毛球的动作及其带来的好处。你可以使用之前列举的与打羽毛球有关的表达和素材，也可以使用在游泳话题中列举的表达和素材。

◎ 回答问题

你已经了解了题目的要求，也掌握了一定数量的英文单词和相关表达，接下来就请用两分钟的时间来回答这道题吧。

◎ 回答范文

I'm going to talk about a time when I played an indoor game with other people.

So, what happened was I wanted to hang out with my friends during the weekend, but the weather was a little rainy, so we decided to play badminton at an indoor badminton court.

We chose badminton because it's an excellent sport. First of all, it's pretty easy to play. All you have to do is hit the ball back and forth across the net. So, compared to other sports, it's not as physically demanding. In fact, if you want to, you can basically just stand at one spot and hit the ball back and forth, which is kind of relaxing in a way.

But usually, when you play badminton, you still get a good cardiovascular workout because you're moving around, jumping around, and using your arms all the time. And if you want to play seriously, then it can get really intense. You'll be running quickly from one side of the court to the other, and you'll often be crouching low or jumping high. And when you spike the ball or hit it far, you have to really swing your arm and wrist. Also, there's a lot of teamwork involved when you're playing two on two. For that reason, playing badminton can be a nice bonding experience.

Anyway, we ended up having a lot of fun playing badminton that day. We played for maybe about an hour or two, with regular breaks in between. Like I said, it was a nice bonding experience and a good stress-relief, and also a fantastic workout.

◎ 范文解析

作者首先表明在一个雨天的周末与一群朋友去室内羽毛球场打羽毛球，这就交代了玩的内容以及和谁一起玩。接下来就需要介绍为何会选择打羽毛球这项运动了。首先，学习打羽毛球并不难（pretty easy to play），动作相对简单，只需要将球打过网（hit the ball back and forth across the net）；其次，打羽毛球有利于身心健康，如有利于心血管健康（a good cardiovascular workout）；最后，打羽毛球是一次不错的增强感情的经历（a nice bonding experience）。

通过这篇范文和前面以游泳为主题的范文，不难发现，如果要介绍一项体育运动，必然包含两部分内容，一是基本动作，二是由它带来的好处，而带来的好处基本都是对身心健康有益。因此，如果考生想以其他体育运动项目为主题来回答问题，要做的就是准备与这些体育运动项目的基本动作相关的表达，而由此项运动带来的好处则基本是相似的。

◎ 表达积累

我们从范文中为考生总结了一些有用的表达，这些表达不仅可以用于描述羽毛球这项运动，还可以用于描述其他运动，对于与体育运动、健康、技能等有关的题目都是适用的。

it's pretty easy to play	很容易玩
move around, jump around	四处走动，到处跳跃
give you a good cardiovascular workout	让你的心血管得到良好的锻炼
a nice bonding experience	不错的增强感情的经历
a good stress-relief	缓解压力的好方法

■■ // 拓展练习 //

根据所掌握的英语词汇及表达，模拟范文，回答以下题目。

Describe a happy experience you had before.

You should say:

　　where you were

　　when it happened

　　what you did

and explain why you were happy about it.

■ // 翻译练习参考答案及拓展练习范文 //

◎ 打羽毛球的动作的句子翻译练习参考答案

1. All you have to do is hit the ball back and forth across the net. So, compared to other sports, it's not as physically demanding.

2. Badminton gives you a good cardiovascular workout because you're still moving around, jumping around, and using your arms all the time.

◎ 打羽毛球的好处的句子翻译练习参考答案

There's a lot of teamwork involved when you're playing two on two. For that reason, playing badminton can be a nice bonding experience.

◎ 拓展练习范文

I want to talk about a happy experience I had playing badminton with my friends at an indoor court last Saturday.

We decided to play badminton because the weather was rainy and we couldn't do our usual outdoor activities. What I love about badminton is that it's a pretty easy sport to play. All you have to do is hit the ball back and forth across the net. So, compared to other sports, it's not as physically demanding. In fact, if you want to, you can basically just stand at one spot and hit the ball back and forth, which is kind of relaxing in a way.

But usually, when you play badminton, you still get a good cardiovascular workout because you're moving around, jumping around, and using your arms all the time. What I find particularly enjoyable about badminton is that it's a great workout that doesn't feel like a workout. When you're caught up in the game, you're not thinking about how much energy you're using. Also, there's a lot of teamwork involved when you're playing two on two.

Anyway, playing badminton that day was a lot of fun. We played for about an hour or two, with regular breaks in between. I was happy about the experience because it was a chance to catch up with my friends and do something active and engaging. It was also a great stress-reliever after a busy week. Playing a sport with others can be a great bonding experience, and I felt closer to my friends after playing badminton with them. Overall, I was happy about the experience because it combined fun, fitness, and socializing in one activity.

话题 3 A FAMOUS ATHLETE（著名的运动员）

说起名人，我们往往会想到著名的企业家、社会各行业有突出贡献的人、明星等，而著名的运动员既是明星，也是对社会有贡献的人。冬奥会和夏奥会举办时，很多人都会在电视机或者手机上观看运动员比赛。在这期间，社交媒体上最活跃的话题也大多与运动员有关。在没有比赛的日子里，运动员们的训练视频、参加的活动也是大家津津乐道的话题。所以，考生如果能掌握与著名的运动员有关的表达和素材，就等于掌握了回答名人类、媒体类、运动类话题的核心内容。

首先，我们来看看有哪些话题与"著名的运动员"有关：

Describe a famous athlete you know.

Describe a famous person in your country.

Describe a famous person you are interested in.

Describe a person in the news who you want to meet.

Describe a person who you follow on social media.

Describe a person who you think is very open.

Describe a person you have seen who is beautiful or handsome.

Describe a popular person.

不难发现，这些话题除了谈论名人本身，也会涉及其他的内容，如知名的程度、喜欢他或她的原因等。接下来我们一起学习一些与运动员有关的词汇和表达。

// 运动员与运动项目 //

夏季奥运会的项目名称大家都比较了解了，从 2022 年开始，冬季奥运会越来越受到人们的关注，参与雪上、冰上运动的人也越来越多。请看以下图片所展示的运动，这些运动在冬季奥运会中十分受欢迎。

- 滑雪
  skiing
- 单板滑雪
  snowboard
- 速度滑冰 / 短道速滑
  speed skating/short track speed skating
- 花滑
  figure skating
- 冰壶
  curling
- 冰球
  ice hockey

■■ // 运动员的成就与受欢迎程度 //

除了需要了解各项运动的英文表达，还要知道怎么去描述运动员。请翻译下列与"著名的运动员"这个话题有关的句子，这些句子可以用来描述运动员的知名度、成就和努力。

1. 原文：她是世界顶尖的女子滑雪运动员之一，最近她参加了北京冬奥会，赢得了三枚奖牌。

翻译：_____

_____

2. 原文：她经常在社交媒体上发布训练视频，这些视频表明要成为一名优秀的滑雪者需要付出很多努力。

翻译：_____

_____

3. 原文：他是中国著名的短跑运动员，他参加过多次奥运会和其他比赛，是世界上最好的短跑运动员之一。

翻译：_____

_____

4. 原文：他是第一个在 10 秒内跑完 100 米的亚洲人，这是非常了不起的。此外，他在奥运会和其他国际比赛中也表现出色，多年来一直名列前茅。

翻译：_____

_____

5. 原文：人们很自然地被他 / 她吸引，是因为他 / 她非常自信和有魅力。

翻译：_____

_____

6. 原文：他 / 她在这里很有名，很受欢迎。他 / 她经常出现在新闻和媒体上，他 / 她在社交媒体上有很多粉丝。

翻译：_____

_____

■■ // 口语练习 //

在掌握了多项运动的英文表达，熟悉了如何描述著名运动员的成就与受欢迎程度之后，接下来就需要将这些内容综合起来，试着用它们来回答口语题目。

◎ 口语例题

Describe a person who you follow on social media.

You should say:

　　who he/she is

　　how you knew him/her

　　what he/she posts on social media

and explain why you follow him/her on social media.

◎ 题目分析

题目要求描述一个你在社交媒体上关注的人，这个人可以是企业家、普通人、演艺圈明星，也可以是著名的体育运动员。在这里，你可以选择"著名的运动员"为回答的主题。接下来，你需要说明人们是怎么知道这个人的，对于运动员来说，大多是通过电视上的比赛被人了解的。随后，你需要对这个运动员的成就和名气进行一番描述，最后表达出你对他或她的喜爱之情及视其为榜样。

◎ 回答问题

你已经了解了题目的要求，也掌握了一定数量的英文单词和表达，接下来就请用两分钟的时间来回答这道题吧。

◎ 回答范文

A person I follow on social media is Eileen Gu. In China, she's known as Gu Ailing.

She's one of the world's top female skiers, and she recently participated in the Beijing Winter Olympics, where she won three medals. She's around 18 years old, and she's half-Chinese, half-American, with her mother being Chinese.

I knew about Eileen Gu because she's often mentioned in social media and she appears in a lot of advertisements. And also, people everywhere were talking about her, especially as the Beijing Winter Olympics got closer. People had high expectations for her, and she quickly became a household name.

On social media, she often posts things like videos of her training, and the videos show that it takes a lot of hard work and dedication to become a great skier. She also posts pictures of her life, like her cats, her school, and her travels. And finally, she's also a model, so she posts a lot of her modelling and promotional pictures. You can tell from her social media that she lives a very interesting and meaningful life.

Anyway, the reason I follow her on social media is because, first of all, I'm curious about her. I want to know more about what she's like and I'm interested in her daily life and what she's doing. What's more, her videos and pictures are very inspiring, especially the ones that show her training. They show that it's important to chase your dreams. And I also enjoy looking at her travel pictures, because you can see lots of beautiful scenery, like snowy mountains and other places.

◎ 范文解析

该范文选择了在 2022 年冬奥会上有突出表现的自由式滑雪运动员谷爱凌为主题，通过描述她在冬奥会上的表现、社交媒体上的热度、大众对她的喜爱来回答问题。

在回答的一开始，先开门见山地点明要谈论的人物是谁，随后介绍这个人物的职业和成就。谷爱凌是世界级顶尖的女子滑雪运动员，注意范文中使用的表达"one of the world's top female skiers"。范文中还有不少关于运动项目和比赛的表达，如描述谷爱凌的奥运会成就用到了"she participated in the Beijing Winter Olympics, where she won three medals"。

除了运动成就，她在社交媒体上也十分受欢迎。她会发布自己的训练视频 (posts things like videos of her training)，这些视频展示了她训练十分努力 (it takes a lot of hard work and dedication to become a great skier)。除了体育训练，她还会发布一些与生活有关的照片和视频 (posts pictures of her life, like her cats, her school, and her travels)。

最后，该范文还提及为何会关注她、喜欢她。关注她是因为对她很好奇（curious about her），希望了解更多关于她的内容（I want to know more about what she's like and I'm interested in her daily life and what she's doing）。喜欢她是因为觉得她很厉害、很努力，她的事迹可以鼓舞人心，在谈及这些内容时，可以使用的词汇及表达有"inspiring""it's important to chase your dreams"等。

◎ 表达积累

我们从范文中为考生总结了一些有用的表达，这些表达不仅可以用于描述谷爱凌，而且稍加改动括号里的内容就可以用来描述其他的运动员。

one of the world's top (female skiers)	世界顶级（女滑雪者）之一
participated in the (Beijing Winter Olympics), where (she won three medals)	参加了（北京冬奥会），获得了（三枚奖牌）
(she's) often mentioned in social media and (she) appears in a lot of advertisements	（她）经常在社交媒体上被提及，（她）出现在很多广告中
people had high expectations for (her)	人们对（她）期望很高
a household name	一个家喻户晓的名字
(she) often posts things like videos of (her) training, and the videos show that it takes a lot of hard work and dedication to become a great (skier)	（她）经常发布训练视频之类的东西，这些视频表明，成为一名优秀的（滑雪者）需要大量的努力和投入
inspiring	鼓舞人心的
it's important to chase your dreams	追逐梦想是很重要的

■ // 拓展练习 //

根据所掌握的英语词汇及表达，模拟范文，回答以下题目。

Describe a famous athlete you know.
You should say:
　　who he/she is
　　how you knew about him/her
　　what he/she has achieved
and explain why he/she is famous.

■ // 翻译练习参考答案及拓展练习范文 //

◎ 运动员的成就与受欢迎程度的翻译练习参考答案

1. She is one of the world's top female skiers, and she recently participated in the Beijing Winter Olympics, where she won three medals.

2. On social media, she often posts things like videos of her training, and the videos show that it takes a lot of hard work and dedication to become a great skier.

3. He is a famous Chinese sprinter who competed in multiple Olympics and other races, and he's one of the best sprinters in the world.

4. He was the first Asian man to run 100 meters in under 10 seconds, which is remarkable. Also, he's done very well at the Olympics and other international competitions, and he's been at the top for many years.

5. People are naturally drawn to him/her because he's/she's quite confident and charismatic.

6. He's/She's quite famous and popular here. He/she appears quite often in the news and media, and he/she has lots of fans on social media.

◎ 拓展练习范文

I'm going to describe a famous athlete I know, and that athlete is Su Bingtian. He's a famous Chinese sprinter who competed in multiple Olympics and other races, and he's one of the best sprinters in the world. In terms of looks, he's not very tall, but he's muscular, like all sprinters are. He also looks confident and has a bright smile. Personality-wise, he's cheerful and nice, and again, he just seems very confident all the time.

I know about Su Bingtian because, well, everyone in China knows who he is. He's quite famous and popular here. He appears quite often in the news and media, and he has lots of fans on social media.

As for what he has achieved, he's done a lot of things. I guess first and foremost, he's one of the best Asian sprinters ever. If I recall correctly, he was the first Asian man to run 100 meters in under 10 seconds, which is remarkable. Also, he's done very well at the Olympics and other international competitions, and he's been at the top for many years.

I guess he's famous mostly because of those achievements. He's done a great job representing China in a field that's traditionally dominated by people of African descent. So, not only are Chinese people and other Asians proud of him, he inspires us because he's beaten the odds. And he was able to get to where he was by training hard every day, which is very admirable. Other than that, I guess people are naturally drawn to him because, as I mentioned, he's quite confident and charismatic.

话题 4 GOOD NEWS（好消息）

收到一个好消息或者坏消息是口语中常见的一类问题，本着"报喜不报忧"的原则，这里将重点落在好消息上面。如果题目涉及坏消息，则可以适当地将好消息中的内容稍作修改，就可以回答问题了。比如原本是获得比赛的胜利，可以将其改成比赛失利，而其他核心内容则保持不变。

好消息可以分成很多种类，可以是自己的好消息、亲朋好友的好消息，也可以是名人的好消息或者某些社会新闻、国际新闻等。获得好消息的方式也有很多，可以是自己从网络、电视上看到的，也可以是别人告知的。获得好消息之后的感受通常是兴奋的、开心的、激动的、令人印象深刻的或鼓舞人心的。

接下来，我们来看看有哪些话题与"好消息"有关：

Describe a piece of good news you heard (from TV or the Internet).

Describe a piece of important news you got through a text message.

Describe a piece of international news you recently heard.

Describe a piece of local news that people were interested in.

Describe a time when you received good news.

不难发现，这些与"好消息"有关的问题多半是与各类新闻有关的。接下来我们将学习一些与好消息相关的表达和素材。

// 好消息的来源与获得消息之后的感受 //

请看以下罗列的与"好消息的来源与获得消息之后的感受"有关的素材，至于好消息的内容，可以使用运动员获得金牌等体育类的新闻。

获取消息的方式

- ·（出现在）当地新闻和国际新闻上
    on the local and international news
- ·通过印刷品或者电子媒体，如报纸、杂志、书籍、社交媒体网站、微信、短信
    through print or electronic media such as newspapers, magazines, books, social media sites, WeChat and text messages
- ·通过广播和电视
    through radio and television
- ·在脸书、推特、微博、抖音等社交媒体上关注她 / 他
    through following a famous person on social media, such as on Facebook, Twitter, Weibo, and TikTok

获得消息之后的感受

- ·非常兴奋
    a lot of excitement
- ·令人印象深刻的
    think it's impressive
- ·鼓舞人心的
    think it's inspiring
- ·为……感到骄傲
    proud of her/him

在掌握了这些与好消息有关的表达之后，我们来完成句子翻译练习。

1. 原文：这一切都出现在当地和国际新闻上，因为一个如此年轻的人能够赢得所有这些奖牌，这是令人印象深刻的。

翻译：_____

_____

2. 原文：我在社交媒体上关注她，她经常发布自己的训练情况。

翻译：_____

_____

3. 原文：人们都为她感到骄傲，她也因此获得了很多粉丝。

翻译：_____

_____

■ // **口语练习** //

在掌握了与"好消息的来源与获得消息之后的感受"有关的表达之后，接下来就需要将这些内容综合起来，试着用它们来回答口语题目。

◎ **口语例题**

> Describe a piece of international news you recently heard.
>
> You should say:
>
> what the news is about
>
> where and when you heard it
>
> what you were doing when you heard the news
>
> and explain how you felt about this piece of international news.

◎ **题目分析**

题目要求你描述一则最近听过的国际新闻。国际新闻涉及的范围非常广泛，包括政治新闻、经济新闻、文化新闻、体育新闻、自然新闻等。其中，相对比较容易描述的是体育新闻。运动员参加国际大型赛事会受到全世界的关注，如奥运会和世界杯。作为观众，你会在电视或网络上看到本国运动员参加比赛、获得奖牌，这不仅是一则国际新闻，更是令人振奋的好消息。

◎ **回答问题**

你已经了解了题目的要求，也掌握了一定数量的英文单词和表达，接下来就请用两分钟的时间来回答这道题吧。

◎ **回答范文**

I'm going to describe a piece of international news I heard, which is when Gu Ailing won gold medals in skiing during the Beijing Winter Olympics. Gu Ailing is also known as Eileen Gu, and she's one of the world's best female skiers. She's really young, and she's half-Chinese, half-American, with her mother being Chinese.

Anyway, Gu Ailing chose to represent China during the Beijing Winter Olympics, and there was a lot of anticipation built up because people were expecting great things, so there was a lot of excitement. And then, once the competition started, she performed extremely well. She was left with two gold medals and one silver for skiing. It was all on local and international news because it was so awesome that someone so young could win all those medals. In addition, she was the first person at the Winter Olympics to win three medals in three separate events.

I think what she did was very inspiring, not just for me, but to many Chinese people. I follow her on social media and she often posts about her training. You can see how hard she works and how passionate she is at skiing. It shows that you can fulfil your dreams if you really dedicate yourself to something. So yeah, people were really proud of her, and she gained lots of fans from it. In addition, I am quite certain that, thanks to her, many more people have taken an interest in skiing, so I think we'll see more Chinese skiers in future competitions. At least I hope so.

◎ 范文解析

该范文选取了谷爱凌在 2022 年冬奥会上获得奖牌的新闻为主题进行描述。选择这则国际新闻的原因很简单，一是可以使用已经学过的关于运动员的表达和素材，二是这一事件广为人知，描述起来比较容易。范文首先简单描述了这则国际新闻是什么，并对谷爱凌的身份进行了描述，随后对她获奖的过程进行了较为详细的介绍，最后表达了得到该消息之后的感受。

◎ 表达积累

我们从范文中为考生总结了一些有用的表达，这些表达不仅可以用于描述谷爱凌的冬奥会之旅，还可以用于回答其他相关的题目。

it was all on the local and international news	当地和国际新闻都报道了
I follow her on social media	我在社交媒体上关注她
inspiring	鼓舞人心的
there was a lot of excitement	大家都很兴奋
be proud of	感到骄傲的

■ // 拓展练习 //

根据所掌握的英语词汇及表达，模拟范文，回答以下题目。

Describe a piece of good news you heard (from TV or the Internet).

You should say:

what the news was about

when you got this news

where you got this news from

and explain why you think it was a good piece of news.

■ // 翻译练习参考答案及拓展练习范文 //

◎ 好消息的来源与获得消息之后的感受的翻译练习参考答案

1. It was all on the local and international news because it was so impressive that someone so young was able to win all these medals.

2. I follow her on social media and she often posts about her training.

3. People were really proud of her, and she gained lots of fans from it.

◎ 拓展练习范文

I'm going to describe a piece of good news I heard, which is when Gu Ailing

扫码听音频

won gold medals in skiing during the Beijing Winter Olympics. Gu Ailing is also known as Eileen Gu, and she's one of the world's best female skiers. She's really young, and she's half-Chinese, half-American, with her mother being Chinese.

Anyway, Gu Ailing chose to represent China during the Beijing Winter Olympics, and there was a lot of anticipation built up because people were expecting great things, so there was a lot of excitement. And then, once the competition started, she performed extremely well. She was left with two gold medals and one silver for skiing. It was all on local and international news because it was so awesome that someone so young could win all those medals. In addition, she was the first person at the Winter Olympics to win three medals in three separate events.

I think what she did was very inspiring, not just for me, but to many Chinese people. I follow her on social media and she often posts about her training. You can see how hard she works and how passionate she is at skiing. It shows that you can fulfil your dreams if you really dedicate yourself to something. So yeah, people were really proud of her, and she gained lots of fans from it. In addition, I am quite certain that, thanks to her, many more people have taken an interest in skiing, so I think we'll see more Chinese skiers in future competitions. At least I hope so.

看完这篇范文，大家心里是不是有个疑惑：这篇范文是不是跟口语练习的范文一样呀？没错，就是同一篇范文。其实这就是我们希望考生掌握的一种技能，即准备自己最有把握的素材和表达，把它们合理地运用到不同的题目中去。这样既可以节约备考的时间，又可以在遇到难题的时候快速找到可用的素材和表达。

话题 5 A RESTAURANT（餐厅）

餐厅是一个人们常去的地方，人们去餐厅可以是为了填饱肚子，也可以是慕名打卡、庆祝生日、庆祝纪念日、放松心情。餐厅有不同种类，有自助的，也有非自助的。餐厅的食物也多种多样，可以是牛排、日料、汉堡、火锅、烧烤等。喜欢某个餐厅可能是因为其食物美味和环境宜人，也可能是因为满意餐厅的服务。掌握了与餐厅有关的表达和素材之后，就能将其应用于回答难忘的经历、地点、服务、食物等话题中。

首先，我们来看看有哪些话题与"餐厅"有关：

Describe a dinner that you really enjoyed.

Describe a meal you invited others to have at your home or in a restaurant.

Describe a party that you attended.

Describe a popular product (e.g. food, handicraft...) made in your region.

Describe a special day when you went out but didn't spend much money.

Describe a time when you ate something for the first time.

Describe a time when you received money as a present.

Describe a time when you were excited.

Describe a time you received good service.

Describe a time you received horrible service.

Describe an important event that you celebrated.

Describe an occasion when many people were smiling.

Describe an occasion when you had to dress up (wear your best clothes).

Describe an unusual meal you had.

无论是题目里提到喜欢的食物、喜欢的餐厅还是聚会庆祝活动，考生都可以使用"餐厅"这个话题来回答。接下来我们将分类学习一些与"餐厅"有关的表达与素材。

// 餐厅与食物 //

民以食为天，食物是生活的必需品，也是餐厅受欢迎的核心。在回答与餐厅有关的题目时，肯定要涉及对食物或菜肴的描述。下面以广受人们喜爱的火锅为例，给出一些相关的表达。

生的食材 (Raw ingredients)
·蔬菜：卷心菜、菠菜、香菇
　　vegetables: cabbage, spinach, mushroom
·豆腐
　　tofu
·海鲜：海藻、对虾、鱿鱼、鱼、蟹或蟹棒
　　seafood: seaweeds, prawns, squid, fish,
　　crab or crab stick
·肉类：牛肉 / 猪肉片、蛋饺、牛肉丸子、牛肚
　　meat: beef/pork slices, egg dumplings, beef
　　balls, beef tripe

汤底 (Soup base)
·两种口味、双拼
　　double flavour
·辣的
　　spicy
·鸡汤
　　chicken soup

蘸酱 (Sauce)
·酸辣蘸酱
　　spicy and sour sauce
·芝麻蘸酱
　　sesame sauce

吃火锅的步骤 (Steps for eating hotpot)
·自己煮食材，把它们放入沸腾的锅里
　　cook the ingredients yourself by putting
　　them in a boiling pot
·用筷子夹住它
　　grab it with your chopsticks
·蘸酱
　　dip it in sauce

在掌握了这些与食物有关的表达之后，我们来完成句子翻译练习。

1. 原文：你会点很多不同的食材，如肉、蔬菜和豆腐。

翻译：_____

_____

2. 原文：你需要自己煮食材，把它们放入桌子上一个沸腾的锅里。

翻译：_____

_____

3. 原文：中国火锅很特别，因为通常你可以选择辣的汤，这可以为所有食物增添额外的味道。

翻译：_____

_____

■ // 餐厅与服务 //

除了好吃的食物，餐厅的服务也是值得关注的。优质的服务和好吃的食物是人们反复光顾一家餐厅的主要原因。一般来说，餐厅的服务可以分为到餐厅前（如预定是否方便）、到餐厅时（如接待或点餐）、就餐时（如上菜、倒酒或饮料、收餐盘）和就餐完毕（如结账速度）。以火锅店为例，我们来学习以下与图片匹配的表达。

去餐馆前 (Before we went to the restaurant)
· 在一个受欢迎的网站上阅读评论，该网站允许用户对餐馆进行评分并发布评论
    read reviews on a popular website that lets users rate restaurants and post reviews
· 预定
    made a reservation

到达餐馆后 (After we arrived at the restaurant)
· 服务员快速引导（顾客）入座
    seated quickly by the server
·（服务员）给我们水和菜单
    provided us with water and the menu
·（服务员）细心、有礼貌
    attentive and polite
· 定期过来看看我们是否准备好点餐了
    came by regularly to check if we were ready to order
· 提供一些很棒的推荐
    provided some great recommendations

点餐后 / 用餐时 (After we finished ordering/when we were eating)
- 上菜很快
    served quickly
- 在用餐过程中给我们续杯
    gave us refills during the meal
- 清理我们桌子上的空盘子
    cleared empty dishes off our table
- 为火锅开火和关火
    turned on the heat for the hotpot and also turned it off
- （火锅）加汤
    added soup

用餐结束 (When we were done with our meal)
- 很快把账单给我们
    let us have the bill quickly
- 分开付
    shared the bill
- 和我们说再见
    said goodbye to us

在掌握了这些与服务有关的表达之后，我们来完成句子翻译练习。

1. 原文：这名评论者说，当她到达餐厅时，他们很快就被服务员安排就座，服务员给他们端来了水和菜单。

翻译：_____

_____

2. 原文：他们点完餐后，食物很快就上来了。

翻译：_____

_____

3. 最后，当他们吃完饭后，服务员很快就把账单拿来了。

翻译：_____

_____

■ // 餐厅与愉快的经历 //

有了美食和周到的服务，在餐厅的就餐经历一定是非常愉快的。除了单纯享受美食与服务，人们还可以在餐厅里庆祝生日、与朋友聚会、和同事聚餐，这些都是愉快的经历。如何描述一次愉快的经历，这通常包括为何会愉快（如食物好吃、服务周到、举办生日会）以及表达这种愉快的心情，请看以下表达。关于食物和服务方面的表达可以参考前面"餐厅与食物"和"餐厅与服务"中的内容，这里不再介绍。

愉快的原因	食物很好吃，很新鲜	delicious, fresh ingredients
	很棒的服务	excellent service
	请我吃饭	treated me to a meal
	拿出生日蛋糕	brought out a birthday cake
	（服务员）帮我们拍照	took a picture of us
	收到礼物，例如……	gave me some presents, like...
表达开心快乐	笑容满面	had a big smile/big smiles on my face/our faces
	相当与众不同的和令人兴奋的	pretty unusual and exciting
	感到很幸运能有一大群朋友	felt very lucky to have my group of friends

在掌握了这些与愉快的经历有关的表达之后，我们来完成句子翻译练习。

原文：这是我第一次在餐厅庆祝生日，所以这很不寻常，也很令人兴奋，我觉得很幸运能有一群朋友。

翻译：_____

_____

■ // 口语练习 //

在掌握了与食物、服务、愉快的经历有关的表达之后，接下来就需要将这些内容综合起来，试着用它们来回答口语题目。

◎ 口语例题

Describe a company where you live that employs a lot of people.

You should say:

　　what it does

　　how many people it employs / what kind of people work there

　　how you knew about it

and explain how you feel about it.

◎ 题目分析

第一眼看到这道题，你可能会觉得雇佣很多人的公司怎么会与餐厅有关联呢？其实餐厅非常符合这个题目的要求，首先餐厅是一种公司，其次餐厅会雇佣很多人，比如服务员和厨师。既然确定了围绕餐厅展开回答，接下来就需要介绍这家餐厅的食物、服务和你就餐的感受。当然，如果不想说餐厅，也可以选择介绍便利店、大型企业（如新媒体企业、IT 巨头）。总之，围绕它们的产品、服务和用户感受展开来谈即可。

◎ 回答问题

你已经了解了题目的要求，也掌握了一定数量的英文单词和表达，接下来就请用两分钟的时间来回答这道题吧。

◎ 回答范文

A company with many employees here is a chain of hotpot restaurants. It's very popular and there are hundreds of their restaurants across the country and they hire thousands of people.

The hotpot restaurant is known for having fresh ingredients that are high quality and not that expensive. They have a good variety of ingredients too—many different kinds of meat, vegetables, and tofu. They also have different types of soup bases you can choose, and they're all quite good. My favourite is probably their spicy soup base.

If you haven't eaten hot pot before, what you do is you cook raw ingredients yourself by putting them in a boiling pot that's normally shared with other people at the table. It's a great bonding experience, which is why hotpot is very popular and the best hotpot restaurants make a lot of money.

I discovered the restaurant years ago when I was reading reviews on a popular website that lets users rate restaurants and post reviews about them. I was using the website to find a hotpot restaurant where I could go to with my friends, and one of the restaurants caught my eye, so I checked its reviews. Most of the reviews were short, but one of them was quite long. It gave a detailed description about how the food was extremely delicious and that the service was excellent. After I read the review, I went to the restaurant with my friends and had a great dinner there.

The restaurant has become very successful these years because it has maintained high standards for its food and service, and this has given it a great reputation with good word of mouth.

◎ 范文解析

该范文在首段非常直接地介绍了这个公司是一家连锁火锅店（a chain of hotpot restaurants），分店众多，还雇佣了非常多的员工。随后介绍了这家火锅店因为价格公道、食材新鲜多样、味道好而出名，这部分主要结合"餐厅与食物"的相关表达展开。最后，根据题目要求，说明了是通过网站上的评论（reviews on a popular website）了解到这家火锅店的，这家店的食物和服务给人留下了深刻的印象。

◎ 表达积累

我们从范文中为考生总结了一些有用的表达，这些表达不仅可以用于描述火锅店，还可以用于回答其他与食物、餐馆有关的题目。

restaurant chain	连锁餐厅
hire thousands of people	雇佣数千人
known for having fresh ingredients	以食材新鲜而闻名
have a good variety of ingredients	有各种各样的食材
a great bonding experience	很棒的增进感情的经历
rake in big bucks	赚很多钱
read the reviews on a popular website where users can rate and post comments about restaurants	在一个很受欢迎的网站上阅读评论，该网站允许用户对餐厅进行评级并发表评论
gave a detailed description about how the food was extremely delicious and that the service was excellent	详细描述了那里的食物非常美味，服务非常好

// 拓展练习 //

根据所掌握的英语词汇及表达，模拟范文，回答以下题目。

Describe a time when you received money as a present.

You should say:

who gave it to you

when you received it

what you did with it

and how you felt about it.

// 翻译练习参考答案及拓展练习范文 //

◎ 餐厅与食物翻译练习参考答案

1. You order lots of different raw ingredients, like meat, vegetables, and tofu.

2. You need to cook the ingredients yourself by putting them in a boiling pot on the table.

3. Chinese hot pot is something that's special because often you can choose for the soup to be spicy, which adds an extra flavour to everything.

◎ 餐厅与服务翻译练习参考答案

1. The reviewer said that when she arrived at the restaurant, they were seated quickly by the waiters, who brought them water and the menu.

2. After they finished ordering, the food arrived quickly.

3. Finally, when they were done with their meal, the waiter quickly brought them the bill.

◎ 餐厅与愉快的经历翻译练习参考答案

It was the first time I celebrated my birthday at a restaurant, so it was pretty unusual and exciting and I felt very lucky to have my group of friends.

◎ 拓展练习范文

Well, it was two years ago for my nineteenth birthday, on a summer night. I was with my closest friends, who treated me to a meal at a hotpot restaurant.

The restaurant was close to downtown, about just twenty minutes from my apartment. I remember taking the subway over there to meet my friends.

It was my first time eating hotpot there. I thought everything was delicious. I really enjoyed the soup and the fresh ingredients, and the service was also excellent. We were seated quickly and the waiters were very attentive and polite, and they came by regularly to check if we were ready to order. We weren't completely sure what to order, so the waiter provided some great recommendations for us. After we finished ordering, the food arrived quickly. At the end of the meal, they even brought out a birthday cake for our celebration. The waiter took a picture of us, which I later put on a wall at home. We all had big smiles on our faces and I looked fantastic because I was dressed up.

Afterwards, my friends gave me gifts, such as a karaoke machine and a pretty hat. One of my friends just gave me some money because he couldn't decide on a good present. Regardless, I was thankful for it and used the money to buy some clothes later. All in all, it was a great experience. It was the first time I celebrated my birthday at a restaurant, so it was pretty unusual and exciting and I felt very lucky to have my group of friends.

话题 6 A TRADITIONAL PRODUCT / FOOD（传统产品 / 食物）

说起与传统有关的东西，我们会想到一些手工制品，比如饰品、衣服、食物、器物，这里选择食物作为代表。传统食物是传统产品中比较容易描述和为人所知的，毕竟民以食为天。在描述某种传统食物时，通常会涉及这种食物的制作流程、食用方法、口味、受欢迎程度及对当地人的意义。因此，掌握与"传统食物"有关的表达和素材对回答相关口语问题有很大的帮助。

首先，我们来看看有哪些话题与"传统食物"有关：

Describe a kind of food people eat during a special event.

Describe a popular product (e.g. food, handicraft...) made in your region.

Describe a time that you bought something in a street market.

Describe a time when you ate something for the first time

Describe a time when you shared something with others (or another person).

Describe a traditional product in your country.

■ // 描述一种传统食物 //

在上一话题"餐厅"的学习中，考生了解了很多描述食物的表达，通过这个话题，考生将学习更多的表达。由于每个人的喜好不同，在回答时考生可以选择自己喜爱的并且熟悉的食物进行描述，但描述的方法和逻辑基本相同。接下来以江南地区广受欢迎的小笼包为例，为考生展示如何对一种传统食物进行描述。

以下表格中所涉及的表达有些仅限于描述小笼包，有些可以用来描述馄饨、包子等类似的食物。至于食物的制作方法，如果能够精确描述肯定是最好的，如果不能，那就把几个主要动作说清楚就好。

整体描述 (What it is)
· 一个有汤的小包子
　　a small soup dumpling
· 一个（皮）非常薄且柔软的圆包
　　a very thin, soft, steamed bun
· 里面有些汤汁
　　there's some soup inside
· 同时包含肉和汤
　　contain both meat and soup together

口味 (Flavour)
· 美味的
　　mouth-watering
· 咸味儿的
　　salty
· 有独特的味道
　　has a unique flavour
· 有柔软的质地
　　has a soft texture

制作及烹饪方法（How to make and cook it）
· 一开始把面团平铺在桌子上，然后把肉或蔬菜放在里面，一边旋转一边包裹起来
　　start with having the bun flat on a table, and then put the meat or vegetables inside and spin it to close it up
· 把它放在蒸屉里蒸
　　steam it in some kind of basket

在掌握了这些与传统食物的外形和制作烹饪方法有关的表达之后，我们来完成句子翻译练习。

1. 原文：小笼包是一种（外皮）很薄很软的圆包，通常里面会有汤和肉，有时可能是蟹肉、猪肉或鸡肉。

翻译：_____

_____

2. 原文：很多饭店都有一个开放式的厨房，你可以在那里看到厨师们做食物，但我从来没有站在那里看他们做很长时间。我想首先要把圆面团铺平在桌子上，然后把肉或蔬菜放进去，旋转它，把它合起来。

翻译：_____

_____

■ // 口语练习 //

掌握了与传统食物的外形、口感、制作及烹饪方法有关的表达之后，接下来就需要将这些内容综合起来，试着用它们来回答口语题目。

◎ 口语例题

> Describe a traditional product in your country.
> You should say:
>   what it is
>   when you tried this product for the first time
>   what it is made of
> and explain how you feel about it.

◎ 题目分析

题目是让你介绍一种你们国家的传统产品，选择食物、用品、饰物或者衣物来回答均可。这里不妨选择小笼包作为主题，它是江南地区很有代表性的食物。在回答过程中，你需要对小笼包进行一个整体的介绍，比如外形和口味，还需要重点介绍小笼包的制作过程和第一次吃小笼包的经历，最后需要描述一下吃小笼包的感受。

◎ 回答问题

你已经了解了题目的要求，也掌握了一定数量的英文单词和表达，接下来就请用两分钟的时间来回答这道题吧。

◎ 回答范文

扫码听音频

If you were to ask me to describe a traditional product in my country, the first one that comes to my mind is Xiao Long Bao.

Xiao Long Bao is basically like a small soup dumpling. It's a kind of very thin, soft, steamed bun and generally there's some soup inside as well as meat—sometimes it could be like, crab, or pork, or chicken, so it definitely varies what's inside the Xiao Long Bao, but generally it's meat. And the way you make it is that you steam it in some kind of basket. And then usually when people order the food, it's like eight at a time, because they're very small. And, they're usually made in dim-sum restaurants or in restaurants that serve cuisine from the Jiang Nan region, like around Shanghai.

I can't recall exactly when I tried it for the first time, but that was when I was a child. And I ate that all my life.

As for how I feel about it, well, I really like it. I think that Xiao Long Bao is mouth-watering. It's salty, has a unique flavour, and has a soft texture. And I also love how it contains both meat and soup together, which is a really satisfying combination that makes it an enjoyable and fun food to eat. Usually you dip it in a sauce, like vinegar, but you can also just eat it without any sauce. So yeah, Xiao Long Bao is a really popular dish in China. Plus, it's usually not very expensive, which means you can eat it quite often.

◎ 范文解析

该范文是围绕小笼包这一传统食物展开的。首先对小笼包进行整体介绍，包括外形、口感、制作方法和烹饪方式。至于第一次吃是什么时候，如果有很清晰的记忆（比如在某个早上在餐厅和朋友或家人一起吃的，餐厅服务很好），那么自然可以进行描述，但如果没有很清晰的记忆，则可以选择粗略地一句话带过。最后，需要谈一下对小笼包这种传统食物的感受。由于对美食的感受都比较接近，所以很多内容都是通用的，比如吃东西的时候很愉悦、食物很对味、食物很特别等。

◎ 表达积累

我们从范文中为考生总结了一些有用的表达，这些表达不仅可以用于描述小笼包，还可以用于描述其他食物。

serve cuisine from	提供……的食物
I ate that all my life	我这辈子基本上都在吃它
mouth-watering	美味的
salty	咸的
has a unique flavour	味道独特
a really satisfying combination that makes it an enjoyable and fun food to eat	这是一个非常令人满意的组合，使它成为一种令人愉悦的和有趣的食物
a really popular dish in China	在中国很受欢迎的一道菜

■ // 拓展练习 //

根据所掌握的英语词汇及表达，模拟范文，回答以下题目。

Describe a popular product (e.g. food, handicraft...) made in your region.
You should say:

　　what it is

　　what it is like

　　how it is made

and explain why it is popular.

■ // 翻译练习参考答案及拓展练习范文 //

◎ 描述一种传统食物的句子翻译练习参考答案

1. Xiao Long Bao is a kind of very thin, soft, steamed bun and generally there's some soup inside as well as meat—sometimes it could be like, crab, or pork, or chicken.

2. Lots of the shops have an open kitchen where you can watch the chefs make the food, but I've never really stood around to watch them make it for a long time. I imagine that it has to start with having the bun flat on a table, and then they probably put the meat or vegetables inside and spin it to close it up.

◎ 拓展练习范文

My area is pretty famous for a type of food call Xiao Long Bao. It's a kind of very thin, soft, steamed bun, and it often has something inside like meat or vegetables. It's really popular in my city. If you walk down just about any street, you'll probably see lots of shops that sell it.

One of the questions wants me to explain how to make it, and I have to be honest and say that I'm not a hundred percent sure. Lots of the shops have an open kitchen where you can watch the chefs make the food, but I've never really stood around to watch them make it for a long time. I imagine that it has to start with having the bun flat on a table, and then they probably put the meat or vegetables inside and spin it to close it up. All this probably needs to be done quickly while it is still hot so that they can create the right shape.

But about the other question, it's pretty easy to explain why it's popular. It's really mouth-watering! But I guess it's more than that because there's a lot of delicious food, right? So, I guess it's popular because, aside from tasting good, it is also usually quite cheap. It's something everyone can enjoy. Personally, I also think it's just an amazing food to eat. It has various layers, and it's warm and really nice.

话题 7 AN EXCITING BOOK（令人激动的书籍）

　　书籍是贯穿我们幼儿时期、学生时期、工作甚至退休时期的一种重要物品。每个年龄阶段都需要阅读，阅读是一种娱乐休闲、精神慰藉，也是获取知识的重要渠道。书籍的内容可以是知识性的、娱乐性的、需要开动想象力的，也可以是纪实的、科幻的、爱情的。此外，如果是小说，书里的内容还可以被改编成戏剧、电视剧或电影。总之，书籍类的话题在雅思口语考试中十分重要，出题频率很高，掌握与书籍有关的表达和素材对于回答相关口语题目有很大的帮助。

　　首先，我们来看看有哪些话题与书籍有关：

Describe a book you read that you found useful.

Describe a film that made you laugh.

Describe a TV program you liked when you were little.

Describe a TV program you like.

Describe a memorable story told by someone.

Describe a movie that you would like to share with your friends.

Describe a time when you needed to use your imagination.

　　阅读以上题目，以书籍为切入点不仅可以回答与书籍有关的题目，还可以回答与电影、电视节目、故事、想象力有关的题目，因为很多小说都会被改编成电影、电视剧，并且阅读小说和创作小说本身也需要丰富的想象力。

■ // 书籍分类与背景知识 //

　　在学习如何描述一本小说之前，先来学习一些与小说有关的背景知识。为了方便介绍，这里以四大名著之一的《西游记》为例。

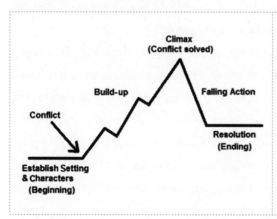

　　小说的英文是"novel"，在字典里的解释是"A novel deals imaginatively with human experience, usually through a connected series of events involving a group of people in a specific setting"，即"小说以富有想象力的方式处理人类的经验，通常通过一系列相关的事件，涉及在一个特定的背景下的一群人"。换句话说，组成小说的元素有情节、人物与场景环境。一本小说最重要的元素就是情节(plot)，情节包含：Beginning（开始/背景交代），Conflict（冲突），Build-up（故事情节逐步发展），Climax（高潮），Falling Action（解答疑问、整理线索、引导解决），Ending（结束/结果）。

小说《西游记》有许多的重要情节，比如"三打白骨精"

除了情节，人物（Character）和场景环境（Scene or Setting）也是小说的重要组成部分。同样以《西游记》为例，唐僧、孙悟空、沙僧、猪八戒和花果山分别是非常关键的人物及场景环境

▌// 介绍一本书 //

在了解了与小说相关的背景知识之后，我们以中国四大名著之一的《西游记》为例讲解如何有效地介绍一本小说。西游记的故事情节跌宕起伏、寓意深刻，人物鲜活，场景设定也非常别致，读起来让人兴奋激动。

首先，我们来了解《西游记》的故事大纲怎样用英文表达。

Journey to the West is a Chinese novel published in the 16th century during the Ming Dynasty. It is regarded as one of the Four Great Classical Novels of Chinese literature, and has been described as arguably the most popular literary work in East Asia.

The novel is based on the legendary pilgrimage of the Tang Dynasty Buddhist monk Xuanzang, who travelled to Central Asia and India to obtain Buddhist sacred texts and returned after many trials and much suffering. The monk is referred to as Tang Sanzang in the novel. The novel retains the broad outline of Xuanzang's own account, *Great Tang Records on the Western Regions*, but adds elements from folk tales and the author's invention: Gautama Buddha gives this task to the monk and provides him with three protectors who agree to help him as an atonement for their sins. These disciples are Sun Wukong, Zhu Bajie, and Sha Wujing, together with a dragon prince who acts as Tang Sanzang's steed, a white horse. The group of pilgrims journeys towards enlightenment by the power and virtue of cooperation.

以上关于《西游记》的英文简介只作背景知识参考，以下表格中涉及的内容才是口语回答中需要完整掌握的表达和素材。

中文奇幻小说	a Chinese fantasy
被认为是经典	is considered a classic
唐朝	Tang Dynasty
（佛教）僧侣	(Buddhist) monk
一群徒弟，包括孙悟空	a group of disciples, including Monkey King
淘气和叛逆的行为（孙悟空的特质）	mischievous and rebellious behaviour
傲慢自大的、骄傲的（孙悟空的特质）	arrogant, prideful
有意思的、搞笑的、笨拙的（其他两个徒弟）	interesting, funny, clumsy
获得一些重要的佛教卷轴（真经）	get some important Buddhist scrolls
冒险	adventure
克服了许多困难 / 障碍	overcome many dangers/obstacles
与很多恶魔作斗争	fight lots of demons
打败了很多敌人	defeat many enemies
以智取胜	outsmart their enemies
在旅途中幸存下来并到达终点	survive the journey and arrive at/reach their destination

在掌握了这些与描述小说有关的表达之后，我们来完成句子翻译练习。

1. 原文：这是一本非常有名的中国奇幻小说。它被认为是一部经典，多年来被改编成不同的电影和电视剧。

翻译：_____

_____

2. 原文：总的来说，有很多动作场面和戏剧性的高潮。我也喜欢那些有趣的主角。

翻译：_____

_____

3. 原文：故事讲的是一个僧侣为了得到一些重要的佛经而长途跋涉。为了做到这一点，他和一群徒弟一起旅行，其中包括孙悟空、猪八戒和沙僧。在他们的旅程中，他们在激烈的战斗中打败了许多敌人，或者以智取胜。最后，这群人在旅途中活了下来，到达了目的地。

翻译：_____

_____

■ // 口语练习 //

掌握了与介绍一本书有关的表达之后，接下来就需要将这些内容综合起来，试着用它们来回答口语题目。

◎ 口语例题

Describe a movie that you would like to share with your friends.

You should say:

    when / where you watched it

    what it was about

    who you watched it with

and why you want to share it with friends.

◎ 题目分析

题目要求描述一部你愿意与朋友分享的电影。你可以介绍一部由热门漫画改编的电影，也可以介绍一部由小说改编的电影。由于小说和电影、电视剧可以共享相当多的表达，所以准备一个关于小说的介绍，不仅可以用于与小说有关的题目，还可以用于与电视剧、电影等有关的题目。

◎ 回答问题

你已经了解了题目的要求，也掌握了一定数量的英文单词和表达，接下来就请用两分钟的时间来回答这道题吧。

◎ 回答范文

I'm going to describe a movie that I like to share with my friends, which is *Journey to the West*.

I watched the movie a few years ago with my family over the weekend when we had nothing to do. We watched it at a movie theatre near the city centre, which is not too far from my house. It usually takes us about twenty minutes to walk there, but we were feeling lazy that day so we just took the subway.

Anyway, the movie is based on a Chinese classic novel that's very famous, and it's been adapted into different movies and TV shows over the years. The story is about a monk who has to go on a long journey in order to get these Buddhist scrolls. To do that, he travels with a group of disciples, which includes the Monkey King, a pig, and a river demon. Throughout their journey, they defeat many enemies in exciting battles, or they outsmart them. In the end, the group survives the journey and reaches their destination.

I really enjoyed the movie because it has a good build-up, followed by an exciting climax and a satisfying resolution. I also enjoyed the group of interesting and funny characters like the Monkey King, who often made me laugh with his mischievous and rebellious behaviour. But even though the movie had funny and exciting moments, it also taught me some things. The

Monkey King was very arrogant and prideful at first, but by the end of the story he had learned to be more humble. That's a useful message because it shows that it's never too late to change and become a better person.

◎ 范文解析

该范文首先提到要推荐的电影的名字是《西游记》，由《西游记》改编的电影有很多不同的名字，但在口语回答中没有必要说得那么详细。随后提到是在何时何地和谁一起看的，这一段的语言组织相对简单，以地点为例，可以借鉴描述餐馆、咖啡馆等的相关表达。接下来是回答的重点，关于电影的主要内容，可以使用描述小说时用到的表达和素材。最后，谈到为何喜欢这部电影的时候也同样可以使用这些表达和素材，比如电影情节跌宕起伏、人物设定有趣且有教育意义等。

总而言之，灵活运用所学的表达是将与描述小说有关的表达运用到讲述电影的题目中去的关键。除此之外，因为创作小说或者阅读小说都需要运用想象力，所以当题目与想象力有关时，也可以使用这个话题的部分表达。

◎ 表达积累

我们从范文中为考生总结了一些有用的句子，这些内容不仅可以用于描述《西游记》，还可以用于描述其他小说，也可以用于描述电影、电视剧。

(The movie) is based on a Chinese classic novel that's very famous.	这部电影是根据一部非常著名的中国经典小说改编的。
It's been adapted into different movies and TV shows over the years.	多年以来，它被改编成不同的电影和电视剧。
It has a good build-up, followed by an exciting climax and a satisfying resolution.	它有一个很好的铺垫，接着是一个令人兴奋的高潮和一个令人满意的结局。
I also enjoyed the group of interesting and funny characters like...	我也很喜欢那群有趣的角色，比如……
It shows that it's never too late to change and become a better person.	它告诉我们，（只要想）改变自己并成为一个更好的人，永远都不晚。

■ // 拓展练习 //

根据所掌握的英语词汇及表达，模拟范文，回答以下题目。

Describe a time when you needed to use your imagination.

You should say:

when it was

why you needed to use imagination

how difficult or easy it was

and explain how you felt about it

■ // **翻译练习参考答案及拓展练习范文** //

◎ **介绍一本书的句子翻译练习参考答案**

1. It's a Chinese fantasy novel that's very famous. It's considered a classic, and it has been adapted into different movies and TV shows over the years.

2. In general, there's a lot of action and a dramatic climax. I also liked that the main characters were interesting and funny.

3. The story is about a monk who has to go on a long journey in order to get some important Buddhist scrolls. To do that, he travels with a group of disciples, which includes the Monkey King, a pig, and a river demon. Throughout their journey, they defeat many enemies in exciting battles, or they outsmart them. In the end, the group survives the journey and reaches their destination.

◎ **拓展练习范文**

A time when I needed to use my imagination was when I had to write a story for one of my classes.

I needed to use my imagination because it was a solo assignment, meaning I couldn't ask my teacher or my friends for ideas. I had to come up with everything myself.

At first, it was quite hard, because I hadn't written a story in a long time. Also, I couldn't really think of anything to write about. In order to draw inspiration, I thought back to one of my favourite stories when I was a kid, which is about a monk who has to go on a long journey to get these Buddhist scrolls. To do that, he travels with a group of disciples, which includes the Monkey King, a pig, and a river demon. Throughout their journey, they defeat many enemies in exciting battles, or they outsmart them. In the end, the group survives the journey and reaches their destination. After thinking back to this story, I decided to include some things I liked about it in my own story. So, I ended up writing an adventure story that has a good build-up, followed by an exciting climax and a satisfying resolution. I also included a group of interesting and funny characters like the Monkey King, who often made me laugh with his mischievous and rebellious behaviour.

I enjoyed writing the story because it was fun to create the different settings and characters, even though—like I said—it was hard to think of the story at first. And, of course, it gave me a sense of accomplishment.

 话题 8 A FAMOUS BUSINESS PERSON（商界名人）

说起名人，可以是体育明星、文娱明星，也可以是商界名人和社会名人。商界名人是比较有特色的一类人群，他们的特征、成就和影响力与文体明星不同，并且与其关联的题目所涉及的范围也很广泛。

首先，我们来看看有哪些话题与"商界名人"有关：

Describe a businessman you admire.

Describe a person who has interesting ideas or opinions.

Describe a book you read that you found useful.

Describe an interesting person from another country.

Describe a foreign person who you have heard of or known that you think is interesting.

Describe a famous person you are interested in.

Describe a person in the news who you want to meet.

Describe a popular person.

Describe a foreign celebrity you want to meet.

浏览以上题目，可以发现"商界名人"这个话题可以应用到各种不同类别的题目中。比如在回答一个你想见的名人时，可以介绍本国的商界名人或国外的商界名人；再比如在描述一本有用的书时，可以介绍某位 CEO 写的创业和管理类书籍。

// 描述"知名" //

对于商界名人，首先要学会使用不同的表达来描述他 / 她很知名。请看以下表格中罗列的英文表达，描述知名除了直接说"他 / 她很有名"，还可以用其他方式。

	家喻户晓的名字	a household name
有名的人	每个人都知道他 / 她是谁	everyone knows who he/she is
	善于推销自己	is good at promoting himself/herself
	在社交媒体上有很多粉丝	has many fans on social media
	经常出现在新闻、媒体和电视节目中	often in the news, media and TV shows
	参加很多重要的会议和活动	attends a lot of important conferences and events

在掌握了这些与"知名"有关的表达之后，我们来完成句子翻译练习。

1. 原文：我知道他 / 她，因为大多数中国人都知道他 / 她——他 / 她基本上是家喻户晓的名字。

翻译：_____

_____

2. 原文：他 / 她出名是因为他 / 她所有的商业成就。

翻译：_____

_____

3. 原文：他 / 她经常出现在新闻、媒体和电视节目中，他 / 她很擅长推销自己。

翻译：_____

_____

■ // 描述性格特征 //

作为商界名人，他们的性格特征往往独树一帜，有着不同于常人的精力、耐力和自信。请看以下表格中的图片及与之匹配的英文表达，这些都是成功商业人士的常见性格特征。

- 有信心的
  confident

- 有魅力的
  charismatic

- 敏锐的头脑
  sharp mind

- 有一个清晰的愿景
  has a clear vision

- 着眼于大局
  sees the big picture

- 着眼于长远
  focuses on the long term

- 发愤图强的，有动力的
  driven

- 专注的
  is focused

・热情的，激情的
　passionate

・精力充沛的
　energetic

・非常活跃的人
　a very active person

・坚持不懈的
　persistent

・坚韧不拔的人
　a tough person

・克服各种苦难
　overcomes many challenges

在掌握了这些与商界名人性格特征有关的表达之后，我们来完成句子翻译练习。

1. 原文：他是一个非常活跃的人，总是忙于一些事情。显然他有一个非常敏锐的头脑，他非常专注，很有动力，有一个明确的长期愿景，这就是他如此成功的原因。

翻译：_____

_____

2. 原文：我很钦佩她，因为我认为她是一个非常坚强的人。她克服了许多挑战，把 ABC 公司从一个小公司发展到今天的大公司。这说明她非常勤奋，有动力，而且聪明。她能够着眼于长远，看到大局。

翻译：_____

_____

▰▰ // 成就与贡献 //

对于商界名人，肯定需要描述他 / 她在商业上的成就及对社会的贡献，由于这部分的内容因人而异，所以考生需要在平时准备一些自己欣赏的企业家的档案资料。下面以一位企业家为例，展示如何描述商界名人的成就与贡献。

请看以下这段关于董明珠的工作与成就的描述，根据括号里的中文完成翻译。

As for what kind of business she does, as I mentioned, she's the ＿＿＿＿（董事长）of Gree Electric（格力电器），which is a company that started by making air conditioning machines. Then, ＿＿＿＿＿＿＿＿＿＿＿＿＿＿＿＿＿＿＿＿＿＿（它扩展到做各种各样的事情），like household appliances. These days, the company is also ＿＿＿＿＿＿＿＿＿＿＿＿＿＿＿（涉足了其他行业），but I can't really remember them all. As the chairman, ＿＿＿＿＿＿＿＿＿＿＿＿＿＿＿＿＿＿＿＿＿＿ ＿＿＿＿＿＿＿（她处理所有的业务运作和长期规划）. Basically, ＿＿＿＿＿＿＿＿＿＿＿＿＿＿＿＿＿＿ ＿＿＿＿＿＿＿＿（她监督着公司的一切）.

She's a very tough person. When she was young, she had to raise a child on her own, and, you know, as a woman, it wasn't as easy to be successful back then. Yet, ＿＿＿＿＿＿＿＿＿＿ ＿＿＿＿＿＿＿＿＿＿＿＿＿＿＿＿＿＿＿＿＿＿＿＿＿＿＿＿＿＿＿（她 克 服了这些挑战，将格力电器从一个小公司发展成为今天的大公司）. It shows that she's extremely hard-working, driven and smart. She's able to focus on the long term and see the big picture. And, finally, from what I know, ＿＿＿＿＿＿＿＿＿＿＿＿＿＿＿＿＿＿＿＿＿＿（她还向慈善机构 捐款），so she seems like a good person who cares about other people.

■ // 口语练习 //

掌握了与商界名人有关的表达之后，接下来就需要将这些内容综合起来，试着用它们来回答口语题目。

◎ 口语例题

Describe a businessman you admire.
You should say:
　　who this person is
　　how you knew about this person
　　what kinds of business this person does
and explain why you admire this person.

◎ 题目分析

关于钦佩的企业家，你心中的答案可能不止一个，他们或引领科技进步，改变人们的生活方式；或服务民生，为社会提供非常多的工作岗位；或带领企业勇于突破，取得骄人的成绩；或热衷于慈善事业和环保事业，诠释责任与担当。这里选择了比较有代表性的女性企业家董明珠，她不仅带领公司不断前行，而且关注慈善，是企业家与杰出女性的代表。

◎ 回答问题

你已经了解了题目的要求，也掌握了一定数量的英文单词和表达，接下来就请用两分钟的时间来回答这道题吧。

◎ 回答范文

So, a businessperson that I admire is Dong Ming Zhu. She is the chairman of Gree Electric, which is a well-known Chinese company.

I know about her because, well, most people in China know about her—she's basically a household name. She's famous because of all her business achievements. Also, she appears quite often in the news, media and TV shows, and she's good at promoting herself.

As for what kind of business she does, as I mentioned, she's the chairman of Gree Electric, which is a company that started by making air conditioning machines. Then, it expanded to doing all sorts of things, like household appliances. These days, the company is also involved in other industries, but I can't really remember them all. As the chairman, she handles all the business operations and long-term planning. Basically, she oversees everything about the company.

Anyway, I admire her a lot because I think she's a very tough person. When she was young, she had to raise a child on her own, and, you know, as a woman, it wasn't as easy to be successful back then. Yet, she overcame these challenges and was able to build Gree Electric from a small business to the huge company that it is today. It shows that she's extremely hard-working, driven and smart. She's able to focus on the long term and see the big picture. And, finally, from what I know, she also donates to charity, so she seems like a good person who cares about other people.

◎ 范文解析

该范文首先对董明珠这一人物进行了整体介绍，她是格力电器股份有限公司的董事长。随后介绍了她在中国的知名度，比如她经常出现在一些电视节目或者广告里。

作为企业家，她的公司业务不仅有空调，还涉及其他各类家电。值得一提的是，在谈到企业家的工作和公司时，如果考生能很清楚地记住具体内容，则可以随便挑选自己熟悉的内容来说，但如果记得不是很清楚，则可以使用类似"I can't really remember them all"的表达。

最后一部分是对董明珠这个人物的性格及一些社会贡献进行描述。作为成功的女性企业家，她必然有着一些突出的性格特点，比如"tough""overcame challenges""extremely hard-working"和"driven and smart"。这些表述本书在之前的部分已经介绍过，它们的使用范围非常广泛，不限于描述企业家，对于任何做事取得成功的人都可以使用这些表达来描述。

◎ 表达积累

我们从范文中为考生总结了一些有用的表达，这些内容不仅可以用于描述董明珠，还可以用于描述其他商界名人。

the chairman of...	某公司的总裁
a household name	家喻户晓的名字
business achievements	商业成就
good at promoting herself	善于推销自己
it expanded to doing all sorts of things	它扩展到做各种各样的事情
the company is also involved in other industries	该公司还涉足其他行业
handles all the business operations and long-term planning	处理所有业务运作和长期规划
oversees everything about the company	监督公司的一切
a very tough person	一个非常坚强的人
overcame these challenges	克服了这些挑战
extremely hard-working, driven and smart	非常勤奋，有上进心和聪明
focus on the long term and see the big picture	着眼于长远，看大局
donates to charity	向慈善机构捐款
cares about other people	关心他人

■ // 拓展练习 //

根据所掌握的英语词汇及表达，模拟范文，回答以下题目。

Describe a foreign person who you have heard of or known that you think is interesting.

You should say:

who the person is

how you knew him/her

what kind of person he/she is

and explain why you think he/she is interesting.

■ // 翻译练习参考答案及拓展练习范文 //

◎ 描述"知名"句子翻译练习参考答案

1. I know about him/her because, well, most people in China know about him/her—he's/she's basically a household name.

2. He's/She's famous because of all his/her business achievements.

3. He/She appears quite often in the news, media and TV shows, and he's/she's good at promoting himself/herself.

◎ 描述性格特征句子翻译练习参考答案

1. He's a very active person. He's always busy with something, and he obviously has a very sharp mind and he's very focused and driven, with a clear vision for the long term, which is why he's so successful.

2. I admire her a lot because I think she's a very tough person. She overcame many challenges and was able to build ABC company from a small business to the huge company that it is today. It shows that she's extremely hard-working, driven and smart. She's able to focus on the long term and see the big picture.

◎ 成就与贡献句子翻译练习参考答案

As for what kind of business she does, as I mentioned, she's the chairman of Gree Electric, which is a company that started by making air conditioning machines. Then, it expanded to doing all sorts of things, like household appliances. These days, the company is also involved in other industries, but I can't really remember them all. As the chairman, she handles all the business operations and long-term planning. Basically, she oversees everything about the company.

She's a very tough person. When she was young, she had to raise a child on her own, and, you know, as a woman, it wasn't as easy to be successful back then. Yet, she overcame these challenges and was able to build Gree Electric from a small business to the huge company that it is today. It shows that she's extremely hard-working, driven and smart. She's able to focus on the long-term and see the big picture. And, finally, from what I know, she also donates to charity, so she seems like a good person who cares about other people.

◎ 拓展练习范文

A foreign person I've heard of who I think is interesting is Mark Zuckerberg. He's a famous businessman, who's known for creating the social media website Facebook. He's one of the richest people in the world, and he's a huge celebrity because he's popular and has many fans on social media.

I know about Zuckerberg because, like I said, he's very famous, so everyone knows who he is. He's basically a household name and is often in the news and social media. He travels a lot and attends many important conferences and events, and his company is involved with many different businesses and industries, so I'm always hearing about him.

As for what kind of person he is, um, he's hard-working, driven and smart. He's able to focus on the long term and see the big picture, which is why he was able to build Facebook from a small business to the huge company that it is today. And, from what I know, he also donates a lot to charity, so he seems like a good person.

Regarding why I think he's interesting, well, it's mostly because he's a modern day genius with lots of unique ideas. For example, he's trying to make virtual reality a bigger thing, and he's doing this by building a virtual world where users can work, play games, and interact with each other using VR headsets. I think that these ideas are interesting because they're ahead of their time and they push human society forward. At the same time, his ideas drive competition and have led to breakthroughs in science and technology.

话题 9　AN OLDER PERSON YOU KNOW（你认识的一位长者）

与人物有关的话题，除了与名人有关的，还有与身边人有关的，题目可以涉及父母、长辈、兄弟姐妹、朋友、同学等。其中与父母、长辈（长者）有关的话题经常出现。

首先来看看有哪些话题与"长者"有关：

Describe a family member you spend the most time with.

Describe a good parent you know.

Describe a person who helped and encouraged you.

Describe a person who often helps others.

Describe a person who taught you a skill when you were a child.

Describe a person who taught you knowledge.

Describe a person who you are happy to know.

Describe a person you know who knows a lot about something.

Describe a person you wanted to be similar to when you were growing up.

Describe an intelligent person you know.

Describe an interesting neighbour you have/had.

Describe an old person who is interesting.

Describe an old person you know and respect.

Describe someone who is older than you that you admire.

Describe someone who is talkative.

阅读这些题目，不难发现除了直接提到长辈的题目，还有一些题目是关于帮助过你或者教过你的人，或者是一个你敬佩和仰慕的人，这些题目可以使用与名人有关的素材来回答，也可以使用与"长者"有关的素材来回答。

// 陪伴与榜样 //

如果要描述一个人，首先需要准备一些描述人的形容词。通常来说，回答时都会使用一些积极向上的词汇，部分词汇在运动员和商界名人话题中已经介绍过，比如"focused""driven""confident""charismatic"。考生还可以根据所需描述的对象准备一些词汇，比如对于长者，常会说他 / 她很会关心人（caring）、很善良和蔼（kind）等。此外，长辈们往往会陪伴自己成长，很多人的童年都是与外公外婆、爷爷奶奶一起度过的，他们会接送你放学、为你准备可口的食物、陪你去公园和儿童乐园等。当他们老了之后，你也会在节假日或者周末去看望他们，陪他们聊天或者带他们出去玩。很多时候，外公外婆、爷爷奶奶也是你生活和工作的榜样，他们的行为也会深深地影响你。接下来，将学习描述这部分内容的表达。

请看以下列出的与长者有关的图片及相关英文表达。

日常生活及一起参与的活动

- 讲过去的故事
  tell the stories of the past
- 一起看电视
  watch TV together
- 一起玩游戏
  play games together
- 公园散步
  take walks at the park

值得学习的优点

- 善良及关心他人
  kind and caring
- 照顾家人
  take care of family
- 帮助他人
  help other people
- 先人后己
  put others before herself/himself

在掌握了这些与长者有关的表达之后，我们来完成句子翻译练习。

1. 原文：我的（外）祖母很健谈，喜欢给我讲过去的故事，这很有趣，因为这就像听到了一个不同的世界。

翻译：_____

_____

2. 原文：我的（外）祖母年轻时很有动力、很专注，所以她在学校表现很好，事业也很成功。

翻译：_____

_____

3. 原文：我的（外）祖母现在仍然有非常敏锐的头脑，她给了我很多很好的建议，比如努力工作和为未来做准备是多么重要。

翻译：_____

_____

4. 原文：我的（外）祖母也教育我照顾好自己身体的重要性，应有足够的睡眠和锻炼，以及健康饮食。

翻译：_____

_____

5. 原文：我的（外）祖母天生就是一个非常善良和关心他人的人，她总是先人后己。

翻译：_____

_____

■ // 口语练习 //

掌握了与长者有关的表达之后，接下来就需要将这些内容综合起来，试着用它们来回答口语题目。

◎ 口语例题

Describe someone who is older than you that you admire.

You should say:

    who this person is

    how you knew this person

    what kind of things you like to do together

and explain how you feel about this person.

◎ 题目分析

题目要求描述一位你崇拜的且比你年长的人。回答这种题目时，大部分考生会想到老师、父母和（外）祖父母。你需要对这个人物的性格、职业、贡献和彼此的相处都进行一番描述。需要注意的是，这里最好不要选择名人，因为答题要点涉及"things you like to do together"，所以还是选择熟悉和亲近的人比较好。

◎ 回答问题

你已经了解了题目的要求，也掌握了一定数量的英文单词和表达，接下来就请用两分钟的时间来回答这道题吧。

◎ 回答范文

Someone who's older than me that I admire is my grandmother. She's in her seventies and she's retired, but she's still a very active person.

As for how I know her, like I said, she's my grandmother, and she's raised me since I was a child. My grandparents live with my family, so we see each other every day.

My grandmother and I do lots of different things together. For example, we both enjoy watching TV and playing games together. Sometimes, we take walks at the park. She's quite talkative and likes to tell me stories of the past, which is interesting because it's like hearing about a different world. It's amazing how things have changed so much.

Regarding how I feel about my grandmother, well, I really admire and respect her. She was very driven and focused when she was young, so she did well in school and had a great career. She did all this while taking care of her family, which is incredible. My grandmother still has a very sharp mind these days and she's given me lots of good advice, like how it's important to work hard and prepare for the future. She's also taught me the importance of taking care of my body, getting enough sleep and exercise, and eating a healthy diet. She's even taught me how to cook some simple but healthy dishes. Beyond that, she inspires me because she's always helping other people, especially my family. For example, she often buys groceries and cooks for us and cleans the house. She does these things because she's just naturally a very kind and caring person who puts others before herself.

◎ 范文解析

该范文首先对自己的（外）祖母进行了概括性的描述，包括年龄、工作状态和最显著的性格特征。随后回答自己是怎么知道她的，显而易见，只要是家里的亲人，都可以说 "raised me since I was a child"。接下来，范文罗列了自己和她一起做的事情，比如一起看电视、听她讲过去的故事等。最后，范文用最大的篇幅描述了自己对她的感情，这其中包含了对她的尊敬和从她身上学习的东西。

◎ 表达积累

我们从范文中为考生总结了一些有用的表达，这些表达不仅可以用于描述（外）祖母，还可以用于描述其他长辈。

in her seventies	她 70 多岁
retired	退休的
a very active person	一个非常活跃的人
she's raised me since I was a child	她从小把我养大
live with my family	和我家人住在一起
do lots of different things together	一起做很多不同的事情
talkative	健谈
tell me stories of the past	给我讲过去的故事

续表

driven and focused	上进和专注
take care of her family	照顾好她的家人
have a very sharp mind	有非常敏锐的头脑
give me lots of good advice	给我很多好的建议
teach me the importance of taking care of my body	教育我照顾好自己身体的重要性
inspire me	激励我
help other people	帮助别人

// 拓展练习 //

根据所掌握的英语词汇及表达，模拟范文，回答以下题目。

Describe someone you really like to spend time with.

You should say:

who this person is

how you knew him/her

what you usually do together

and explain why you like to spend time with him/her.

// 翻译练习参考答案及拓展练习范文 //

◎ 陪伴与榜样句子翻译参考答案

1. My grandmother is quite talkative and likes to tell me stories of the past, which is interesting because it's like hearing about a different world.

2. My grandmother was very driven and focused when she was young, so she did well in school and had a great career.

3. My grandmother still has a very sharp mind these days and she's given me lots of good advice, like how it's important to work hard and prepare for the future.

4. My grandmother has also taught me the importance of taking care of my body, getting enough sleep and exercise, and eating a healthy diet.

5. My grandmother is just naturally a very kind and caring person who puts others before herself.

◎ 拓展练习范文

Someone who I really like to spend time with is my grandmother. She's in her seventies and she's retired, but she's still a very active person.

As for how I know her, like I said, she's my grandmother, and she's raised me since I was a child. My grandmother lives with my family, so I see her every day.

My grandmother and I do lots of different things together. For example, we both enjoy watching TV and playing games together. Sometimes, we take walks at the park. She's quite talkative and likes to tell me stories of the past, which is interesting because it's like hearing about a different world.

As for why I enjoy her company, well, first of all, she's fun to be around. As I said, we do lots of different things together. We also have silly conversations, and we joke around with each other all the time. She doesn't take herself too seriously, and knows how to have fun. However, at the same time, we're also able to have deeper, more serious conversations. And we're able to do that because my grandmother is a great listener. For example, she never interrupts when I speak and she isn't judgmental at all. At the same time, she is quite honest if I ask her for advice, which means that I'm able to trust her and share my troubles and worries with her. All in all, I really value the time I spend with her. She's someone I respect and admire a lot because she's naturally a very kind and caring person who puts others before herself.

话题 10 A LIBRARY（图书馆）

细数城市里的建筑，图书馆往往是极具特色的，有些图书馆是由历史保护建筑改建而成的，有些则是当代建筑大师的杰出作品。每个人都有在图书馆里看书的经历，因为那是一个非常安静、适合学习、适合思考、适合保持清醒的地方。

首先，我们来看看有哪些话题与"图书馆"有关：

Describe a quiet place you like to spend your time in.

Describe a part of a city or town you enjoy spending time in.

Describe a place where you are able to relax.

Describe a public building you enjoyed visiting.

Describe a crowded place you went to.

Describe a place (not your home) where you read and write.

Describe a historical building you have seen and want to learn more.

Describe a new public place you would like to visit.

Describe a newly built public facility (such as parks, cinemas, etc.) that influences your city.

Describe a place in your city or town that you like to visit with your friends.

Describe a new development (such as new roads, shopping centres) that appeared in your town or city.

Describe an indoor or outdoor place where it was easy for you to study.

Describe a public place that you think needs improvements.

Describe a building you like.

Describe a place where you often visit with your friends or family.

通过这些题目，不难发现图书馆这个话题既可以与城市的建筑物有关，也可以与一个安静的学习地点有关，还可以与你喜欢或者不喜欢的一栋建筑物有关。

// 外观与设施 //

要描述图书馆，首先需要知道怎么介绍其外观和设施。在介绍的先后顺序上，一般选择由外及里的顺序，如它的外观非常现代、它是一栋历史文化保护建筑，随后再说一下这个图书馆有什么特别的地方。考生可以想象自己走进一座图书馆，它的整体设计很精美，有很多楼层和空间，有明亮的窗户，馆内还装饰着漂亮的绘画和雕塑。

请看以下与外观和设施有关的图片及相关英文表达。

· 有趣的建筑和设计
　　interesting architecture and design
· 有几个楼层且空间很大
　　there are several floors and a lot of space
· 明亮的照明 / 灯光很亮
　　bright lighting/the lighting is bright
· 到处都是有趣的雕塑和绘画
　　there are interesting sculptures and paintings everywhere

在掌握了这些与外观和设施有关的表达之后，我们来完成句子翻译练习。

原文：当你走向图书馆时，你首先注意到的是它有趣的建筑和设计。当你走进去的时候，你会发现有几个楼层，空间很大。灯光明亮，到处都是有趣的雕塑和绘画。

翻译：＿＿＿＿＿＿＿＿＿＿＿＿＿＿＿＿＿＿＿＿＿＿＿＿＿＿＿＿＿＿＿＿＿＿＿＿＿＿

＿＿＿

// 适合读书学习 //

图书馆因其安静、馆藏书籍多、空间宽敞明亮，成为最佳的学习地点之一。无论是学校的图书馆还是社区、城市的图书馆，总能见到人们埋头学习的身影。

请看以下罗列的与"图书馆适合读书学习"有关的图片及相关英文表达。

- 有一个良好的学习环境
  have a good study environment
- 有许多桌子和椅子
  there are lots of tables and chairs
- 不会被……分心
  don't get distracted by...
- 帮助你更好地集中注意力
  help you focus better
- 被学习的人包围会让你也想学习
  being surrounded by other people who are studying makes you want to study too

- 有各种各样的书可供外借
  there are all kinds of books available for borrowing
- 也有电脑、Wi-Fi、打印和复印设备
  there are also computers, Wi-Fi, and printing and copying equipment

在掌握了这些与"图书馆适合读书学习"有关的表达之后，我们来完成句子翻译练习。

1. 原文：我喜欢去图书馆，因为那里有很好的学习环境。那里有很多桌椅，甚至还有沙发，（环境）非常安静。你不会被电视或室友之类的事情分心，所以这有助于你更好地集中注意力。此外，周围都是学习的人，会让你也想学习。

翻译：_____

_____

2. 原文：如果你在寻找信息，有各种各样的书可以借阅，包括电子书和音频。还有电脑、无线网络、打印和复印设备。

翻译：_____

_____

▰ // 适合休闲放松 //

除了去图书馆学习，人们还经常把它当作放松心情的好去处，可以去里面阅读一些杂志、翻翻旧报纸、看看小说，甚至打个盹。现在很多展览也会在图书馆举办，所以周末也可以去图书馆看展览。很多图书馆的一楼都有咖啡店，去那里喝杯咖啡也不失为一种放松。

请看以下罗列的与"图书馆适合休闲放松"有关的图片及相关英文表达。

· 放松
　　relax
· 阅读一些杂志、报纸或者小说
　　read some magazines, newspapers or novels
· 打个盹
　　take a nap
· 去旁边的咖啡店（买杯咖啡）让自己清醒一下
　　go to a nearby coffee shop to refresh yourself

· 在图书馆里举办的展览
　　exhibitions held in the library

在掌握了这些与"图书馆适合休闲放松"有关的表达之后，我们来完成句子翻译练习。

1. 原文：当你需要休息的时候，你可以在那里放松。如果你感到无聊，你可以读一些杂志、报纸或小说。如果你觉得困了，你可以打个盹，或者去附近的咖啡店放松一下。

翻译：_____

_____

2. 原文：有时候，图书馆里甚至会举办展览，那些展览总是很有趣。

翻译：_____

_____

▰ // 口语练习 //

掌握了与图书馆的外观与设施、适合读书学习、适合休闲放松有关的表达之后，接下来就需要将这些内容综合起来，试着用它们来回答口语题目。

◎ 口语例题

Describe a quiet place you like to spend your time in.

You should say:

　　where it is

　　how you knew it

　　how often you go there

　　what you do there

and explain why you like the place.

◎ 题目分析

题目要求描述一个你喜欢的安静的地方。图书馆通常是人们第一时间会想到的主题。你需要描述这个图书馆在哪里，你是怎么知道它的，多久去一次图书馆及在里面做什么。最后，你需要解释为何会喜欢这个图书馆。

◎ 回答问题

你已经了解了题目的要求，也掌握了一定数量的英文单词和表达，接下来就请用两分钟的时间来回答这道题吧。

◎ 回答范文

A quiet place I like to spend time in is my university's library. It's located in the middle of my university, so it's in a convenient location.

And I know about the place because, well, all students know about the university library. It's an important part of the university.

I go to the library a few times a week and I mainly go there to study or relax.

I like the place because, first of all, it's beautiful. As you walk to the library, the first thing you notice is its interesting architecture and design. And when you walk in, you'll notice that there are several floors and a lot of space. The lighting is bright, and there are interesting sculptures and paintings everywhere.

I also like going to the library because it has a good study environment. There are lots of tables and chairs—even sofas—and it's very quiet. You don't get distracted by things like the TV or your roommates, so it helps you focus better. Also, being surrounded by other people who are studying makes you want to study too.

If you're looking for information, there are all kinds of books available for borrowing, including electronic books and audio. There are also computers, Wi-Fi, and printing and copying equipment.

And finally, when you need a break, you can relax there. If you're bored, you can read some magazines, newspapers or novels. If you feel sleepy, you can take a nap or go to a nearby coffee shop to refresh yourself. Oh, and sometimes, there are even exhibitions held in the library, and those are always interesting to see.

◎ 范文解析

该范文一开始介绍了图书馆的位置，即坐落在大学的中央。如果想要介绍城市里的图书馆，可以说"The library is near the city centre, about just ____ minutes from my apartment. I remember taking the subway over there."只要是描述城市里的某个地点，考生都可以使用类似的句子。对于图书馆，无论是校内的还是校外的，几乎所有人都会知道它的存在。至于去图书馆的频率，则因人而异，记住表达"___ times a week"就可以了。最后，谈及去图书馆的目的，无非就是学习和放松，只要掌握前面介绍的表达，就可以非常完美地回答这个问题了。

◎ 表达积累

我们从范文中为考生总结了一些有用的表达，这些表达可以用于描述学校的图书馆或者社会上的图书馆，稍加修改也可以用于描述一个安静的、适合学习和休闲的咖啡馆。

be located in...	位于……
in a convenient location	在一个（交通）便利的地方
a few times a week	一周几次
go there to study or relax	去那里学习或放松
the first thing you notice is its interesting architecture and design	首先你会注意到它那有趣的建筑和设计
there are several floors and a lot of space	有几个楼层，空间很大
The lighting is bright, and there are interesting sculptures and paintings everywhere.	灯光明亮，到处都是有趣的雕塑和绘画。
has a good study environment	有良好的学习环境
If you're bored, you can read some magazines, newspapers or novels.	如果你感到无聊，你可以读一些杂志、报纸或小说。

■ // 拓展练习 //

根据所掌握的英语词汇及表达，模拟范文，回答以下题目。

Describe a building you like.

You should say:

   where it is

   what it is used for

   what it looks like

and explain why you like it.

■ // 翻译练习参考答案及拓展练习范文 //

◎ 外观与设施句子翻译练习参考答案

As you walk to the library, the first thing you notice is its interesting architecture and design. And when you walk in, you'll notice that there are several floors and a lot of space. The lighting is bright, and there are interesting sculptures and paintings everywhere.

◎ 适于读书学习句子翻译练习参考答案

1. I like going to the library because it has a good study environment. There are lots of tables and chairs—even sofas—and it's very quiet. You don't get distracted by things like the TV or your roommates, so it helps you focus better. Also, being surrounded by other people who are

studying makes you want to study too.

2. If you're looking for information, there are all kinds of books available for borrowing, including electronic books and audio. There are also computers, Wi-Fi, and printing and copying equipment.

◎ **适合休闲放松句子翻译练习参考答案**

1. When you need a break, you can relax there. If you're bored, you can read some magazines, newspapers or novels. If you feel sleepy, you can take a nap or go to a nearby coffee shop to refresh yourself.

2. Sometimes, there are even exhibitions held in the library, and those are always interesting to see.

◎ **拓展练习范文**

A building I like is my university library.

It's located in the middle of my university, so it's in a convenient location. My university itself is close to the city centre.

As for what it's used for, the library is mainly a place where students can study or relax. Usually, I go there myself to study between classes or after classes.

And… what it looks like? Well, it's beautiful. As you walk to the library, the first thing you notice is its interesting architecture and design. And when you walk in, you'll notice that there are several floors and a lot of space. The lighting is bright, and there are interesting sculptures and paintings everywhere.

Besides its looks, I like going to the library because it has a good study environment. There are lots of tables and chairs—even sofas—and it's very quiet. You don't get distracted by things like the TV or your roommates, so it helps you focus better. Also, being surrounded by other people who are studying makes you want to study too.

If you're looking for information, there are all kinds of books available for borrowing, including electronic books and audio. There are also computers, Wi-Fi, and printing and copying equipment.

And finally, when you need a break, you can relax there. If you're bored, you can read some magazines, newspapers or novels. If you feel sleepy, you can take a nap or go to a nearby coffee shop to refresh yourself. Oh, and sometimes, there are even exhibitions held in the library, and those are always interesting to see.

话题 11 A SHOPPING MALL（购物中心）

在城市的各类建筑中，购物中心也是非常有特色的。有些城市将历史文化建筑改造成购物中心，更多的购物中心则代表了城市特色和当代特色。与图书馆不同，购物中心更注重其商业性和娱乐性。

首先，我们来看看有哪些话题与"购物中心"有关：

Describe a building you like.

Describe a crowded place you went to.

Describe a new development (such as new roads, shopping centres) that appeared in your town or city.

Describe a part of a city or town you enjoy spending time in.

Describe a place in your city or town that you like to visit with your friends.

Describe a place where you often visit with your friends or family.

Describe a tall building in your city you like or dislike.

这些题目有些也可以用"图书馆"话题中的相关表达来回答，所以在回答问题时，建议考生选择自己喜欢的和擅长的话题进行描述。

■ // 位置与建筑外观 //

对于购物中心的位置，考生可以参考前面"餐厅"话题中介绍过的表达。建筑的外观可以是现代风格的，也可以是古典风格的，考生可以根据自己的喜好选择一种作答，该部分表达可以参考前面"图书馆"话题中介绍过的表达。

请看以下罗列的与"购物中心的位置与建筑外观"有关的表达。

地理位置	· 位于市中心或市中心附近 　　is located in/near the city centre · 离我住的地方不远 　　not too far from where I live · 乘坐地铁或公交车 　　take the metro or bus
建筑外观	· 又高又大 　　tall and large · 新颖且现代 　　new and modern · 建筑物内部干净且采光很好 　　the inside of the building is clean and well-lit

在掌握了这些与"购物中心的位置与建筑外观"有关的表达之后，我们来完成句子翻译练习。

1. 原文：商场位于市中心附近，离我住的地方不太远，所以如果天气好的话，我有时会步行去那里。

　　翻译：_____

_____

2. 原文：一共有六层，建筑物内部干净且采光很好。

　　翻译：_____

_____

// 布局与功能 //

谈及购物中心的布局，可以按自下而上或者自上而下的顺序来进行介绍。购物中心的功能是回答的重点，要说清楚人们来到这里可以做什么。可以单独介绍它的功能，也可以结合布局一起介绍，比如谈到顶楼的布局时可以说顶楼设有电影院，人们可以在那里看电影。

请看以下罗列的与"购物中心的布局与功能"有关的图片及其相关表达。

布局

· 有有用的问询台、清晰的标志和很多电梯
　　there are helpful information desks, clear signs, and lots of elevators
· 大多数楼层都有不同的商店和饭店
　　most of the floors are filled with different stores and restaurants
· 在顶楼有一家电影院
　　there's a movie theatre on the top floor

功能

· 去购物、吃饭、看电影
　　go to shop, eat, or even watch a movie
· 如果你想吃东西，这里有很多选择
　　if you want to eat, there are many options
· 售卖各种各样的东西，如化妆品、珠宝、衣服、鞋子、电子产品，甚至还有一个超市
　　the stores sell all kinds of things, like cosmetics, jewellery, clothes, shoes, electronics, and there's even a supermarket
· 和我的朋友或家人去那里看一部新的电影
　　go there with my friends or family to watch a new movie

在掌握了这些与"购物中心的布局与功能"有关的表达之后，我们来完成句子翻译练习。

1. 原文：尽管商场相当大，但很容易找到方向，因为有有用的问询台、清晰的标志和很多电梯。

翻译：_____

_____

2. 原文：如果你想吃东西，有很多选择，包括日本菜、中餐和快餐。

翻译：_____

_____

3. 原文：除了吃，你当然也可以购物。大部分楼层都是不同的商店，出售各种各样的东西，如化妆品、珠宝、衣服、鞋子、电子产品，甚至还有一个可以买食品杂货的超市。

翻译：_____

_____

// 口语练习 //

掌握了与购物中心的位置与建筑外观、布局与功能有关的表达之后，接下来就需要将这些内容综合起来，试着用它们来回答口语题目。

◎ 口语例题

Describe a tall building in your city you like or dislike.

You should say:

　　where it is

　　what it is used for

　　what is looks like

and explain why you like or dislike it.

◎ 题目分析

题目要求描述一栋城市里你喜欢或者讨厌的高层建筑。一般来说购物中心所在的楼宇都属于高层建筑，而且谈及喜欢或者讨厌的原因也比较容易。如果想换别的主题，那么图书馆也是一个不错的选择。在确定了主题之后，考生需要在回答中谈及这个建筑的位置、外观、功能及喜欢或讨厌它的理由（这些理由往往与建筑的外观和功能有关）。

◎ 回答问题

你已经了解了题目的要求，也掌握了一定数量的英文单词和表达，接下来就请用两分钟的时间来回答这道题吧。

◎ 回答范文

A tall building in my city that I like is a shopping mall that I visit sometimes.

The mall is located near the city centre, which is not too far from where I live, so I sometimes walk there if the weather is nice. But if the weather is too hot or rainy, then I take the metro or bus instead.

Anyway, the mall is where people go to shop, eat, or even watch a movie. If you want to eat, there are many options, including Japanese food, Chinese food, and fast food. Normally, the eating area is crowded with people during lunch and dinner time, so it can be hard to find a seat. Aside from eating, you can also shop, of course. Most of the floors are filled with different stores that sell all kinds of things, like cosmetics, jewellery, clothes, shoes, electronics, and there's even a supermarket where you can buy groceries. There's also a movie theatre on the top floor. Sometimes, I go there with my friends or family to watch a new movie.

As for what the mall looks like, it's tall and large and also very new and modern. There are six floors, and the inside of the building is clean and well-lit. And even though the mall is quite big, it's easy to navigate because there are helpful information desks, clear signs, and lots of elevators.

Finally, I like the shopping mall because it's a great place for people to spend their free time. Like I said, you can do anything there, whether it's eating, shopping, or watching a movie.

◎ 范文解析

该范文首先介绍购物中心位于市中心附近，紧接着说从住的地方去那边的距离不算远，走路或坐车都可以。此处用于介绍地理位置的表达和句子是最常见的组合，配合着从住处到某地的距离可以让建筑的地理位置更清晰、更直观。随后，作者介绍了购物中心的功能和外观。从功能上说，餐馆和菜系是比较容易描述的。至于整个购物中心的设计和结构，作为当代的建筑，"new and modern""clean and well-lit"是非常通用的表述，此外就是购物中心特有的问询台"information desk"。

◎ 表达积累

我们从范文中为考生总结了一些有用的表达，这些内容可以用于描述购物中心等商业场所或建筑。

is located near the city centre	位于市中心附近
is filled with different stores	充满了不同的商店
tall and large and also very new and modern	它又高又大，也非常新颖和现代
clean and well-lit	干净明亮
there are helpful information desks, clear signs, and lots of elevators	有有用的问询台、清晰的标志和很多电梯

■ // 拓展练习 //

根据所掌握的英语词汇及表达，模拟范文，回答以下题目。

Describe a part of a city or town you enjoy spending time in.

You should say:

　　where it is

　　what it is like

　　what you do there

and explain why you enjoy spending time there.

■ // 翻译练习参考答案及拓展练习范文 //

◎ 位置与建筑外观句子翻译练习参考答案

1. The mall is located near the city centre, which is not too far from where I live, so I sometimes walk there if the weather is nice.

2. There are six floors, and the inside of the building is clean and well-lit.

◎ 布局与功能句子翻译练习参考答案

1. Even though the mall is quite big, it's easy to navigate because there are helpful information desks, clear signs, and lots of elevators.

2. If you want to eat, there are many options, including Japanese food, Chinese food, and fast food.

3. Aside from eating, you can also shop, of course. Most of the floors are filled with different stores that sell all kinds of things, like cosmetics, jewellery, clothes, shoes, electronics, and there's even a supermarket where you can buy groceries.

◎ 拓展练习范文

A part of a city I enjoy spending time in is a shopping mall that I visit sometimes.

The mall is located near the city centre, which is not too far from where I live, so I sometimes walk there if the weather is nice. But if the weather is too hot or rainy, then I take the metro or bus instead.

As for what the mall looks like, it's tall and large and also very new and modern. There are ten floors, and the inside of the building is clean and well-lit. And even though the mall is big, it's easy to navigate because there are helpful information desks, clear signs, and lots of elevators.

Anyway, I enjoy shopping, eating, or watching a movie in the shopping mall. If I want to eat, there are many options, including Japanese food, Chinese food, and fast food. Normally, the eating area is crowded with people during lunch and dinner time, so it can be hard to find a seat. Aside from eating, I can also shop, of course. Most of the floors are filled with different stores that sell all kinds of things, like cosmetics, jewellery, clothes, shoes, electronics, and there's even a supermarket where I can buy groceries. There's also a movie theatre on the top floor. Sometimes, I go there with my friends or family to watch a new movie.

Finally, I like the shopping mall because it's a great place for people to spend their free time. Like I said, I can do anything there, whether it's eating, shopping, or watching a movie.

话题 12 A JOURNEY（旅行）

旅行是生活中非常重要的一种休闲方式。与旅行有关的表达和素材，比如为什么去旅行、目的地是哪里、和谁一起、使用何种交通工具、旅行中发生了什么事情等都可以运用到其他的口语话题中去。

首先，我们来看看有哪些话题与"旅行"有关：

Describe a bicycle/motorcycle/car trip you would like to go on.

Describe a car journey you enjoyed.

Describe a journey that you went on by car.

Describe a long car journey you went on.

Describe a long walk you had.

Describe a special day that made you happy.

Describe a time when you were excited.

Describe a trip that you plan to go on in the near future.

Describe a trip that you went on by public transportation.

Describe an expensive activity that you enjoy doing occasionally.

Describe a time when the vehicle you took broke down in your travel.

Describe a time when you got bored when you were with others.

Describe something interesting your friend has done but you haven't.

Describe something you enjoyed doing with a group of people.

Describe an important journey that was delayed.

Describe an occasion when you lost your way.

Describe a time when you looked for information on the Internet.

与旅行有关的题目非常多，基本上都会涉及交通工具（bicycle/motorcycle/car trip, public transportation）、旅行内容（an expensive activity）、旅行时的感受（excited, made you happy, got bored）及旅行时遇到的问题（delayed, looked for information on the Internet）。

■ // 交通工具 //

说起旅行，人们首先会想到坐什么交通工具出行，可以自驾、坐火车、坐飞机、坐船等。选择何种交通工具往往和距离、时间、费用、旅行内容等有关。即使题目中没有提到交通工具，考生也不可避免地会在回答中提到，比如在回答"Describe a trip that you plan to go on in the near future"这一问题时就一定会说到选择何种交通工具去旅行。

针对不同的交通工具，会有不同的与优势相关的表达。请看以下与旅行中使用的交通工具有关的图片及其相关表达。

火车

· 因为更便宜、更方便，所以坐火车

   take a train because it's cheaper and more convenient
· 沿途有美丽的风景和自然风光

   there's beautiful scenery and nature along the way
· 比坐飞机便宜

   it's cheaper than a plane

飞机

· 因为更快捷，所以坐飞机

   take a plane because it's faster
· 坐飞机去海外旅行

   travel abroad by plane

在掌握了这些与"不同交通工具的优势"有关的表达之后，我们来完成句子翻译练习。

1. 原文：这个城市在我所在的城市的南面，开车大约需要 2 小时，坐火车大约需要 30 分钟。我们决定乘坐火车，因为火车更快，我们想尽快到达那里。

   翻译：_____

_____

2. 原文：我想开车去，因为沿途风景很美。

   翻译：_____

_____

■ // 旅行的内容 //

旅行的内容是此类题目的核心部分，一般来说，可分为城市观光购物、文化之旅、乡村休闲和极限运动四类。旅行的内容因人而异，差别很大，这里只给出相对简单且能够普遍运用的表达和素材。

请看以下表格中与旅行的内容有关的图片及相关表达。

	·去所有别人推荐的景点 　go to all the scenic spots that were recommended by others ·去著名的旅游景点，比如…… 　go to the famous tourist spots like... ·参观古老的寺庙和建筑 　visit ancient temples and buildings ·参观博物馆和公园 　visit museums and parks ·去百货商店购物，并在许多不同的本地餐馆吃饭 　go shopping at department stores and eat at many different local restaurants
	·远离城市 　get away from cities ·享受大自然的景色并欣赏郊外风光 　enjoy the views of nature and see the countryside ·沿途有许多树木、野花和小溪 　there are lots of trees, wild flowers, and streams along the way ·感觉非常平静和放松 　feel very peaceful and relaxing ·一次（培养）亲密关系的体验 　a good bonding experience

在掌握了这些与"旅行的内容"有关的表达之后，我们来完成句子翻译练习。

1. 原文：当我们到达这个城市时，我们去了所有别人推荐的旅游景点。例如，我们参观了古老的寺庙和建筑，以及著名的博物馆和公园。我们还去了百货商店购物，在许多不同的本地餐馆吃饭。晚上，我们回到市中心附近的酒店。

翻译：_____

_____

2. 原文：我们可以享受大自然的景色并欣赏郊外风光，这非常棒，因为我们在大城市的时间太久了。

翻译：_____

_____

■ // 口语练习 //

掌握了与旅行有关的表达之后，接下来就需要将这些内容综合起来，试着用它们来回答口语题目。

◎ 口语例题

Describe a long walk you had.

You should say:

 when this happened

 where you walked

 who you were with

and explain how you felt about this long walk.

◎ 题目分析

题目要求描述一次你走远路的经历。如果要去一个很远的地方，在没有交通工具的情况下，人们通常会选择走路，但这种经历比较难描述。再仔细分析，不难想到徒步旅行非常符合这个题目的要求，并且有丰富的内容可以回答，比如发生的时间和地点、旅途的风景和心情等。

◎ 回答问题

你已经了解了题目的要求，也掌握了一定数量的英文单词和表达，接下来就请用两分钟的时间来回答这道题吧。

◎ 回答范文

I'm going to describe a long walk I had, which was when I went hiking with my family.

This happened about a few years ago during summer. My family and I used to go hiking almost every summer, so it was kind of like a family tradition.

As for where I went hiking, well, first we took a train to a village that was about two hours away from my city. The village is a pretty popular tourist destination, and it's a beautiful place. The next day, we went hiking in the nearby mountain.

And again, I was with my family during the entire trip—specifically, my mom and dad. They both enjoy hiking and nature a lot.

Anyway, after we arrived at the mountain, we started hiking right away. I can't remember exactly how many kilometres we walked, but it took us at least several hours. I remember that the weather was great that day. It was sunny, but not too hot because we were in the mountains. Also, the scenery was excellent. There were lots of trees, wild flowers, and streams along the way. I guess, all in all, it felt very peaceful and relaxing. And even though we walked a lot, it wasn't that tiring because we took breaks and stopped to take pictures every now and then. Oh yeah, we also got a little lost in the middle of the walk, but we were able to find our way by looking at the map on our cell phones. So yeah, overall, it was a very enjoyable walk and a good bonding experience.

◎ 范文解析

该范文开门见山地说明这个"long walk"就是一次"hiking",它发生在某个夏天,全家人一起去徒步远足。为了让整个描述更丰富,首先说搭乘什么交通工具去到这个远足的地方,随后描述这个地方的大致环境。由于是和家人一起远足的,所以这部分不需要添加过多的故事。范文的重点是描述远足时看到的风景和遇到的事情。关于风景的描述可以比较笼统,比如天气好、树木茂密、有山有水等。至于远足中遇到的事情,可以是迷路之类的小插曲。最后,范文提到了整个旅程的心情和感受。

◎ 表达积累

我们从范文中为考生总结了一些有用的表达,这些内容可以用于描述徒步旅行,也可以用于描述去乡村山野的旅行。

go hiking	去徒步旅行
take a train	坐火车
a pretty popular tourist destination	一个非常受欢迎的旅游目的地
the scenery was excellent	风景好极了
There were lots of trees, wild flowers, and streams along the way.	沿途有许多树木、野花和小溪。
peaceful and relaxing	平静和放松的
enjoyable	令人愉快的
a good bonding experience	一次（培养）亲密关系的体验

▓ // 拓展练习 //

根据所掌握的英语词汇及表达,模仿范文,回答以下题目。

Describe a bicycle/motorcycle/car trip you would like to go on.

You should say:

　　who you would like to go with

　　where you would like to go

　　when you would like to go

and explain why you would like to go by bicycle/motorcycle/car.

■ // **翻译练习参考答案及拓展练习范文** //

◎ **交通工具句子翻译练习参考答案**

1. The city is to the south of my city, and it's about a 2-hour drive by car or a 30-minute ride by train. We decided to take the train because it's faster and we wanted to get there as soon as possible.

2. I want to travel there by car because there's beautiful scenery along the way.

◎ **旅行的内容句子翻译练习参考答案**

1. When we arrived at the city, we went to all the scenic spots and tourist places that were recommended by others. For example, we visited ancient temples and buildings, along with famous museums and parks. We also went shopping at department stores and ate at many different local restaurants. At night, we would return to our hotel close to the city centre.

2. We would get to enjoy the views of nature and see the countryside, which is nice because we spend so much time in big cities.

◎ **拓展练习范文**

I'm going to describe a car trip I'd like to go on.

I would like to go on the trip with my close friends or family because I'm more comfortable with them and it would be more fun. It has also been a long time since we've done a car trip.

We could go to a city or a scenic spot that's close enough so that we could just drive there. I guess we could go to Suzhou, which is close to my city. It's a popular tourist spot that's known for its canals, and it also has a lot of history and culture. I've been there before and really enjoyed the experience, so I would love to visit again.

As for when I would like to go on the trip, I guess when everyone is free. Nowadays, we're all quite busy with school or work, so it probably has to be during summer or winter vacation if it's with my friends. And if it's with my family, then it probably has to be during a national holiday.

And finally, I want to go there by car because there's beautiful scenery along the way. We would get to enjoy the views of nature and see the countryside, which is nice because we spend so much time in big cities. Also, the car trip itself would also be fun. We could talk and catch up on things, so it would be a good bonding experience. And, like I mentioned, we haven't gone on a car trip in a while, so it's about time we did it again.

 话题 13 WATER ENVIRONMENT（水环境）

水是生命之源，它与人们的生活息息相关。人们在日常生活中需要清洁的水，休闲旅行也喜欢去有水的地方；人类的生存环境离不开江河湖海，社会的工业生产也离不开水。

我们来看看有哪些话题与"水环境"有关：

Describe a change that can improve your local area.

Describe a good law in your country.

Describe a law on environmental protection.

Describe a place you visited that has been affected by pollution.

Describe an important river/area of water in your country.

Describe a leisure activity near/on the sea that you want to try.

Describe a place where you often visit with your friends or family.

Describe an unforgettable bike trip.

纵观以上题目，虽然直接与"水环境"有关的题目不多，但其涉及的范围很广泛，可以与水污染及环保有关，也可以与水边的活动有关。回答这类题目需要融合不同的话题，使用不同的表达和素材。

// 水污染 //

水污染是环保中非常重要的一个话题。水污染的源头、危害和一些解决方法是其中比较重要的部分。造成水污染的原因有自然的和人为的，而后者是最主要的。人们排放的污染物、废料、废弃物及人类活动造成的酸雨等都对海洋和湖泊造成了巨大的污染。由于水资源受到了污染，水中的生物也会受到伤害，人类的健康同样也会受到威胁。为了防止水污染，人们在加大宣传并完善相关法律的同时，也在通过科技手段解决水污染问题。

请看以下表格中罗列的与水污染的原因、影响及控制方法有关的图片及其相关表达。

水污染的原因 (Causes of Water Pollution)

- 产生有毒废料（如化学品或杀虫剂）
  produce a lot of toxic waste (for example, chemicals and pesticides)
- 将有毒废料倒入河流
  dump toxic waste into rivers

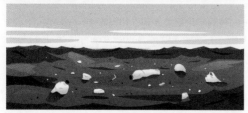

- 吸管、塑料袋和其他人们用过一次就扔掉的垃圾
  straws, plastic bags, and other junk that people use once and then throw away

87

水污染的影响 (Effects of Water Pollution)

- 破坏自然环境
  destroy the natural environment
- 水生动物会吃垃圾或者被垃圾卡住
  aquatic animals eat trash /garbage /waste or get stuck in trash/garbage

- 当有毒废料进入食物或者饮用水中时，会对人们的身体健康造成损害
  when toxic waste gets into our food or our drinking water, it can harm us

控制水污染的方法 (How to Control Water Pollution)

- 政府可以制定环境法律与政策，以防工厂污染水
  governments can create environmental laws and policies that prevent factories from polluting water
- 为了执行这些法律，他们可以对违规者处以罚款和监禁
  to enforce these laws, they could punish offenders with fines and jail

- 垃圾分类
  waste sorting/garbage sorting
- 回收利用和重复使用，如重复使用塑料袋
  recycle and reuse (for example, reuse plastic bags)

在掌握了这些与水污染有关的表达之后，我们来完成句子翻译练习。

1. 原文：曾经有一个案例，一些生产化学品和杀虫剂的公司被发现向河流中倾倒垃圾。政府以违反法律为由对他们处以数百万人民币的罚款。

翻译：＿＿＿＿＿＿＿＿＿＿＿＿＿＿＿＿＿＿＿＿＿＿＿＿＿＿＿＿＿＿＿＿＿＿＿＿

＿＿＿＿＿＿＿＿＿＿＿＿＿＿＿＿＿＿＿＿＿＿＿＿＿＿＿＿＿＿＿＿＿＿＿＿＿＿

2. 原文：我们可以通过重复使用塑料袋、正确地回收垃圾来减少塑料垃圾。

翻译：＿＿＿＿＿＿＿＿＿＿＿＿＿＿＿＿＿＿＿＿＿＿＿＿＿＿＿＿＿＿＿＿＿＿＿＿

＿＿＿＿＿＿＿＿＿＿＿＿＿＿＿＿＿＿＿＿＿＿＿＿＿＿＿＿＿＿＿＿＿＿＿＿＿＿

// 与水有关的休闲活动及运动 //

当水环境得到治理，山川、湖泊、大海变得怡人，人们是很愿意到水边进行活动的，比如游泳、散步、骑车、钓鱼或沿着湖泊徒步旅行。

根据图片想一下我们能在水边或者水里参与的活动吧。

可以通过一个故事来记忆这些可以在水边或者水里进行的活动：早晨起床，人们首先去游泳，这可以让人们清醒；然后去湖里抓鱼；用抓来的鱼和自带的食物（如水果、面包、沙拉等）准备一个湖边野餐；吃完午饭，人们会休息一下，随后在太阳下山前去湖边的山里徒步或者去湖边骑车

根据以上提示，写一段话，描述在水边或者水里进行的活动。

■ // 口语练习 //

掌握了与水资源有关的表达之后，接下来就需要将这些内容综合起来，试着用它们来回答口语题目。

◎ 口语例题

Describe a law on environmental protection.

You should say:

what it is

how you first learned about it

who benefits from it

and explain how you feel about this law.

◎ 题目分析

题目要求描述一则环境保护法律。考生可以选择空气保护、水保护、森林保护、动物保护等法律，这其中对水资源和空气的保护相对比较简单。在描述时，需要对这则法律做大致的介绍，介绍污染的原因、污染的危害及怎样做到法律上的保护。

◎ 回答问题

你已经了解了题目的要求，也掌握了一定数量的英文单词和表达，接下来就请用两分钟的时间来回答这道题吧。

◎ 回答范文

Okay, so the law I'm going to describe is an anti-water pollution law. Basically, the law makes it illegal for people to dump their waste into rivers. The law is mostly targeted at businesses that produce a lot of toxic waste in their factories.

I first learned about this law while reading the news. There was a case where some companies that make chemicals and pesticides were caught dumping their waste into rivers. The government responded by fining them millions of RMB for breaking the law. It was a landmark case because of the heavy fines and because the people who were responsible were sentenced to prison.

Regarding who benefits from this law, well, I guess everyone benefits. People who like to swim in rivers benefit from having cleaner rivers to swim in, and people who eat fish from rivers or drink from rivers won't get poisoned. It also has an economic impact because rivers provide tourism for many towns next to rivers. Cleaner rivers attract more tourists to these places, which boosts the income of the people living there. Finally, rivers are home to many animals, so this law helps keep them alive, not just fish but also endangered species like river dolphins and turtles.

I feel great about this law because it has a positive effect on so many lives. As I mentioned, both people and animals benefit greatly from it. Also, I think that companies have been getting away with water pollution for too long. They deserve to be punished heavily for putting profits over safety.

◎ 范文解析

该范文首先表明这个法律是 "anti-water pollution law"，即防治水污染法。随后，简单介绍了该法律的主要内容是 "makes it illegal for people to dump their waste into rivers"，即 "使得往水里倾倒污染物和垃圾变得违法"。接下来，对该法律的来源和背景进行介绍，一般来说，人们通常通过新闻媒体了解与法律相关的资讯。然后，作者对保护水环境的重要性和好处进行介绍，即山清水秀不仅对人的健康有利，对动植物有利，还会让这个地方吸引更多的游客。

◎ 表达积累

我们从范文中为考生总结了一些有用的表达，这些内容同样适用于对其他环境保护法律的介绍。

The law is mostly targeted at...	这项法律主要针对的是……
illegal	非法
a landmark case	具有里程碑意义的案件
heavy fines	高额罚款
were sentenced to prison	被判入狱
has a positive effect on	有积极的影响
They deserve to be punished heavily for putting profits over safety.	他们把利润置于安全之上，应该受到严厉的惩罚。

■ // 拓展练习 //

根据所掌握的英语词汇及表达，模拟范文，回答以下题目。

Describe a place where you often visit with your friends or family.
You should say:
　　where the place is
　　how you knew the place
　　how you go there
and explain why you like to visit it.

■ // 翻译练习参考答案及拓展练习范文 //

◎ 水污染句子翻译练习参考答案

1. There was a case where some companies that make chemicals and pesticides were caught dumping their waste into rivers. The government responded by fining them millions of RMB for breaking the law.

2. We could reduce plastic waste by reusing plastic bags and recycling our garbage properly.

◎ 与水有关的休闲活动及运动翻译练习参考答案

We wake ourselves up by going for a swim. It's really nice and refreshing to swim early in the morning. After the swim, we normally go fishing to catch fish for lunch. Then we have a nice picnic by the lake, eating not just the fish we caught but other things we brought too, like fruit, bread, and salad. After lunch, we take an afternoon nap, and after waking up from that, we go hiking or bicycling by the lake before sunset. During sunset, we take beautiful pictures of the lake. And that's basically a typical day we spend at the lake.

◎ 拓展练习范文

I'm going to talk about a place I often visit with my family, which is a lake that's not far from my city. The lake used to be polluted by factories many years ago, but because of anti-water pollution laws, it's been clean for years.

I know about the place because, well, my parents have taken me there many times over the years. I'm not sure how they knew about the place, but they probably heard about it from friends or coworkers.

It only takes about an hour to get there by car, which means we're able to go there quite often. I'm pretty sure you can also reach the place by bus or train, but we just prefer to drive.

Anyway, I like to visit the place because it's beautiful and we can easily spend an entire weekend there on a camping trip. After we arrive, we're usually a little tired and just rest and relax, but the next morning we wake ourselves up by going for a swim. It's really nice and refreshing to swim early in the morning. After the swim, we normally go fishing to catch fish for lunch. Then we have a nice picnic by the lake, eating not just the fish we caught but other things we brought too, like fruit, bread, and salad. After lunch, we take an afternoon nap, and after waking up from that, we go hiking or bicycling by the lake before sunset. During sunset, we take beautiful pictures of the lake. And that's basically a typical day we spend at the lake.

 话题 14 LANGUAGE LEARNING（语言学习）

与语言学习相关的题目出现次数不少，题目可以是纯粹的与语言学习有关的题目，也可以是

喜欢的学科或课程，还可以是想学习的一门技能。

首先，我们来看看有哪些题目与"语言学习"有关：

Describe a course that impressed you a lot.

Describe a subject that you like most.

Describe a subject you used to dislike but now have an interest in.

Describe a thing you did to learn another language.

Describe an ambition that you have not yet achieved.

Describe an interesting subject you learned at school.

在这些题目中，需要特别指出的是关于"ambition"的题目，考生可以选择不同的目标，比如学会游泳、骑车或者考上某所大学，当然也可以选择学习一门语言。这些题目看似宽泛且抽象，但只要掌握了一定的表达和素材，回答起来并没有那么难。

语言学习的内容和方法

语言学习不限于学习一门语言，还可以是学习学校里的一门课程，其内容涉及单词、语法、听说读写各方面。

请看以下表格中罗列的与语言学习的内容和方法相关的图片及其表达。

语言学习之读写学习

· 学习语法规则
  learn grammar rules
· 写作文
  write essays
· 阅读文章和小说并为其写摘要
  read articles and novels and write summaries
· 练习阅读理解
  practice reading comprehension

语言学习之听口学习

· 与以英语为母语的人交谈
  have conversations with a native English speaker
· 帮助我们纠正发音，并教我们一些地道的表达和短语
  help correct our pronunciation and give us some native expressions and phrases

语言课程的整体描述

· 定期完成家庭作业、小测验和考试
  regularly have homework assignments, quizzes, and tests

在掌握了这些与语言学习的内容和方法有关的表达之后，我们来完成句子翻译练习。

1. 原文：这门课程真的能帮助学生学习英语，因为它涵盖了英语的所有不同领域，所以我们在知识上没有那么多的缺漏。

翻译：_____

_____

2. 原文：我们学习很多语法规则，然后通过写文章来练习它们。

翻译：_____

_____

3. 原文：我们阅读文章和小说，并为它们写摘要，这有助于练习我们的阅读理解和写作。

翻译：_____

_____

4. 原文：我们练习与以英语为母语的人对话，这很有帮助，因为她帮助我们纠正发音，给我们一些地道的表达和短语。

翻译：_____

_____

■ // 语言学习的用途 //

语言学习的用途广泛，除了用于读书和求职，在日常生活中也有广泛应用。请看以下与语言学习的用途有关的表达。

对我的未来有帮助，比如我的入学考试和未来工作	help me in the future, like for my entrance exams and my future job
使用我的英语技能来帮助预订酒店和有导游带领的旅游	use my English skills to help book hotels and guided tours
与当地人交流及问路	communicate with the local people and ask for directions

在掌握了这些与语言学习的用途有关的表达之后，我们来完成句子翻译练习。

原文：我很感激我学到的东西，因为它们会在未来帮助我，比如我的入学考试和我未来的工作。

翻译：_____

_____

■ // 口语练习 //

掌握了与语言学习的内容、方法和用途有关的表达之后，接下来就需要将这些内容综合起来，试着用它们来回答口语题目。

◎ 口语例题

Describe a thing you did to learn another language.

You should say:

    what language you learned

    what you did

    how it helped you learn the language

and explain how you felt about it.

◎ 题目分析

题目要求描述你为了学习一门外语所做的事情。这道题非常契合前面介绍的表达和素材，你可以在回答中加入所学语言的内容（听说读写）、用了什么学习方法（比如和外教对话、上课）、有什么效果。至于学习语言的感受，可以说学习语言之后的用途（工作、升学和旅游）。

◎ 回答问题

你已经了解了题目的要求，也掌握了一定数量的英文单词和表达，接下来就请用两分钟的时间来回答这道题吧。

◎ 回答范文

One thing I did to learn another language was to take a course for it. The language I learned was English.

The course helped me learn English because it covered all the different areas of English so that we didn't have that many gaps in our knowledge. For example, we learned lots of grammar rules and then practiced them by writing essays. We also read articles and novels and wrote summaries for them, which helped us practice both reading comprehension and writing. For speaking, we practiced having conversations with a native English speaker, which was helpful because she helped correct our pronunciation and gave us some native expressions and phrases. And finally, we regularly had homework assignments, quizzes, and tests, which pushed us to practice and review the things we were taught.

I thought that taking the course was very useful. Like I said, it covered all the different areas of English, and it pushed me to really learn English. I could feel my English improving throughout the course. By the end of it, I could read, speak, and write quite well. I am grateful for the things I learned because they will help me in the future, like for my entrance exams and my future job. Even for travelling, it will be a big help. For example, if my family and I were to travel to the UK, I could use my English skills to help book hotels and guided tours. Once we get there, I would be able to communicate with the local people and ask for directions.

◎ 范文解析

该范文开门见山地指出"我通过报了一个语言课程来学习这门外语"。随后，范文从学习语言的几个方面入手来说明这个课程怎么帮助学习外语，比如学习语法（grammar rules）并进行写作练习，阅读不同的文章和小说并为此写摘要（summaries），和母语为英语的人对话（have conversations with a native speaker）来练习听力与口语。介绍完如何学习，还需要描述一下学习语言的好处，比如有助于未来的入学考试和工作（entrance exams and future job），以及去英国旅游等。

◎ 表达积累

我们从范文中为考生总结了一些有用的表达，这些内容不仅可以用于描述英语学习，稍加修改还可以用于描述其他语言的学习。

it covered all the different areas of English	它覆盖了英语（学习）的方方面面
learned lots of grammar rules and then practiced them by writing essays	学了很多语法规则，然后通过写文章来练习
read articles and novels and wrote summaries for them	阅读文章和小说，并为它们写摘要
practiced having conversations with a native English speaker	练习与以英语为母语的人对话
helped correct our pronunciation and gave us some native expressions and phrases	帮助纠正我们的发音，给我们一些地道的表达和短语
regularly had homework assignments, quizzes, and tests	定期安排家庭作业、测验和测试
pushed us to practice and review the things we were taught	督促我们练习和复习所学的知识
help me in the future, like for my entrance exams and my future job	在将来能帮到我，比如我的入学考试和我未来的工作
use my English skills to help book hotels and guided tours	用我的英语技能帮助预定酒店和有导游带领的旅游
communicate with the local people and ask for directions	与当地人沟通和问路

■ // 拓展练习 //

根据所掌握的英语词汇及表达，模拟范文，回答以下题目。

> Describe an ambition that you have not yet achieved.
> You should say:
>> what it is
>>
>> why you haven't achieved it
>>
>> what you are doing about it now
> and explain how you feel about it.

■ // 翻译练习参考答案及拓展练习范文 //

◎ 语言学习的内容和方法句子翻译练习参考答案

1. The course really helps students learn English because it covers all the different areas of English so that we don't have that many gaps in our knowledge.

2. We learn lots of grammar rules and then practice them by writing essays.

3. We read articles and novels and write summaries for them, which helps us practice both reading comprehension and writing.

4. We practice having conversations with a native English speaker, which is helpful because she helps correct our pronunciation and gives us some native expressions and phrases.

◎ 语言学习的用途句子翻译练习参考答案

I am grateful for the things I learned because they will help me in the future, like for my entrance exams and my future job.

◎ 拓展练习范文

An ambition that I haven't achieved yet is to become really good at English.

The reason I haven't achieved this yet is simply because I haven't spent enough time learning and practicing English. I think that to get good at anything, you must spend a lot of time doing it.

To change this, I have been taking an English course. The course really helps students learn English because it covers all the different areas of English so that we don't have that many gaps in our knowledge. For example, we learn lots of grammar rules and practice them by writing essays. We also read articles and novels and write summaries for them, which helps us practice both reading comprehension and writing. For speaking, we practice having conversations with a native English speaker, which is helpful because she helps correct our pronunciation and gives us some native expressions and phrases. And finally, we regularly have homework assignments, quizzes, and tests, which pushes us to practice and review the things we were taught.

By doing this course, I can already feel my English improving a lot. I really want to get better at English because it will help me in the future, like for my entrance exams and my future job. Even for travelling, it will be a big help. For example, if my family and I were to travel to the UK, I'll be able to use my English skills to help book hotels and guided tours. Once we get there, I'll be able to communicate with the local people and ask for directions.

话题 15 SCIENCE AND MATH（科学与数学）

除了语言，科学与数学也是非常重要的学习领域，有些与课程和爱好有关的题目没有办法使用语言学习来回答，就需要使用科学与数学的学科素材来回答。

首先，我们来看看有哪些题目与"科学与数学"有关：

Describe a subject that you like most.

Describe a subject you used to dislike but now have an interest in.

Describe a useful skill you learned in a math class from your primary/high school.

Describe an area of science (physics, biology, psychology, etc.) that interests you.

Describe an interesting subject you learned at school.

Describe an interesting talk or lecture.

有些题目本身就限定了需要用与数学有关的素材来回答。除此之外，由于数学在一部分人眼里是有趣且有用的，在另一部分人眼里是讨厌且枯燥的，所以很适合用来回答"like/dislike"之类的题目。

■ // 数学学习的内容与用途 //

由于学科之间差异巨大，考生平常要注意积累自己喜欢的学科的相关素材。这里选择数学为主题进行介绍，因为数学是大部分人都熟悉的课程，贯穿小学到高中，半数以上的大学课程的基础也是数学。学习一些与数学课程相关的描述可以帮助考生回答一系列的口语题目。

请看以下表格中罗列的与基础数学学习有关的图片及其相关表达。

基础数学课（即算数课 arithmetic）的内容

· 加、减、乘、除
　　addition, subtraction, multiplication, and division
· 乘法表
　　multiplication table
· 有定期的小测验和考试
　　have regular quizzes and tests

算数课老师

- 很擅长教学
  be quite good at teaching
- 相当严格
  pretty strict

算数的用途

- 日常生活中有实际价值
  has practical value in daily life
- 在初中和高中学习更高级的数学，比如代数、几何、微积分
  learn more advanced math subjects in middle school and high school, like algebra, geometry, and calculus

在掌握了这些与数学学习的内容与用途有关的表达之后，我们来完成句子翻译练习。

1. 原文：老师将题目写在黑板上，告诉我们如何解答这些题目，有时会要求学生来解答这些题目。然后，我们将自己练习。

翻译：_____

_____

2. 原文：我们有定期的小测验和考试，这有助于我们记住学习的内容。

翻译：_____

_____

3. 原文：当我和朋友们分摊餐费时，我把这些菜的费用加起来，然后按人分摊。

翻译：_____

_____

4. 原文：当我计算买东西后剩下多少钱时，我会用减法。

翻译：_____

_____

5. 原文：这些基本的数学技能在我们初中和高中学习高级数学科目时非常有用，比如代数、几何和微积分。

翻译：_____

_____

■ // 口语练习 //

掌握了与数学学习的内容与用途有关的表达之后，接下来就需要将这些内容综合起来，试着用它们来回答口语题目。

◎ 口语例题

Describe a useful skill you learned in a math class from your primary/high school.

You should say:

what the skill was

how you learned it

who taught you

and explain why it was useful to you.

◎ 题目分析

题目要求描述一种你在学校学到的技能。一说到技能，考生可能会想到语言、计算机、手工等，但其实算术也是一种技能，而且这种技能的学习从幼儿时代就开始了，贯穿整个学生时代。接下来，需要介绍这门学科包含哪些内容、怎样学习以及是由谁教授的。说完这些，需要继续描述为何觉得它有用，一般来说，无论是语言、文史、数理化，用处都包含两方面，一是可以帮助自己在学术上更有成就，二是帮助自己找到更好的工作。

◎ 回答问题

你已经了解了题目的要求，也掌握了一定数量的英文单词和表达，接下来就请用两分钟的时间来回答这道题吧。

◎ 回答范文

A useful skill I learned from math class was arithmetic.

Arithmetic is about addition, subtraction, multiplication, and division. It's one of the required subjects that all primary students have to learn.

The way we learned it was simple. My teacher would write questions on the blackboard and show us how to do these questions, sometimes calling on students to do them. Then, we would practice on our own. So yeah, we mainly learned by doing lots and lots of practice questions, as well as memorizing things like the multiplication table. We also had regular quizzes and tests, which helped us remember the information.

As I mentioned, I was taught arithmetic by my primary school teacher. She was a nice woman who was quite good at teaching, though she could also be pretty strict sometimes. She made sure that we eventually became good at arithmetic, and I'm happy that I had her for a teacher.

Anyway, arithmetic is useful to me because it has a lot of practical value in daily life. For example, when I share the costs of meals with friends, I add up the costs of the dishes and then divide it by person. And when I'm calculating how much money I have left after I buy something, I use subtraction. It's the same when I'm calculating my budget or savings. Aside from this, these basic math skills were very useful when I learned more advanced math subjects in middle school and high school, like algebra, geometry, and calculus. And I'm sure they'll be useful if I take math-related courses in university, like accounting, finance, computer science, or engineering.

◎ 范文解析

该范文介绍的一种在学校学到的有用技能是算术。首先，介绍算术包含哪些内容，即比较基础的加减乘除。算术作为基础数学，是在小学完成学习的，学习的过程是老师讲解、学生做题、考试测验等。至于是谁教的，那必然是老师，范文用了一些形容词来描述算术老师，比如"nice"和"pretty strict"。最后，范文用最多的篇幅来介绍算术的有用之处，一方面算术对生活有极大的帮助，另一方面算术是未来学习数学的基础。

◎ 表达积累

我们从范文中为考生总结了一些有用的表达，这些内容不仅可以用于描述算术，还可以用于描述其他理工类学科。

one of the required subjects that all primary students have to learn	所有小学生必须学习的必修科目之一
My teacher would write questions on the blackboard and show us how to do these questions, sometimes calling on students to do them.	我的老师会在黑板上写问题，然后告诉我们如何解答这些问题，有时还会叫学生上去做题
practice on our own	自己练习
learned by doing lots and lots of practice questions	通过做大量的练习题来学习
has a lot of practical value in daily life	在日常生活中有很大的实用价值
these basic math skills were very useful when I learned more advanced math subjects in middle school and high school	当我在初中和高中学习更高级的数学科目时，这些基本的数学技能是非常有用的（句子中的 math 可以被替换成其他学科名词）

■ // 拓展练习 //

根据所掌握的英语词汇及表达，模拟范文，回答以下题目。

Describe an area of science (physics, biology, psychology, etc.) that interests you.
You should say:

what it is

when you knew about it

how you learn it

and explain why you are interested in it.

■ // 翻译练习参考答案及拓展练习范文 //

◎ 数学学习的内容与用途句子翻译练习参考答案

1. The teacher writes questions on the blackboard and shows us how to do these questions, sometimes calling on students to do them. Then, we will practice on our own.

2. We have regular quizzes and tests, which helps us remember the information.

3. When I share the costs of meals with friends, I add up the costs of the dishes and then divide it by person.

4. When I'm calculating how much money I have left after I buy something, I use subtraction.

5. These basic math skills are very useful when we learn more advanced math subjects in middle school and high school, like algebra, geometry, and calculus.

◎ 拓展练习范文

An area of science that interests me is biology.

Biology is basically the study of life. It ranges from the study of very small and simple organisms to large and complex organisms. And in the process, you learn about things like evolution and the ecosystem.

I first started learning about biology when I was in high school. It's one of the required subjects that all students have to learn. At first, I wasn't really a fan of biology because I had to memorize a lot of small details, like the parts of a cell structure and their functions, and it just seemed a little boring. But after a while, we started learning about more complicated organisms and how they interact with each other. This allowed me to see the value in learning about biology: when you learn biology, you gain a deeper understanding of the world. In other words, it broadens your horizons.

Also, I think there is a lot of practical value in learning biology, because sometimes we had to do experiments and projects. These taught me how to think critically and logically, and it also encouraged me to explore and ask questions. So, not only did this make me a better thinker, it also gave me a better mindset about the world. These are very important lifelong skills.

As for how we learned biology, well, sometimes we had lectures, other times we watched videos, and finally, like I said, we had to do experiments and projects. There were many quizzes, tests, and homework assignments, which helped us learn and remember the information.

话题 16　AN INTERESTING vs. A BORING JOB
（有意思的工作与无聊的工作）

工作是我们永远绕不开的话题，可以描述工作的内容、回报、未来的职业发展，也可以描述工作是否有趣或是否热爱工作，总之，考生需要准备一些关于工作的方方面面的实用表达，既有对这个工作的优势的表达，也有对这个工作表示不满的表达。

首先，我们来看看有哪些口语题目与"工作"有关：

Describe a job that you would not like to do in the future.

Describe a perfect job you want to do in the future.

Describe a person whose work is useful to the society.

Describe a short term job you want to have in a foreign country.

Describe an interesting job that you want to have in the future.

Describe your grandparent's job.

与工作有关的题目都非常直接，往往会涉及是否有用、是否有趣、是否喜欢这些方面。

// 教师工作的职责和意义 //

教师是大部分人都比较熟悉的一个职业，所以这里以教师为例展开讨论，分析教师的各种职能及这份工作的积极意义。教师的主要职责是教书育人，不仅给学生传授新知识、帮助学生拓展视野，还影响着学生的各类发展。

请看以下表格中罗列的与教师工作的职责和意义有关的表达。

教书	·教给我们（某门学科的）各种概念/知识 　teach us all kinds of concepts/knowledge about... ·解释（概念/知识）清晰 　explain things clearly ·使课堂更有趣、更放松 　make class more interesting and relaxed

续表

育人	・教我们如何独立思考 　　teach us how to think for ourselves ・牵着我们的手，引导我们 　　hold our hands or guide us ・给你生活的目标 　　give you a purpose in life ・激励我们更加努力 　　inspire us to be more hard-working
总结：对社会有着 巨大的贡献	・教育年轻一代 　　educate the younger generation ・塑造社会的未来 　　shape the future of society ・通过教授我们重要的技能和知识，帮助我们为未来的工作做好准备 　　help prepare us for our future jobs by teaching us important skills and 　　knowledge

在掌握了这些与教师的工作职责和意义有关的表达之后，我们来完成句子翻译练习。

1. 原文：我的数学老师教我们关于数学的各种概念，他能够清楚地解释这些，所以我们能够理解有难度的概念。

翻译：_____

_____

2. 原文：教师帮助教育年轻的一代，他们有一天会成为世界的领导者。

翻译：_____

_____

3. 原文：他们教我们重要的技能和知识，帮助我们为未来的工作做好准备。

翻译：_____

_____

4. 原文：我非常喜欢数学课，所以我决定主修一个与数学相关的课程领域。

翻译：_____

_____

■ // 教师工作的难处与挑战 //

任何事物都有正反面。教师工作非常有意义，同时也有很多难处和挑战。教书职能要求教师有足够的学科知识或者跨学科知识储备。育人职能要求教师有一定的心理学知识、有极大的爱心和耐心，愿意奉献和付出。教师还要有社会贡献，所以教师的压力是巨大的。

请看以下表格中罗列的与教师工作的难处与挑战有关的表达。

| 教书的压力与挑战 | · 负责许多学生的教育工作
  responsible for the education of many students
· 成为你所在领域的专家，并善于解释
  be an expert in your subject and be good at explaining things
· 有很多耐心
  have a lot of patience |

| | · 做一个好的向导
  be a good guide
  励他们努力学习
  think for themselves and inspire them to work hard
  候，你必须为下一节课做计划、批改家庭作业及回答家长
  teaching, you have to plan for your next lessons, grade
  answer parents' questions. |

"_____" 有关的表达之后，我们来完成句子翻译练习。

保他们正在学习重要的技能和知识，为他们的未来

_____

_____

人。你应该是一个很好的向导，教他们独立思考，激

_____

_____

_____

下来就需要将这些内容综合起来，试着用它们来回

e society.

ul to the society.

◎ 题目分析

题目要求描述一个人，其工作对社会有用，这非常容易让人想到人类灵魂的工程师——教师，

当然考生也可以描述医生、军人、工人等。如果以教师为主题，考生可以使用非常多前面学过的表达和素材，比如语言学习、数理化学习及人物类话题中的短语和句子，这会使回答变得轻松简单。

◎ 回答问题

你已经了解了题目的要求，也掌握了一定数量的英文单词和表达，接下来就请用两分钟的时间来回答这道题吧。

◎ 回答范文

I'm going to talk about a person whose work is useful to society, and that person is my high school math teacher, whose name is Tom.

I've known him since my second year of high school, when he became my math teacher.

Anyway, my math teacher teaches us all kinds of concepts about math, and he's able to explain things clearly so that we're able to understand hard concepts. Also, he is a funny person and he likes to joke around with us, which makes class more interesting and relaxed.

As for why I think his work is useful to society, well, I think there are many reasons why teachers in general serve an important role in society. First, they're helping to educate the younger generation, who will one day become the leaders of the world. So, in a way, they are shaping the future of society. Second, they help prepare us for our future jobs by teaching us important skills and knowledge. We will carry this knowledge for the rest of our lives. But besides giving us knowledge, good teachers also teach us how to think for ourselves. This is important because we won't always have someone to hold our hands or guide us. In addition, teachers can give you a purpose in life. For example, I enjoyed my math class so much that I decided to major in a math-related field. And finally, good teachers inspire us to be more hard-working. They push us and challenge us to take responsibility for our future. That's why I truly believe that teachers are some of the most important people in society.

◎ 范文解析

该范文介绍了一位数学老师。作者在介绍数学老师时使用了不少前面话题中学过的与数学有关的表达和素材，比如上课的方式及老师的一些性格特征。范文的重点是介绍"为何他的工作对社会有用"，一是教育年轻一代（educate the younger generation），二是帮助年轻一代准备未来工作所需的技能（help prepare us for our future jobs），三是起到激励的作用（inspire us）。

◎ 表达积累

我们从范文中为考生总结了一些有用的表达，这些内容不仅可以用于描述数学老师，也可以用于描述其他学科的老师。

teaches us all kinds of concepts about...	教我们关于……的各种概念
is able to explain things clearly	能把事情解释清楚

续表

a funny person	一个有趣的人
likes to joke around with us	喜欢和我们开玩笑
makes class more interesting and relaxed	使课堂更有趣和轻松
serve an important role in society	在社会中发挥重要作用
they're helping to educate the younger generation	他们正在帮助教育年轻一代
they are shaping the future of society	他们正在塑造社会的未来
they help prepare us for our future jobs by teaching us important skills and knowledge	他们教我们重要的技能和知识，帮助我们为未来的工作做好准备
teach us how to think for ourselves	教我们如何独立思考
hold our hands or guide us	牵着我们的手或指引我们
teachers can give you a purpose in life	老师能给你人生的目标
good teachers inspire us to be more hard-working	好老师激励我们更加努力
They push us and challenge us to take responsibility for our future.	他们鞭策我们，挑战我们，让我们为自己的未来负责。

■ // 拓展练习 //

根据所掌握的英语词汇及表达，模拟范文，回答以下题目。

Describe a job that you would not like to do in the future.

You should say:

　　what is the job

　　why you don't want to do it

and explain how you feel about the job.

■ // 翻译练习参考答案及拓展练习范文 //

◎ 教师工作的职责和意义句子翻译练习参考答案

1. My math teacher teaches us all kinds of concepts about math, and he's able to explain things clearly so that we're able to understand hard concepts.

2. Teachers help to educate the younger generation, who will one day become the leaders of the world.

3. They help prepare us for our future jobs by teaching us important skills and knowledge.

4. I enjoyed my math class so much that I decided to major in a math-related field.

◎ 教师工作的难处与挑战句子翻译练习参考答案

1. You are responsible for the education of many students, and you have to make sure that they're acquiring important skills and knowledge that will prepare them for their future.

2. Teaching is not just about giving information to children. You're supposed to be a good guide, teaching them to think for themselves and inspiring them to work hard.

◎ 拓展练习范文

A job I wouldn't want to do in the future is to be a teacher.

There are lots of reasons why I don't want to be a teacher. I guess, first of all, it's because being a teacher is a lot of responsibility. You are responsible for the education of many students, and you have to make sure that they're acquiring important skills and knowledge that will prepare them for their future. To do that, you need to be an expert in your subject and be good at explaining things. This can sometimes be challenging because students can be disruptive or not pay attention, so you need to have a lot of patience. Also, teaching is not just about giving information to children. You're supposed to be a good guide, teaching them to think for themselves and inspiring them to work hard. And finally, when you're not teaching, you have to plan for your next lessons, grade homework, and answer parents' questions. What this means is that your work hours can be very long, and you don't really get to have a healthy work-life balance. So yeah, I think that being a teacher is very tough, and they're not even paid that well for the work they do.

Even though I don't want to be a teacher, I really respect teachers and what they do. They definitely serve a very important role in society because they educate the younger generation, who will one day become the main workforce and leaders of the country. In other words, teachers basically shape the future of society. They are that important.

话题 17 CELL PHONES & THE INTERNET（手机和互联网）

手机与互联网是人们获取信息的重要途径。手机除了可以打电话、发短信，还可以通过互联网连接各种新闻、娱乐、交友程序。只要有网络，手机几乎可以联通天下，完成很多事情。手机与互联网结合为人们的生活带来了颠覆性的改变，同时也带来了一些挑战。

首先，我们来看看有哪些题目与"手机和互联网"有关：

Describe someone or something that made a lot of noise.

Describe an application (program) you usually use on your phone.

Describe something you bought that was difficult to use at first.

Describe a product or application which is based on artificial intelligence.

Describe an important technological product you bought.

Describe something useful you borrowed from others.

Describe something lost by others but found by you.

Describe a time that you spent a lot of money on something.

Describe something given to you that you really need.

Describe something you own but want to replace.

Describe something important you lost in the past.

Describe a piece of technology (not computer related) you like to use.

Describe an advertisement that made you buy something.

Describe a rule at your school that you agree or disagree with.

Describe an occasion when you forgot something important.

Describe an occasion when you could not use your mobile phone.

Describe a time you borrowed something from your friends or family.

Describe the time when you received your first phone.

Describe a time that you saved money for something.

Describe a time you were pleased with your mobile phone.

与"手机和互联网"有关的口语题目非常多。有些是非常直接地要求描述手机，比如 "Describe a piece of technology (not computer related) you like to use"；有些则与手机使用的场景有关，比如"Describe a rule at your school that you agree or disagree with"。

// 手机的功能与应用 //

在这短短十多年里，以前只能打电话和发短信的手机变得非常智能，功能非常强大。如今的手机功能齐全、内存很大，可以拍摄、编辑各类高清照片和视频，可以处理各种文案，还可以监测健康。这里主要罗列手机最重要的三种功能：沟通、休闲娱乐、购物支付。

整体描述

· （手机）支持 5G 通信
    (cell phone) has 5G
· 访问无线网络
    access Wi-Fi
· 拍摄高清照片
    take high-definition photos
· 内存很大
    lots of storage space

沟通

· 与朋友和家人交流
  communicate with friends and family
· 允许我们互相发短信
  allows us to text each other

休闲娱乐

· 休闲时使用手机
  use my phone for leisure
· 用手机玩游戏
  play games on my phone
· 用手机看有趣的视频
  watch funny or interesting videos on my
  cell phone
· 打发时间的有趣方式
  a fun way to pass time

购物支付

· 支付
  pay for something
· 通过我的手机支付
  pay through my cell phone
· 从各种餐馆订餐
  order food from all kinds of restaurants
· 使我的生活更方便
  makes my life much more convenient

在掌握了这些与手机的功能与应用有关的表达之后，我们来完成句子翻译练习。

1. 原文：在我的生活中，我用手机做很多日常的事情。

翻译：_____

_____

2. 原文：每当我需要支付一些东西，我都通过我的手机。如果我需要坐地铁，我也会用手机支付。但是如果是雨天，我就可以通过手机叫到出租车。

翻译：_____

_____

3. 原文：我经常用手机点餐。你可以从各种餐馆点餐，而且通常送货很快。

翻译：_____

_____

// 使用手机带来的危害 //

　　长时间使用手机会对健康造成危害：长期低头看手机对脖子有害，容易得颈椎病；一直盯着手机屏幕容易造成眼疲劳；晚上不睡觉看手机会导致睡眠质量下降。通过手机上网会接触到一些假消息或不适合青少年的内容。如果是学生，上课偷玩手机会影响学习。

　　请看以下表格中的图片及与之匹配的英文表达。

	・造成健康问题 　　cause health problems ・眼疲劳 　　eyestrain ・骨骼和肌肉的健康状况不佳 　　poor bone and muscle health ・睡眠紊乱 　　sleep disorders
	・接触到暴力的或不合适的内容 　　be exposed to violent or inappropriate content ・假新闻 / 消息 　　fake news/information
	・自控能力差 　　poor self-control ・不能阻止自己查看微信 　　not able to stop myself from checking WeChat ・影响学生的成绩 　　affect students' grades

　　在掌握了这些与"使用手机带来的危害"有关的表达之后，我们来完成句子翻译练习。

1. 原文：因为我的自制力很差，无法阻止自己查看微信，所以不带手机有助于我专注于课堂。

翻译：_____

_____

2. 原文：我的很多同学基本上都沉迷于手机，这影响了他们的成绩。

翻译：_____

_____

3. 原文：手机确实会导致健康问题，比如眼睛疲劳和睡眠障碍。

翻译：_____

_____

■ // 口语练习 //

掌握了与手机有关的表达之后，接下来就需要将这些内容综合起来，试着用它们来回答口语题目。

◎ 口语例题

Describe a product or application which is based on artificial intelligence.

You should say:

　　what it is

　　what it is used for

　　how it is used

and what you think of it.

◎ 题目分析

题目要求描述一个基于人工智能的产品和应用，手机就非常符合题目要求。手机的面部识别和指纹识别系统与人工智能有关，手机中安装的程序也与人工智能有关。手机和手机中安装的程序可以根据实际情况进行描述，由它们带来的好处或危害基本一致，可以使用相同的表达和素材。

◎ 回答问题

你已经了解了题目的要求，也掌握了一定数量的英文单词和表达，接下来就请用两分钟的时间来回答这道题吧。

◎ 回答范文

I'm going to talk about a product that's based on artificial intelligence, and that's my cellphone. Currently, I'm using a Huawei phone, and I've had it for a few years. It has 5G, a good camera, and lots of storage space.

As for what it's used for, well, a variety of things. First of all, it's used to help me communicate with friends and family. Here in China, we use an app called WeChat, which allows us to text each other. Sometimes, I use my phone to call other people too. It depends on the situation, like how urgent it is.

Aside from communication, I also use my phone for leisure. For example, sometimes I play games on my phone. It's a fun way to pass time on my way home while in the subway. When I'm not playing games, I like to watch funny or interesting videos on my cell phone. Sometimes, I even take videos or pictures myself and send them to friends or family. My cellphone is able to take high-definition photos.

And finally, I use my cellphone for many daily things in my life. Whenever I need to pay for something, I do it through my cell phone. And if I need to take the metro, I also pay through my cellphone. But if the weather is rainy, then I might get a taxi through my cell phone. Other than that, I use my phone quite often to order food. You're able to order from all kinds of restaurants, and the delivery is usually pretty fast. So, all in all, I really like my cell phone because it makes my life much more convenient.

◎ 范文解析

该范文以人们经常使用的智能手机为主题展开回答。首先简单介绍了手机的品牌和功能。其次详细地描述了手机的用途，第一是沟通 (communication)，第二是娱乐 (leisure)，第三是日常生活中的支付功能 (pay for something)。为了让每一个用途描述得更饱满，作者添加了例子，比如沟通功能使用微信作为例子，娱乐功能使用玩游戏、看视频、拍照作为例子，支付功能使用坐地铁、打出租车作为例子。

◎ 表达积累

我们从范文中为考生总结了一些有用的表达和句子，这些内容可以用于描述互联网、手机及手机中安装的程序等题目。

It has 5G, a good camera, and lots of storage space.	它有 5G 网络，一个很好的摄像头，还有很大的存储空间。
help me communicate with friends and family	帮助我与朋友和家人沟通
allows us to text each other	让我们可以互相发短信
use my phone for leisure	休闲时用手机
play games on my phone	用我的手机玩游戏
pass time on my way home	在我回家的路上打发时间
watch funny or interesting videos on my cell phone	在我的手机上看有趣的视频
take videos or pictures myself and send them to friends or family	自己拍视频或照片，发给朋友或家人
take high-definition photos	拍摄高清照片
use my cellphone for many daily things in my life	在我的生活中使用我的手机做很多日常的事情
pay for something	支付

续表

pay through my cellphone	通过手机支付
get a taxi through my cell phone	用我的手机叫一辆出租车
use my phone quite often to order food	经常用我的手机点食物
order from all kinds of restaurants	从各种餐厅点餐
it makes my life much more convenient	它使我的生活更方便

■ // 拓展练习 //

根据所掌握的英语词汇及表达，模拟范文，回答以下题目。

Describe a rule at your school that you agree or disagree with.

You should say:

    what the rule is

    why the rule is needed

    how people would be punished if the rule was violated

and explain why you agree or disagree with this rule.

■ // 翻译练习参考答案及拓展练习范文 //

◎ 手机的功能与应用句子翻译练习参考答案

1. I use my cell phone for many daily things in my life.

2. Whenever I need to pay for something, I do it through my cell phone. And If I need to take the metro, I also pay through my cell phone. But if the weather is rainy, then I might get a taxi through my cell phone.

3. I use my phone quite often to order food. You're able to order from all kinds of restaurants, and the delivery is usually pretty fast.

◎ 使用手机带来的危害句子翻译练习参考答案

1. I have poor self-control, and I wouldn't be able to stop myself from checking WeChat, so not having my cell phone with me helps me focus on the class.

2. Many of my classmates basically have become addicted to their cell phones and it has affected their grades.

3. It's true that cell phones can cause health problems, like eyestrain and sleep disorders.

◎ 拓展练习范文

I'm going to talk about a rule at my school, which is that students are not allowed to bring their cell phones to the campus.

According to my school, this rule is needed to protect students' eyes and make sure that they're focused on the class. It's supposed to also help prevent students from becoming addicted to the internet as well as being exposed to inappropriate content.

Students who violate the rules will be required to write a note pledging not to repeat the offense in the future. In certain schools, when students break the rules, their cell phones are taken away and only returned at the end of the school day.

On one hand, I somewhat agree with the rule because I have poor self-control, and I wouldn't be able to stop myself from checking WeChat, so not having my cell phone with me helps me focus on the class. Many of my classmates also have poor self-control. In fact, some of them still bring their cell phones to class and find all kinds of ways to not get caught. They basically have become addicted to their cell phones and it has affected their grades. And I guess it's also true that cell phones can cause health problems, like eyestrain and sleep disorders.

However, I still think that the rules should be relaxed a little. I think that cell phones should be allowed on campus, just not during class. And I guess the main reason is that cell phones help us relax in between classes and during lunch. Also, if there's a family emergency, it's important for family members to be able to reach us.

🔊 话题 18 AN ITEM OF CLOTHING（衣着）

衣食住行与人们的日常生活息息相关，口语考试自然也少不了"衣着"这个话题。关于日常穿着，需要考生直接描述衣服的时候比较少，很多时候需要考生描述一些配饰，比如围巾、帽子或项链。

首先，我们来看看有哪些题目与"衣着"有关：

Describe a gift that took you a lot of time to prepare/choose.

Describe a gift you would like to buy for your friend.

Describe a piece of clothing you enjoy wearing.

Describe a present you received which was made by hand.

Describe an item of clothing that someone gave you.

Describe something you received for free.

Describe a product you bought recently that made you happy.

Describe a thing that you bought and felt pleased about.

Describe something that you can't live without (not a computer / phone).

Describe a time that you bought something in a street market.

Describe a special thing you took home from a tourist attraction.

这些题目中除了个别题目直接提到了"clothing"，其余的题目大多与"gift"有关。围巾或帽子是非常不错的回答对象，一来容易描述，二来确实也是人们经常赠送的礼物，并且围巾、帽子这种配饰可以手工制作，送人比较有意义。

■ // 围巾的质地、样式与用途 //

围巾是日常生活中经常使用的配饰，如果要描述它，就不可避免地要提及它的质地、样式和用途。从质地上说，可以是丝绸的、羊毛的、化纤的；从样式上说，有条纹的、格子的、长条的、方形的；而用途除了装饰就是保暖。围巾可以是自己购买的一样单品，也可以是旅游纪念品、他人赠送的礼品，抑或是亲手制作的爱心礼物。

请看以下与围巾的质地、样式、用途有关的图片及其相关表达。

围巾的质地与样式

· 舒服柔软，由羊毛制成
  soft and comfortable, made of wool

· 条纹围巾
  striped scarf

· 格子围巾
  plaid scarf

围巾的用途

· 把围巾围在我的脖子上
  wrap the scarf around my neck
· 保护我免受寒冷
  protect me from the cold
· 保持温暖
  keep me warm

在掌握了这些与"围巾的质地、样式与用途"有关的表达之后，我们来完成句子翻译练习。

1. 原文：这条围巾是纯灰色的，看起来很漂亮。它很长，很适合我。它也是用非常柔软舒适的材料做的——我想是羊毛做的。我觉得这条围巾非常御寒。

翻译：_____

_____

2. 原文：我觉得在寒冷的天气里没有围巾我是活不下去的，比如秋天和冬天。寒冷的天气会持续好几个月，我非常需要戴围巾，因为它能很好地保护我免受寒冷。

翻译：_____

_____

3. 原文：出门之前，我会把围巾围在脖子上，这样可以保暖。当我在室内的时候，如果太热我就把它脱下来。

翻译：_____

_____

■■ // 口语练习 //

掌握了与围巾有关的表达之后，接下来就需要将这些内容综合起来，试着用它们来回答口语题目。

◎ 口语例题

Describe an item of clothing that someone gave you.

You should say:

    what the clothing was

    who gave it to you

    when you got it

and explain why this person gave you the clothing.

◎ 题目分析

题目要求描述别人给你的一件服饰。根据题目要求，这件服饰需要符合"别人给你"这个前提，收到的礼物就符合这个要求。围巾既是一种服饰，又很符合"别人给你"这个要求（比如生日礼物）。因此，考生只需要将围巾的款式、用途、是谁送的、在什么场合送的说清楚就可以很好地完成这个问题了。

◎ 回答问题

你已经了解了题目的要求，也掌握了一定数量的英文单词和表达，接下来就请用两分钟的时间来回答这道题吧。

◎ 回答范文

An item of clothing that someone gave me was a scarf.

The scarf has a plain grey colour, and it looks quite nice. It is pretty long and it fits me quite well. It is also made of very soft and comfortable material—I think it's made of wool. I would say that the scarf does a very good job of protecting me from the cold.

I got the scarf from my friend. Her name is Jenny and I've known her for many years. We are very close. Anyway, she bought the scarf for me a few years ago as a Christmas gift, and I wear it all the time during fall and winter, which can last for many months. I think it's really something I can't live without during cold weather.

As for why my friend bought me the scarf, well, like I said, it was a Christmas gift. But she didn't do it just because of tradition. I think she also wanted to show me that she cares about me a lot and that she values our friendship. I really appreciate her kindness and I thanked her for her gift. And of course, I also gave her a gift too. I gave her a karaoke machine because she likes to sing. She told me that she chose a scarf instead of something else because the weather was getting cold. And even though I already had a scarf, she noticed that I had been wearing it for many years and it was getting old and worn out. So yeah, I thought that she chose the perfect gift.

◎ 范文解析

该范文在确定了以围巾为主题之后，首先对围巾的样式、质地、穿戴感受和用途做了一个简单的介绍；随后对围巾的来历做了比较详尽的描述，即围巾是朋友送的圣诞礼物，这个礼物非常棒，可以抵御冬天的寒冷；接着范文着重强调了收到礼物的经历。对于这部分的描述，考生可以根据个人的经历展开，可以和范文一样是互换的圣诞礼物，也可以是生日礼物、新年礼物、升学礼物、升职礼物。将重点放在这部分有一个明显的好处，那就是"言之有物"，毕竟比起描述物品，描述经历会更简单、更有表述的内容。

如果想介绍另一种服饰，在使用类似的表达和素材的前提下，可以选择夹克衫（jacket）作为主题，因为它和围巾有许多共同点，比如舒适柔软、采用条纹或格子的样式、能够抵御寒冷。

◎ 表达积累

我们从范文中为考生总结了一些有用的表达和句子，这些内容可以用于描述围巾、帽子、手套等衣物。

It is also made of very soft and comfortable material.	它也是由非常柔软和舒适的材料制成的。
as a Christmas gift	作为圣诞礼物
I wear it all the time during fall and winter, which can last for many months.	在持续好几个月的秋天和冬天，我总是戴着它。
something I can't live without during cold weather	在寒冷的天气里我离不开的东西
She cares about me a lot and she values our friendship.	她很关心我，也很珍惜我们的友谊。

■ // 拓展练习 //

根据所掌握的英语词汇及表达，模拟范文，回答以下题目。

> Describe something that you can't live without (not a computer / phone).
> You should say:
>> what it is
>> what you do with it
>> how it helps you in your life
> and explain why you can't live without it.

■ // 翻译练习参考答案及拓展练习范文 //

◎ 围巾的质地、样式与用途句子翻译练习参考答案

1. The scarf has a plain grey colour, and it looks quite nice. It is pretty long and it fits me quite well. It is also made of very soft and comfortable material—I think it's made of wool. I would say that the scarf does a very good job of protecting me from the cold.

2. I don't think I can live without my scarf in cold weather, like during fall and winter. The cold weather can last for many months, and I pretty much need to wear a scarf because it does a very good job of protecting me from the cold.

3. Before I go outside, I wrap it around my neck and it keeps me warm. When I'm indoors, I take it off if it gets too warm.

◎ 拓展练习范文

I'm going to describe something I can't live without, which is my scarf.

The scarf has a plain grey colour, and it looks quite nice. It is pretty long and it fits me quite well. It is also made of very soft and comfortable material—I think it's made of wool. I got the scarf from my friend Jenny as a Christmas gift. Even though I already had a scarf, she noticed that I had been wearing it for many years and it was getting old and worn out. So, she bought me a new scarf, which I really appreciated.

Anyway, what I do with the scarf is simple. Before I go outside, I wrap it around my neck and it keeps me warm. When I'm indoors, I take it off if it gets too warm. The scarf is easy to carry around with me and is easy to store. I also hardly notice it after wearing it for a while.

I don't think I can live without my scarf in cold weather, like during fall and winter. The cold weather can last for many months, and I pretty much need to wear a scarf because it does a very good job of protecting me from the cold. This is important because being cold makes me not want to go outside. Aside from that, the scarf is a reminder of my friend's kindness. As I said, she gave it to me as a gift, and sometimes when I put the scarf on, I'm reminded of her, and it fills me with a different kind of warmth.

话题 19 AN IMPORTANT EVENT（重要的事件）

跨年、守岁、生日、婚礼、毕业典礼等重要事件是人们生活中最值得庆祝的。重要的日子可以和家人或朋友一起度过，也可以独自一人度过。重要日子里发生的事情可以是充满欢乐的，也可以是欢乐中带点无聊的。

首先，我们来看看有哪些口语题目与"重要的事件 / 日子"有关：

Describe a special day that made you happy.

Describe a time when someone visited your home.

Describe a time when you waited for something special that would happen.

Describe a time when you were excited.

Describe a time you were sleepy but had to stay awake.

Describe an important event you celebrated.

Describe something you enjoyed doing with a group of people.

这类题目的问法比较单一，但需要注意题目中表达心情和状态的词，比如"happy" "excited" "sleepy / stay awake"。

// 庆祝活动 //

说到重要的事件，除了考试、毕业、面试、结婚等，考生很容易想到节日。而在众多的节日中，新年是比较好准备的素材。庆祝新年不受种族或喜好的影响，人们为庆祝新年而做的准备和参与的活动也大都相同。

请看以下罗列的与庆祝新年有关的图片及其相关表达。

在家庆祝新年

· 和我的家人在家里庆祝除夕
  celebrate New Year's Eve with my family at home
· 观看电视节目，其中有许多明星也在庆祝即将到来的新年
  watch a TV show that features lots of celebrities who are also celebrating the coming New Year
· 讨论一些事情，比如我们的新年计划是什么
  discuss things like what our New Year's resolutions are

在外庆祝新年

· 和朋友出去玩
  hang out with friends
· 去听音乐会
  go to a concert

庆祝新年一定要有的仪式感

· 告别过去的一年，迎接新的一年
  say goodbye to the previous year and welcome a new one
· 倒计时
  a countdown
· 祝彼此新年快乐
  wish each other a Happy New Year
· 通过短信祝朋友新年快乐
  wish friends a Happy New Year over text messages

在掌握了这些与庆祝活动有关的表达之后，我们来完成句子翻译练习。

1. 原文：我们坐在客厅里，观看一个电视节目，里面有很多明星也在庆祝即将到来的新年。

翻译：_____

_____

2. 原文：我有时会和朋友出去玩，甚至去听一场音乐会来庆祝新年。

翻译：_____

_____

3. 原文：你会感到兴奋，因为这是一个新的开始，也因为有倒计时，你可以在电视上看（倒计时），也可以和周围的人一起（倒计时）。

翻译：_____

_____

4. 原文：随着倒计时的临近，这种期待的感觉越来越强烈。

翻译：_____

_____

5. 原文：终于到了午夜，我们互祝新年快乐，我也通过短信祝朋友们新年快乐。

翻译：_____

_____

■ // 口语练习 //

掌握了与庆祝新年有关的表达之后，接下来就需要将这些内容综合起来，试着用它们来回答口语题目。

◎ 口语例题

Describe an important event you celebrated.

You should say:

    what the event was

    when it happened

    who attended the event

and explain how you feel about the event.

◎ 题目分析

题目要求描述你庆祝的一次重要事件。这类题目容易让人联想到庆祝新年或者守岁，因为这是人们最熟悉的也是人人都经历过的。你可以说与家人或朋友一起庆祝新年，也可以说一个人度过。至于这其中发生的事情，可以选择的素材非常广泛。

◎ 回答问题

你已经了解了题目的要求，也掌握了一定数量的英文单词和表达，接下来就请用两分钟的时间来回答这道题吧。

◎ 回答范文

I'm going to describe an important event I celebrated, which was New Year's Eve. This happened just last year, and I remember that I celebrated the event with my family at home. The entire time, we just sat in the living room and watched a TV show that featured lots of celebrities who were also celebrating the coming New Year. In other years, I would sometimes celebrate the New Year by hanging out with friends or even going to a concert, but other times I would also just stay at home.

Anyway, it was an important event because, you know, the New Year happens only once a year. You're basically saying goodbye to the previous year and welcoming a new one. So, you feel excited because it's a new start and also because there's a countdown, which you see on TV or you do it/ this with the people around you. It also feels quite special because you're celebrating a once-a-year event with your family or friends, which brings you closer to them.

While waiting for the event, I remember feeling a little impatient. There definitely was a sense of anticipation that grew stronger as the countdown got closer. I also felt excited because of the New Year's TV show, which was pretty dramatic. At the same time, I felt at peace with my family around me. We talked about the TV show and also discussed things like what our New Year's resolutions were. When it finally hit midnight, we wished each other a Happy New Year, and I also wished my friends a Happy New Year over text messages.

◎ 范文解析

该范文描述的是跨年的经历。首先，作者谈到跨年是与家人一起的，在家里观看了跨年的电视直播节目。当然，跨年也可以和朋友一起，比如去看演唱会。跨年的心情是"excited"。跨年必做的事情有倒计时 (countdown)、做新年计划 (New Year's resolutions)、零点时分发祝福短信 (wished my friends a Happy New Year over text messages) 等。

◎ 表达积累

我们从范文中为考生总结了一些有用的表达和句子，这些内容可以用于描述庆祝新年或者春节。

celebrate the event with my family at home	和我的家人在家里庆祝这一事件
celebrate the New Year by hanging out with friends or even going to a concert	和朋友出去玩，甚至去听一场音乐会来庆祝新年
You're basically saying goodbye to the previous year and welcoming a new one.	你基本上是在告别过去的一年，迎接新的一年。
It's a new start.	这是一个新的开始。
a countdown	倒计时
You're celebrating a once-a-year event with your family or friends, which brings you closer to them.	你正在和你的家人或朋友庆祝一年一度的活动，这会让你和他们更亲近。
There definitely was a sense of anticipation that grew stronger as the countdown got closer.	毫无疑问，随着倒计时的临近，一种期待的感觉越来越强烈。
I felt at peace with my family around me.	有家人在身边，我感到很平静。
New Year's resolutions	新年计划
When it finally hit midnight, we wished each other a Happy New Year, and I also wished my friends a Happy New Year over text messages.	终于到了午夜，我们互祝新年快乐，我也通过短信祝福我的朋友新年快乐。

■ // 拓展练习 //

根据所掌握的英语词汇及表达，模拟范文，回答以下题目。

Describe a time when you waited for something special that would happen.

You should say:

　　what you waited for

　　where you waited

　　why it was special

and explain how you felt while you were waiting.

■ // 翻译练习参考答案及拓展练习范文 //

◎ 庆祝活动句子翻译练习参考答案

1. We sat in the living room and watched a TV show that featured lots of celebrities who were also celebrating the coming New Year.

2. I would sometimes celebrate the New Year by hanging out with friends or even going to a concert.

3. You feel excited because it's a new start and also because there's a countdown, which you see on TV or you do with the people around you.

4. There definitely was a sense of anticipation that grew stronger as the countdown got closer.

5. When it finally hit midnight, we wished each other a Happy New Year, and I also wished my friends a Happy New Year over text messages.

◎ 拓展练习范文

I'm going to describe a time I waited for something special, which was when I waited for the New Year on New Year's Eve.

This happened just last year, and I remember that I waited with my family at home. The entire time, we just sat in the living room and watched a TV show that featured lots of celebrities who were celebrating the coming New Year. In other years, I would sometimes celebrate the New Year by hanging out with friends or even going to a concert, but other times I would also just stay at home.

Anyway, it was a special occasion because, you know, the New Year happens only once a year. You're basically saying goodbye to the previous year and welcoming a new one. So, you feel excited because it's a new start and also because there's a countdown, which you see on TV or you do with the people around you. It also feels special because you're celebrating a once-a-year event with your family or friends, which brings you closer to them.

As for how I felt while waiting, I would say that I felt a little impatient. There definitely was a sense of anticipation that grew stronger as the countdown got closer. I also felt excited because of the New Year's TV show, which was pretty dramatic. At the same time, I felt at peace with my family around me. We talked about the TV show and also discussed things like what our New Year's resolutions were. All in all, I really tried to treasure the moment, which is why I still remember it clearly.

话题 20　AN ANIMAL (PANDA) 动物（熊猫）

与动物有关的口语题目不算多，但却具有一定的特殊性，因为这类题目不能用其他素材来代替。考生可以选择猫、狗、熊猫来准备素材，它们都是大家比较熟悉的宠物或珍稀动物。

首先，我们来看看有哪些话题与"动物"有关：

Describe a time when you got close to wild animal.

Describe a time you saw an interesting animal.

Describe a toy you had/liked in your childhood.

Describe an interesting animal.

纵观这几道题目，如果以熊猫为主题则可以覆盖所有的题目，"toy"也可以是熊猫玩偶，同样可以使用熊猫主题来回答。而如果以宠物猫或狗为主题的话，就不适用于"wild animal"这道题了。综上，我们以熊猫为主题来准备动物类话题的相关素材。

// 介绍熊猫 //

说起动物，很多人第一时间会想到猫或狗，但它们可能不太适合回答与野生或动物园动物有关的话题。动物园里的明星动物当属熊猫，纪念品店里有很多熊猫玩偶，野外保护区里也有熊猫的身影。

请看以下罗列的与熊猫有关的图片及其相关表达。

关于熊猫的描述（外形、动作、食物）

· 拥有黑白皮毛
  have black and white fur
· 眼睛、耳朵、四肢覆盖黑色的皮毛
  black fur around their eyes, ears, and limbs
· 行动缓慢
  move slowly
· 笨拙的
  clumsy
· 吃竹子
  eat bamboo

关于动物园里熊猫生活环境的描述

- 在一个有很多竹子和树木的大围栏里
  in a large enclosure with lots of bamboo and trees
- 有很大的空间活动
  have lots of space to move around

对熊猫的喜爱

- 感到惊奇
  was amazed / it was amazing
- 亲眼看到熊猫是不一样的（感受）
  it was different seeing pandas in person
- 观看熊猫是令人轻松愉悦的
  watching the pandas was very relaxing
- 在礼品店买了一个熊猫玩偶
  bought a panda doll in the gift shop

在掌握了这些与熊猫有关的表达之后，我们来完成句子翻译练习。

1. 原文：熊猫在一个很大的围栏里，里面有很多竹子和树木，所以它们有很多活动空间。

翻译：_____

_____

2. 原文：熊猫有黑白相间的皮毛，眼睛、耳朵和四肢都覆盖着黑色的皮毛。

翻译：_____

_____

3. 原文：当我看到熊猫时，它们基本上只是在吃饭、睡觉或玩耍。

翻译：_____

_____

■■ // 口语练习 //

掌握了与熊猫有关的表达之后，接下来就需要将这些内容综合起来，试着用它们来回答口语题目。

◎ 口语例题

Describe a time you saw an interesting animal.

You should say:

  who it was

  where you saw it

  what it did

and explain why you think it was interesting.

◎ 题目分析

  题目要求描述一种你看到过的有趣的动物，根据题目要求，你可以描述猫、狗、熊猫等大家比较熟悉的动物。答题时除了要说明是什么动物，还要讲清楚是在哪里看到它的、它在干什么，并用比较长的篇幅介绍为何你认为这种动物是有趣的。

◎ 回答问题

  你已经了解了题目的要求，也掌握了一定数量的英文单词和表达，接下来就请用两分钟的时间来回答这道题吧。

◎ 回答范文

A time I saw an interesting animal was during my visit to a zoo.

This happened when I was in middle school, when my class went on a field trip. And even though it happened years ago, I still remember it clearly.

Anyway, so we went on a field trip to the zoo, where we saw pandas. The pandas were in a large enclosure with lots of bamboo and trees, so they had lots of space to move around. We weren't really allowed to get close, but we still got a pretty good view of them, and I was amazed when I saw them. I had seen pictures of pandas before, but it was different seeing them in person. Pandas look very strange. They have black and white fur, with black fur around their eyes, ears and limbs. They're also kind of big and move slowly. When I saw the pandas, they were basically just eating, sleeping, or playing. The ones that were playing looked quite clumsy, but it was also very cute. Oh, and there were also all kinds of pandas there, including adults and small cubs.

Watching the pandas was very relaxing. They seemed like such peaceful animals, which is amazing because they're also bears, and bears are normally quite dangerous. But pandas eat bamboo instead of meat, so they're harmless. And because I liked them so much, I bought a panda doll in the gift shop afterwards. It has been on my bedside for many years now, and it still reminds me of the time I saw pandas.

◎ 范文解析

  该范文首先指出看到的有趣的动物是熊猫，是在动物园里看到的；接下来，范文描述了动物园熊猫馆的环境，随后介绍了熊猫的样子、行为和各种引人注目的点；最后提到看熊猫的心情是十分放松的。熊猫的外形和行为符合"interesting"这一题目要求，光是看熊猫吃饭和玩耍都可以看很久。

◎ 表达积累

我们从范文中为考生总结了一些有用的表达和句子，这些内容可以用于描述熊猫或者部分动物园的动物。

in a large enclosure with lots of...	在一个有很多……的地方（省略号处可以填写树木、花草、石头等词，用于描述动物所处的环境）
They had lots of space to move around.	他们有很大的活动空间。
got a pretty good view of them	看得很清楚
I was amazed when I saw them.	当我看到它们时，我很惊讶。
It was different seeing them in person.	亲眼见到它们是不一样的。
They seemed like such peaceful animals.	它们似乎是很平和的动物。（peaceful 可以被替换成其他形容动物特征的形容词）
...are normally quite dangerous	……通常都很危险（省略号处可以填写某种动物）

■ // 拓展练习 //

根据所掌握的英语词汇及表达，模拟范文，回答以下题目。

Describe a time when you got close to a wild animal.

You should say:

　　what it is

　　where you saw it

　　who you were with

and explain how you felt about this experience.

■ // 翻译练习参考答案及拓展练习范文 //

◎ 介绍熊猫句子翻译练习参考答案

1. The pandas were in a large enclosure with lots of bamboo and trees, so they had lots of space to move around.

2. They have black and white fur, with black fur around their eyes, ears, and limbs.

3. When I saw the pandas, they were basically just eating, sleeping, or playing.

◎ **拓展练习范文**

A time I got close to a wild animal was during my visit to a conservation and research centre for pandas.

This happened when I was in my university, when my class went on a field trip. And even though it happened years ago, I still remember it clearly.

Anyway, so we went on a field trip to the conservation and research centre, where we saw pandas. The pandas were in a large enclosure with lots of bamboo and trees, so they had lots of space to move around. We weren't really allowed to touch the pandas, but we still got a pretty good view of them, and I was amazed when I saw them. I had seen pictures of pandas before, but it was different seeing them in person. Pandas look very strange. They have black and white fur, with black fur around their eyes, ears, and limbs. They're also kind of big and move slowly. When I saw the pandas, they were basically just eating, sleeping, or playing. The ones that were playing looked quite clumsy, but it was also very cute. Oh, and there were also all kinds of pandas there, including adults and small cubs.

Watching the pandas was very relaxing. They seemed like such peaceful animals, which is amazing because they're also bears, and bears are normally quite dangerous. But pandas eat bamboo instead of meat, so they're harmless. And because I liked them so much, I bought a panda doll in the gift shop afterwards. It has been on my bedside for many years now, and it still reminds me of the time I saw pandas.

补充题目及范文

除了以上与话题有关的口语题目，还有一些口语题目及其范文值得学习。本节选取了雅思口语 2022 年度的一些代表题目[①]，按照人物、地点、事物、事件分类，考生在阅读范文的过程中会发现许多表达和素材与前文有重复，这也从侧面说明了本书中提到的素材与表达能灵活运用到各类口语题目中。

---

① 更多新题及范文可以登录"启德i备考"小程序查看与学习。

■ // 人物类 //

◎ 明星 / 有创造力的人

1. Describe a creative person whose work you admire.
   You should say:
       who he/she is
       how you knew about him/her
       what creative things he/she has done
   and explain why you think he/she is creative.

A creative person whose work I admire is Jay Chou. He's a really popular singer and he's been successful for many years. I think he's in his forties now. In terms of personality, he's quite cheerful and nice. He also seems quite outgoing based on all the interviews and media appearances I've seen of him.

As for how I knew about him, well, I've seen him on TV shows quite often, and I've also seen some of his music performances. Also, like I said, he's very famous, so everyone in China knows who he is. He has lots of fans on social media, and he's often in the news and media.

Um, there are many creative things that Jay Chou has done. For example, he's acted in a number of movies, and he's involved with other artistic projects as well, but since he's primarily a musician, his most creative works are in music. I guess you could say that he's known for being a pioneer in music.

I think he's creative because his songs are quite unique and innovative. They combine traditional and modern instruments, which is really interesting to listen to. Also, some of his songs are slow and emotional, while his other songs are fast and upbeat. So, overall, he's a flexible and versatile musician, and he isn't limited to just one style. That's all made possible since he's willing to explore and think outside the box. I respect that mentality because it takes bravery and courage. Many other singers just stick to one style forever, or don't write their own songs.

2. Describe a person you only met once and want to know more about.
   You should say:
       who he/she is
       why you want to know more about him/her
       when you met him/her
   and explain how you feel about him/her.

A person I met only once and want to know more about is Jay Chou. He's a really popular singer and he's been successful for many years. I think he's in his forties now. In terms of personality, he's seems very nice and mature, based on all the interviews and media appearances I've seen of him.

I want to know more about Jay Chou because, first of all, I would like to understand how he thinks. His songs are known to be unique and innovative. They combine traditional and modern instruments, which is interesting to listen to. And some of his songs are slow and emotional, while his other songs are fast and upbeat. So basically, I would like to know how he's able to create such music. It would be fascinating to understand his thought process. Also, I would like to know how he's able to stick to his dreams for so long. From what I know, he's been making music for a long time. I wonder how he's able to motivate himself.

Anyway, I met Jay Chou when I went to one of his concerts. It was during a holiday, and he was performing in our city. There were thousands of people in the stadium, so it was very crowded. I wasn't able to get a good view of him, but it was still a great experience.

As for how I feel about him, well, I admire him a lot. Like I said, he's a nice person and he's extremely talented. If there's a chance, I hope that I can meet him again.

◎ 时尚人士

3. Describe a person who is fashionable.

You should say:

who he/she is

what job he/she does

what kind of dresses he/she wears

and explain why he/she likes fashion.

A person who is fashionable is Jay Chou. He's a very famous and successful singer who's also considered a fashion icon. He has a nice and outgoing personality, and he seems like a cool person based on all the media appearances I've seen of him.

As I said, Jay Chou is a singer, and he's released lots of successful and award-winning albums. He's known for being a pioneer in music and has released a lot of creative and unique songs, like songs that combine traditional and modern music. He has an open mind, which also shows in his fashion. Aside from singing, Jay Chou has also acted in several movies and often appears on TV shows, like music competitions or variety shows.

Just like his music, Jay has a wide variety of dressing styles. Sometimes, he wears clothes that look cool, like the kind that rappers and hip-hop artists wear, which fits him because he also likes to rap in his music. But other times, he wears fancy and colourful clothes, like the kind that you might see on a fashion runway. I've seen him wear both types of clothes.

As for why he likes fashion, well, I can't read his mind, but I would guess because fashion allows him to express himself to the world, just like his music, but in a different way. He also has his own fashion label, which allows him to design his own clothes and exercise his creativity. Artistic people like him tend to be drawn to all sorts of art, not just music but also fashion.

◎ 聪明人 / 商人

4. Describe a person who solved a problem in a smart way.

You should say:

who this person is

what the problem was

how he/she solved it

and explain why you think he/she did it in a smart way.

I'm going to describe a person who solved a problem in a smart way. I'm not sure exactly who the person was, but it was the person who created the first food delivery app.

The problem was that, in the past, if people wanted to eat a meal, they would often have to make it themselves, which was a hassle because they would have to buy the ingredients, cook the meal, and then wash the dishes afterwards. It's also very time-consuming, and we don't have a lot of time, especially in modern society where it's normal for men and women to have full-time jobs. Food delivery existed before, but it required you to call up the restaurant and then order that way, and when the food delivery person arrived, you had to pay by cash.

Now, with the food delivery app, it's much simpler. You can browse through hundreds of restaurants that are in your area and order from any of them. And it's super easy and quick to do that, taking just a few minutes at most. You also pay directly after ordering, so there's no need to prepare cash and change. Then, you just wait from the comfort of your home for the food to arrive, which usually takes just 30 minutes to an hour at most.

I think that the solution is smart because it combines technology with traditional food delivery to make everything faster and more convenient. Most kids in China these days are able to order food themselves. That's how integrated food delivery apps have become in our lives.

◎ 普通人 / 朋友

5. Describe a person who impressed you most when you were in primary school.

You should say:

who he/she is

how you knew him/her

why he/she impressed you most

and how you feel about him/her.

The person who impressed me the most when I was in primary school was probably my class representative in fifth grade.

I got to know her because we were in the same class, and interacted every day at school. Over time, we became good friends.

Anyway, she really impressed me because she was extremely smart and intelligent. She just seemed to know everything, and was a quick learner. She was also super focused and driven, and she obviously had a clear vision for her future. All these characteristics combined made her one of the top students in my class. Even at a young age, I recognised that she would have a bright future, and I was inspired by her to push and challenge myself.

Beyond this, she was also an excellent leader. As the class representative, she seemed mature beyond her years. Firstly, she was very confident, but not arrogant. Secondly, she was good with people because she was very polite and treated everyone with respect. She was also a great listener. For example, she never interrupted when you spoke and wasn't judgemental at all. At the same time, she was quite honest. This meant that I could trust her and share my troubles and worries with her. Of course, she was also open to sharing her own thoughts and feelings, so I felt a strong connection with her.

All in all, I really value the time I spent with her. She's someone I respect and admire a lot, and, even though we lost contact after primary school, to this day I still look up to her and think of her from time to time.

◎ 喜欢摆弄花草的人 / 老人

6. Describe a person you know who loves to grow plants (e.g. vegetables / fruits / flowers etc.).

You should say:

    who this person is

    what he/she grows

    where he/she grows them

and explain why he/she enjoys growing plants.

I'm going to describe a person I know who likes to grow plants, and that person is my grandmother. My grandmother is a retired nurse, and I'm quite close with her. She currently lives with my grandfather in the same city that I live in. I often visit them when I'm free, like during weekends or holidays, because I just really enjoy spending time with them.

Anyway, my grandmother grows lots of different kinds of plants. I can't really name them all, since I'm not an expert on plants, but there are all kinds of flowers, shrubs, and even small trees, such as bonsai. I think she really enjoys having a large variety of plants.

And, as for where she grows them, she puts them in pots around the house, but also in the balcony of her apartment. It really helps make her place seem more welcoming. It's like a good decoration that also helps improve the air.

And finally, I think she enjoys growing plants because, well, first of all it gives her something to do. Watering the plants and moving them in and out of the sunlight is like a comfortable routine for her. And of course, she is very fond of the plants themselves. She thinks plants are beautiful and loves taking care of them and watching them grow. I think it gives her a certain sense of satisfaction to take care of something and see it become something beautiful and healthy. Oh, and plants are also pretty cheap and easy to take care of, meaning it's a perfect hobby for old people.

// 地点类 //

◎ 城市

7. Describe a new place you visited.
You should say:
     where the new place is
     when you went there
     why you went there
and explain how you feel about the place.

I'm going to describe a new place I visited, which was a nearby city.

The city is located to the south of my city, and it's about a 2-hour drive by car—or a 30-minute ride by train. I visited the city with my family, and we decided to take the train because it's faster than driving, and we wanted to get there as soon as possible.

We went to the city during a national holiday last year, and we spent about three to four days there.

As for why we went there, well, the holiday was quite long—like about a week—and we wanted to go travelling instead of staying at home the whole week. In other words, we wanted to experience something new. There were many different options, but we decided to go there because, like I said, it's pretty close to our city—you didn't have to fly there—and we had heard good things about the place. It has a great reputation in general and it's a popular place for tourists to go.

Anyway, we ended up having a great time there. We went to all the scenic spots and tourist places that were recommended by others. For example, we visited ancient temples and buildings, along with famous museums and parks. We also went shopping at department stores and ate at many different local restaurants. The food was delicious and usually not that expensive. So yeah, it was a very fun experience and I really liked the city. If I have the chance, I hope to visit again one day.

8. Describe a city that you think is interesting.

You should say:

where it is

what the city is famous for

why it is interesting

and explain how you feel about it.

I'm going to describe a city that I think is interesting, which is Shanghai.

Shanghai is a city that is located in the east side of China—near the coast, like many big cities in China. It's also next to a major river.

Anyway, Shanghai is famous for being very modern and developed, and it's basically the financial centre of China. It has a great reputation in general and it's a popular place for tourists to go.

Shanghai is an interesting city mainly because there are lots of things to do there and lots of famous scenic spots and tourist places. For example, as a tourist, you can visit ancient temples and buildings, along with famous museums and parks. Some of the most famous places in the city include The Bund, the Jade Buddha Temple, and Yuyuan Garden. These are all amazing and beautiful places. And if you want to have fun, you can also go to Disneyland and easily spend a whole day there. Besides going to tourist hotspots, you can go shopping at department stores and eat at different local restaurants. The food is delicious and usually not that expensive.

So yeah, overall, I would say that Shanghai is a really interesting city with lots of history and culture, and there are many things that you can do there. I think that everyone should visit the city at least once in their life and see the attractions in person. Sometimes, the tourist places can be very crowded, but I think that it's still worth it.

◎ 旅游推荐

9. Describe a place in your country or part of your country that you would like to recommend to visitors/travellers.

You should say:

what it is

where it is

what people can do there

and explain why you would like to recommend it to visitors/travellers.

I'm going to describe a place in my country that I would recommend to travellers, which is the city of Shanghai.

Shanghai is a city that is located in the east side of China—near the coast, like many big cities in China. It's also next to a major river.

Shanghai is famous for being very modern and developed, and it's basically the financial centre of China. It has a great reputation in general and it's a popular place for tourists to go.

There are lots of things to do there and lots of famous scenic spots and tourist places. For example, as a tourist, you can visit ancient temples and buildings, along with famous museums and parks. Some of the most famous places in the city include The Bund, the Jade Buddha Temple, and Yuyuan Garden. These are all amazing and beautiful places. And if you want to have fun, you can also go to Disneyland and easily spend a whole day there. Besides going to tourist hotspots, you can go shopping at department stores and eat at different local restaurants. The food is delicious and usually not that expensive.

So yeah, overall, I would say that Shanghai is a really interesting city with lots of history and culture, and there are many things that you can do there. I think that everyone should visit the city at least once in their life and see the attractions in person. Sometimes, the tourist places can be very crowded, but I think that it's still worth it.[1]

◎ 乡村

10. Describe a place in a village that you visited.

You should say:

where it is

when you visited this place

what you did there

and explain how you feel about this place.

I'm going to describe a place in a village that I visited.

The village is somewhat close to my city, about a 2-hour drive by car—or a 30-minute ride by train. I visited the village with my family, and we chose to drive there.

We went to the village during a national holiday last year, and during the trip, we spent a few hours at a famous temple in the village.

The temple is a popular tourist destination, so there were lots of people there. I mainly just walked around the temple and admired its beauty. The temple is pretty old, so the architecture is very unique and interesting. Being inside the temple is almost like being in a different world. I also enjoyed looking at all the beautiful artwork, like the paintings and statues. There were many, many Buddha statues and their sizes ranged from medium to large. Some of the largest statues were amazing to look at, and I couldn't help but wonder how they were able to make them.

Besides admiring the view, I also spent some time reading descriptions and introductions in the temple. Those descriptions really helped me understand the history and importance of the temple. While I was doing all this, my parents were praying to the Buddha statues. And as we were getting

---

① 这个题目的范文跟上一题几乎一样，只在开头部分做了调整。这再一次说明了相同的素材和表达可以合理地运用到不同的口语题目中去。

ready to leave, we bought some souvenirs, like bracelets for good luck and positive energy.

Anyway, I really enjoyed visiting the temple. I felt very peaceful and relaxing. It's something people need in this busy world. If I have the chance, I hope to visit again one day.

◎ 咖啡店

11. Describe a café you like to visit.

You should say:

　　where it is

　　what kinds of food and drinks it serves

　　what you do there

and explain why you like to go there.

I'm going to describe a café I like to visit. The café is quite close to my school, just about a five-minute walk away. My school is located near a pretty populated area in the city, so the café always has lots of customers, and it's been there for a long time.

As for what kind of food and drinks it serves, there are all kinds. For coffee, you can get lattes, mochas, espressos, Americano, cappuccino and others. For snacks, you can get sandwiches, bread, wraps, and even salad. They're all quite tasty and pretty cheap. I normally just get a latte, but sometimes I also buy bread if I'm hungry.

Anyway, I like to go to the coffee shop right after school, usually with my friends, and we just hang out there and drink coffee. It's a great way for us to relax and relieve some stress before we move on with our day. Sometimes, we also do homework there together, and we help each other out.

Finally, as for why I like to go there, I think it's mostly because of the atmosphere of the coffee shop. It's pretty quiet and serene, even though there are often lots of people. The sense of peace I feel allows me to take my mind off school, but if I want to work on homework, the environment is also perfect for that because there aren't many distractions. And I guess the final reason is that the coffee itself is pretty good. Like I mentioned, it's cheap and tasty, and it also gives me an energy boost for the rest of the day.

◎ 常去的熟人的家

12. Describe the home of someone you know well and that you often visit.

You should say:

　　whose home it is

　　how often you go there

　　what it is like

and explain how you feel about the home.

For this topic, I'm going to describe my grandparent's home.

My grandparents are in their seventies and they are retired. My grandfather is a former teacher, and my grandmother is a former nurse. They've been taking care of me since I was a child, so I'm quite close to them and I try to visit them at least once a week—usually during weekends, and of course, during all the holidays.

Their apartment is in the Pudong district, which is an area in the east side of Shanghai. I also live in Pudong, but it's a large district so it usually takes me about half an hour to travel to their place.

As for what their apartment is like, well, it's not very big but it's still quite comfortable. There's a kitchen, a living room, and a bedroom. It's a pretty old apartment, but my grandparents keep it clean and well-maintained. They have interesting decorations on the wall and bookshelves, and they keep lots of plants in the house and on the balcony so that it feels nice and peaceful. In Chinese, we would say that the place has good feng shui.

The apartment is also a part of a large apartment complex with a nice garden downstairs. Usually, there are lots of children and other old people walking around, and the atmosphere is pretty lively. My grandparents have lots of other friends in the apartment complex, so they're never really lonely.

Anyway, I really enjoy visiting my grandparents at their apartment. I've been there so often that it's almost like a second home to me.

◎ 房子

13. Describe a house or an apartment you would like to live in.

You should say:

what it is like

where it would be

why you would like to live in this house / apartment

and explain how you feel about this house / apartment.

I'm going to describe an apartment that I would like to live in.

My dream apartment would be a new and modern apartment that's located near a safe and convenient location, like in the city centre. It would be right next to a subway station and bus stop, which you could walk to in less than five or ten minutes. There would also be lots of restaurants and cafés close by. And for shopping and entertainment, it would be close to supermarkets, convenience stores, department stores, and movie theatres. For exercising, there would be a gym or a park within walking distance, as well as good hospitals.

As for the apartment complex, there would be good facilities, like its own gym, a swimming pool, and a beautiful garden.

The apartment itself would be clean and modern, with lots of space, especially in the living room so that I could entertain my friends there or something. The bedroom would also be big, and there would be a separate kitchen and bathroom, as well as a balcony where I could enjoy nice views of the city.

I think I would be very happy if I could live in this apartment because it would really improve my quality of life. Where I live right now, some things aren't that convenient. I don't live that close to the city centre, so I often have to travel long distances to reach other parts of the city. Also, there aren't many good restaurants nearby. As for my apartment itself, it's not very big, so it would be nice to have more space.

// 事务类 //

◎ 技能

14. Describe a skill that you learned from older people.
    You should say:
        what the skill is
        who you learned it from
        how you learned it
    and explain how you feel about it.

A skill I learned from older people was how to ride a bike.

I can't remember exactly when I learned it, but it happened when I was really young, maybe around 5 to 7 years old. I learned how to ride a bike from my parents, and they encouraged me to learn it because riding a bike is an essential skill. It allows you travel to nearby places quickly and it's also a great way to get some exercise.

As for how I learned it, like I said, my parents taught and guided me. They bought me a bike with training wheels, and after I became comfortable with riding it, they took off the training wheels, and I learned how to ride a normal bicycle. I remember it was a struggle at first because it was something completely new and unfamiliar to me, and I had to learn how to conquer my fears of falling down, especially when learning how to ride a two-wheel bicycle. But eventually, I was able to do it. Altogether, it took me several months to not only learn the basics but also become good at riding a bike.

Afterwards, I felt happy and proud of myself, and I felt like I had grown up a little. Also, it was satisfying to know that I had learned a useful skill that would stay with me for the rest of my life. I'm very thankful that my parents taught me how to ride a bike. It would have been slower and much more frustrating without their help, and it's possible that I would have given up.

15. Describe a skill that was difficult for you to learn.

You should say:

when you learned it

why you learned it

how you learned it

and explain how you felt when you learned it.

A skill that was difficult for me to learn was how to ride a bike.

I can't remember exactly when I learned it, but it happened when I was really young, maybe around 5 to 7 years old, and I probably learned it during summer or spring when the weather was nice. Altogether, it took me several months to not only learn the basics but also become good at riding a bike.

I learned how to ride a bike because I saw other kids riding bikes and it looked fun, so I wanted to learn it. I'm pretty sure my parents encouraged me to learn it too, since riding a bike is an essential skill. It allows you travel to nearby places quickly and it's also a great way to get some exercise.

As for how I learned it, well, my parents taught and guided me. They bought me a bike with training wheels, and after I became comfortable with riding it, they took off the training wheels, and I learned how to ride a normal bicycle. I remember it was a struggle at first because it was something completely new and unfamiliar to me, and I had to learn how to conquer my fears of falling down, especially when learning how to ride a two-wheel bicycle. But eventually, I was able to do it.

Afterwards, I felt happy and proud of myself, and I felt like I had grown up a little. Also, it was satisfying to know that I had learned a useful skill that would stay with me for the rest of my life.

◎ 电脑

16. Describe something in your home you broke and then repaired.

You should say:

what it is

how you broke it

how you repaired it

and explain how you felt about it.

I'm going to describe something in my home that I broke and repaired, which was my computer.

My computer was quite old. I had it for many years, and it was pretty reliable. But one day, my computer broke down, and I couldn't start it. I don't know why that happened, and I was very confused. I was just using my computer normally and I don't think I downloaded a virus or anything.

Anyway, after trying multiple times to turn on my computer, I became more and more desperate. At first, I considered taking my computer to a computer repair shop, but I didn't want to pay a lot of money or wait for hours or days for my computer to be fixed. Also, I was worried about safety because my computer contained private documents and sensitive information. That's why I decided to try to fix it myself first before going to the computer repair shop. I started searching on my phone for what to do in this situation, how to restart my computer, things like that. There were many different online articles that suggested different solutions, and I tried them one by one. In the end, one of the methods finally worked for me, and I was able to start my computer normally.

I would say that the whole experience felt very stressful. Like I said, I had lots of important files in my computer, and I wasn't sure if I would be able to fix it. It was a big relief when I finally fixed my computer, and I was proud of myself too.

◎ 玩具

17. Describe a toy you liked in your childhood.

You should say:

what kind of toy it is

when you received it

how you played it

and explain how you felt about it.

Okay, so a toy I got in my childhood was a teddy bear. It looked like a typical teddy bear, with soft, brown fur, black eyes, and a black nose. It was one of my favourite toys, and I would always take it with me wherever I went.

As for when I got it, my mother bought the teddy bear for me as a gift when I received a good score on my first test in primary school. I had wanted that teddy bear for a long time, but my mother said she wouldn't buy it for me unless I did well on the first test. Well, I eventually did, so after school one day, she took me to a toy store and bought the toy for me.

I remember being incredibly excited and hugging the toy the moment I received it. I cherished the stuffed animal for a long time and even made up stories for it. It was a very simple toy, but it was fun because I could use my creativity and imagination. After I grew up and no longer played with stuffed animals, I gave the teddy bear to my younger cousin, who still has it on her bedside to this day.

And last of all, I still feel rather fond of that teddy bear. It was one of my first stuffed animals, and it brought me a lot of comfort and security as a child. Now, it serves as a sort of family memento, and I'm sure it brought the same joy to my cousin as it did to me.

◎ 蛋糕

18. Describe a special cake you received from others.

You should say:

when it happened

where it happened

who you got the cake from

and explain why it's a special cake.

I'm going to describe a cake that I received from others.

It was a cake that I got during my last birthday, and it happened at home. I got the cake from my parents, who brought the cake out after dinner.

The cake was special because, first of all, it looked beautiful. It was decorated with fancy dressings on the top and the sides, and there were fruits on the top too, like strawberries, cherries, and blueberries. Also, the cake was huge—I was surprised by its size. It was tall, round, and had many layers. And finally, I remember that it smelled quite nice.

In some ways, the situation itself also made the cake special. You only have your birthday once a year, and that's normally the only time you receive a cake. When my parents brought out the cake, I felt very loved.

Before we started eating the cake, we took some pictures first, which I still have. I was sitting down with my parents and grandparents behind me and the cake in front of me, and I had a big smile on my face. Afterwards, I made a wish and blew out the candles. I think I wished for happiness for me and my family.

After blowing out the candles, we sliced the cake into pieces and we started eating them. I remember that the cake was delicious. It had a sweet taste and a creamy texture, and the fruits tasted fresh too. But because the cake was so big, we couldn't finish it all and had to put the leftovers in the refrigerator.

◎ 漂亮的物品 / 传家宝

19. Describe an object that you think is beautiful.

You should say:

what it is

where you saw it

what it looks like

and explain why you think it is beautiful.

I'm going to describe an object that I think is beautiful, which is a jade bracelet that's been kept in my family for generations.

It's a very special piece of jewellery that was originally my grandmother's. She received it from her own mother as a birthday gift when she turned eighteen and was preparing to leave her hometown to work in another province. Eventually, she gave it to my mother on her wedding day. I remember my mother wearing the jade bracelet almost every day when I was a child. Now, she wears it mostly on special occasions, like during the Spring Festival or family reunions.

As for what it looks like, well, it's a bracelet, so it's round and goes around your arm or wrist. It's also completely made of jade, which is a type of hard stone that's green—like a mix of different shades of green. Oh, and it also looks very smooth and shiny. So even though there is nothing fancy about it, it looks very elegant. And finally, it looks very sturdy, as if it could last for another thousand years.

I think the bracelet is beautiful not just because of the way it looks, but also because of the meaning behind it. Jade traditionally symbolizes good luck and fortune, and it's supposed to protect the person who wears it. And because this bracelet has been passed down from mother to daughter throughout the years, it represents motherly love. In any case, it's definitely one of the most cherished possessions in my family.

// 事件类 //

◎ 讨论

20. Describe an interesting discussion you had with your friend.
    You should say:
        what the discussion was about
        what opinions you and your friend had
        why you think the discussion was interesting
    and explain how you felt about it.

An interesting discussion I had with my friend was about what we wanted to do in the future—specifically, what kind of career we wanted to have.

I told my friend that I wanted to become an accountant. I explained that it would be a very stable career and that the salary would be pretty good. At the same time, I would be contributing to society in a useful way, because accountants are needed for businesses to run smoothly. My friend, on the other hand, said that she wanted to become a professional artist. She's quite talented at art, and she was also passionate about it. She understood that it would be harder to make a good living as an artist, but she wanted to try anyway.

I thought the discussion was interesting because my friend and I got to learn more about each other and our hopes for the future. I thought that my friend was brave for choosing to follow her dreams even though she knew it wouldn't be easy. It was also an interesting discussion because my friend's situation is quite common in society. For example, many people are interested in art or music or literature, but they end up in fields like finance, IT, or sales.

I feel like this is a pretty big problem in society. Even though I'm not a very artistic person and I'm not interested in becoming an artist, I still recognize that art and other similar fields actually have a lot of value for society. People like my friend shouldn't have to make such a hard decision.

◎ 困难的决定

21. Describe a difficult decision that you once made.

You should say:

what the decision was

when you made your decision

how long it took to make the decision

and explain why it was difficult to make.

I'm going to describe a difficult decision I once made, which was what to study for college.

I made the decision in my final year of high school because that's when students have to apply to universities and declare a major.

I remember that it took me quite some time to make my final decision—maybe over a month—and I didn't make the decision until I had discussed it carefully with my family and friends. We went over all the pros and cons, advantages and disadvantages, and so on. My family and friends were very patient and helpful the whole time, and I couldn't have made the decision without their input.

Anyway, the reason it was such a difficult decision to make is that I just wasn't sure what I wanted to study. I was interested in multiple subjects, but didn't really feel a strong passion for anything. What made things even more complicated was that, I not only had to weigh my interest in a field, I also had to consider its earning potential. For example, I enjoyed certain arts subjects, like English literature, but it's harder to earn money from them. On top of that, I felt pressured to make the right decision, because it's something that could affect the rest of my life. It's true that you can change careers even when you're an adult, but it means you have to start over again, which will delay your career development. In the end, I chose to study finance because it has good earning potential while still being somewhat interesting to me.

◎ 早起

22. Describe a time when you got up early.

You should say:

when it was

what you did

why you got up early

and explain how you felt about it.

I'm going to describe a time I got up early, which was when I went to the hospital.

It happened last year, around winter. I had gotten sick, so I needed to visit the hospital. The night before my visit, I went to sleep earlier than usual, and woke up at around 7 a.m. I remember that when I woke up, it was still a little dark outside.

After I got up, I brushed my teeth, dressed up, ate breakfast, and then left the house. Before I left, I made sure to bring everything that I needed for the hospital.

As for why I got up early, well, the closest hospital opens early here at around 8 in the morning, and there are normally lots of people there, so if you don't want to wait in line for a long time, then you need to get there as soon as possible.

Anyway, I felt tired after I got up early that day because I didn't really get enough sleep the night before, but I felt a little better after I dressed up and had breakfast. When I arrived at the hospital, I was glad that I had got up early because there were already quite a few people there. I think I did end up getting checked up faster because of my early arrival. And I guess, all in all, I didn't really mind getting up early because I don't go to the hospital that often, maybe just once a year. However, next time I'll make sure to go to bed even earlier than I did.

◎ 善待不喜欢的人

23. Describe a time you were friendly to someone you didn't like.

You should say:

when and where it happened

who he/she was

why you didn't like this person

and explain why you were friendly to him/her on that occasion.

I'm going to describe a time when I was friendly to someone I didn't like.

It happened during Spring Festival last year at my grandparent's house. It's basically a family tradition for us to go eat there. Sometimes we have hotpot, and other times, just lots of different Chinese dishes.

Anyway, the person I was friendly to was my uncle. He's my father's younger brother, and he's probably in his fifties. I think he works in finance, and I've known him since I was a kid.

During the family gathering last year, he was acting kind of rude. I would even say that he was being disrespectful because he was asking a bunch of nosy questions about my life, many of which were just too personal. After a while, I got really annoyed.

But regardless of how I was feeling, I had to act friendly to him because, well, it was a large family gathering, so I was surrounded by other relatives, including my grandparents. If I acted rude or unfriendly, then it would ruin the mood and everyone would be mad at me. I especially didn't want my grandparents to be disappointed in me. Not to mention, in our culture, you're expected to respect your elders, so it's like a taboo to act unfriendly towards a family member older than you. Because of these reasons, I had to act bright and cheerful to my uncle, even though it was fake. I guess it's just something I have to endure, but it's really not that bad, since it's just once or a few times a year.

◎ 为家人骄傲

24. Describe a time when you felt proud of a family member.

You should say:

when it happened

who the person is

what the person did

and explain why you felt proud of him/her.

I'm going to describe a time I felt proud of a family member, which was when my cousin got good grades for an exam.

This thing happened last year when he took an exam for one of his classes.

The person is, as I said, my cousin. He's a few years younger than me and he's in high school. He looks tall and skinny, and he wears glasses. We've known each other since childhood because we're family, and I would say that we're pretty close. He has a bright and cheerful personality and everyone in my family likes him.

Anyway, what my cousin did was he scored well on an important exam. I think he got one of the highest scores in his class, which is not an easy thing to do, but he managed to do it. Afterwards, he posted about his results in our family WeChat group, which is how I learned about it. We all said congratulations to him and we were all super proud of him.

As for why we felt proud, it's because we knew that he had prepared diligently and had worked extremely hard for his exam results. He did struggle with the exam at first, but he spent hours every day preparing for it. It must have been exhausting and stressful, but he never gave up. So yeah, he deserved to do well and we were all just really happy to hear the results. It meant that he had a promising future. In fact, it inspired me to be more hard-working and driven in my own studies.

◎ 塑料废品

25. Describe a time when you saw a lot of plastic waste (e.g. in a park, on the beach etc.).

You should say:

where and when you saw the plastic waste

why there were a lot of plastic waste

what you did after you saw them

and explain what your thoughts were about this.

A time I saw a lot of plastic waste was when I visited a nearby river.

This happened a few years ago when my family and I went on a sightseeing trip over the holidays. On the way, we visited a famous river, which is a hotspot for tourism. When we first arrived, everything seemed fine. At a glance, the river was breathtaking and the surrounding scenery was gorgeous as well. But when I looked more closely at the river, I noticed that there was actually a lot of plastic waste floating around in it.

I would guess that the plastic was most likely thrown into the river by other tourists, and maybe even dumped by people who lived nearby. Regardless of who did it, it definitely spoiled the natural beauty of the place. I think that, as responsible citizens, we should do our part to protect nature whenever possible. This means not littering and making sure that we throw our trash in trash cans instead of into the river or on the street. And if there aren't any trash cans around, then we should just take our trash with us.

It was disappointing to see that people lacked the common decency to do this. River pollution harms not just the scenery but also the marine life that lives in these rivers. I'm pretty sure that every year, thousands if not millions of fish are killed by river pollution. So yeah, I just hope that people can learn to become more responsible. And it would also help if the local government cleaned the river more often.

◎ 失约

26. Describe a time when you forgot/missed an appointment.

You should say:

what the appointment was for

who you made it with

why you forgot/missed it

and explain how you felt about the experience.

I'm going to talk about a time when I missed an appointment.

This happened about a year ago, when I made an appointment with my dentist for cleaning my teeth. Normally, I get my teeth cleaned about once a year because it helps prevent cavities and it's good for oral hygiene. And I usually book at the same clinic every year. It's not very expensive and has pretty good service and also isn't that far from where I live.

But this clinic is also very busy, so you have to book ahead of time. I made my appointment over their online app about a week beforehand. It's pretty easy and simple to do that. You just press a few buttons and choose a time. However, if you miss your reservation, then it just skips over you and you won't be able to get a checkup that day because, like I said, it's a very busy place with a fixed schedule. They are quite strict about that.

Anyway, I ended up missing the appointment because on that day I was busy with something, and by the time I left for the clinic, I was already running a little late. Then, I was stuck in a traffic jam on the way to the clinic, so I ended up being late by about half an hour and missed my appointment.

I felt pretty bad about it, but I also knew that it was completely my fault. It reminded me that I need to manage my time better and to always leave early whenever I have an important appointment.

SPEAKING

第四章 Part 3 口语题库及素材库

　　雅思口语 Part 3 是整个口语考试中最难的部分，其难点在于：Part 3 的题目是根据考生在 Part 2 的回答而定的，更加深入，回答要求较高，而且考生没有现场准备时间。本章我们将以 Part 3 的题目特色、答题策略、相关的表达与素材为切入点，帮助考生备考 Part 3。

　　本章包括如下内容：Part 3 口语题库及素材库使用指南，Part 3 的答题策略，Part 3 核心话题及相关表达与素材，Part 3 补充话题及相关表达与素材，以及 Part 3 特殊话题及相关表达与素材。其中尤其要关注 Part 3 的答题策略与 Part 3 核心话题及相关表达与素材这两部分的内容。

CHAPTER FOUR

Part 3 口语题库及素材库使用指南

在正式进入 Part 3 口语题库及素材库的学习之前，我们首先介绍一下本部分内容的使用指南。

首先，介绍 Part 3 的**答题要素、题目类型、答题结构**，帮助考生了解不同类型的题目，在学习初期掌握答题的结构和方法。注意，在使用过程中不要**生搬硬套**，尽量使用自己熟悉的方式。

其次，介绍一些**提升流利度**的方法，熟记这些方法并在日常的练习中多加运用可以帮助考生在考场上缓解压力、深入思考、提高回答的质量。

需要说明的是，以上内容仅供参考，如果考生有自己熟悉的答题方式和方法，可以使用自己熟悉的。雅思口语考试没有唯一正确的答题模板或答题方法，只要充分回答考官的提问就可以。

学习了 Part 3 的答题策略之后，接下来最重要的内容是 Part 3 的核心话题及相关表达与素材。由于 Part 3 的核心话题涉及非常多的题目及素材库，为了方便考生学习和掌握内容，我们首先分 5 个步骤为考生讲解**口语题库及素材库的使用方法**，然后罗列了 **Part 3 核心话题及相关表达与素材、Part 3 补充话题及相关表达与素材以及 Part 3 特殊话题及相关表达与素材**。

Part 3 的答题策略

在学习 Part 3 涉及的各类话题之前，先介绍一些答题的策略，主要包括以下内容：

★ 五大答题要素；

★ 应急策略；

★ 三大题目类型与答题结构；

★ 提升流利度的方法。

// 五大答题要素 //

在组织雅思口语 Part 3 的答案时，考生可以根据需要使用不同的答题要素，主要包括：**回答问题、解释、举例、比较和对立观点**。除"回答问题"这个要素必须在答案中首先出现且不可省略以外，其余要素可自由使用且顺序随意。

◎ 回答问题

无论是什么问题，考生首先要做的必须是**回答问题**。考生可以选择直截了当地回答问题，例如：

Question: Do you agree that schools should teach children how to manage money?

Answer: <u>Yes</u>, I think schools should teach children money management skills.

Answer: <u>I definitely agree</u> with that.

当然，也可以不那么直截了当地回答问题，例如：

Question: Why do you think some people like trying new things?

Answer: Well, <u>there are many possible reasons</u>.

Question: What kinds of books do Chinese people like reading?

Answer: Well, <u>it depends</u> on the person, but…

◎ 解释

当给出回答之后，考生需要对其进行扩展，一个常见的方法就是添加**解释**。这里需要明确一点，解释不仅指**解释回答**，还包含**说明原因**。

Question: Why do some people like to stay up late?

Response: I think there are various reasons. <u>One reason is that some people just don't feel tired at night</u>.

Response: Some people like to stay up late <u>because they just don't feel tired at night</u>.

📝 **练习**

请回答下面这道题，试着在你的回答中加入解释，可尝试使用下列词汇：*different value / skills / deserve / unfair / become unmotivated / become lazy*。

Question: Some people say it would be better for society if everyone got the same salary. What do you think about that?

Response: _____

_____

◎ 举例

扩展的另一个常用方法是**举例**。例子的长短随意，可以是单独的句子，由词组"For example"或"For instance"引导，也可以跟在主句后面，由"such as"或"like"引导。请看下面的例子：

Question: Why do some people like to stay up late?

Response: Some people like to stay up late because they just don't feel tired at night. <u>For example, one of my friends is a night owl. He's always up until 1 or 2 in the morning, and he's usually just playing with his mobile phone. He told me that he feels more energetic at night, and that it's hard for him to fall asleep</u>.

Response: Some people like to stay up late because they just don't feel tired at night, <u>like my friend John, who doesn't go to bed until 2 in the morning</u>.

📝 **练习**

请回答下面这道题，试着在你的回答中加入例子，可尝试使用下列词汇：*unhealthy / obese /*

eyestrain / exposed / inappropriate content / socially isolated。

Question: Do you think the free-time activities children do today are good for their health?

Response: _____

_____

◎ 比较

除了解释和举例，考生也可以通过**比较**来扩展回答。虽然这个方法用得比较少，但有时很有效，尤其是在不知道还有什么能解释和举例的时候。给出一个比较可以让回答更充分，也可以延长回答的时间。因此，平时应该有意识地训练一下如何做比较。一般来说，可以使用 "In comparison""By contrast""Compared to (sth.)" 或 "Without (sth.)" 来引出比较的内容。

Question: Why do some people like to stay up late?

Response: Some people like to stay up late because they just don't feel tired at night, like my friend John, who doesn't go to bed until 2 in the morning. <u>By contrast, I have another friend who goes to bed really early because she has class early in the morning and she's really disciplined.</u>

📝 练习

请回答下面这道题，试着在你的回答中加入比较，可尝试使用下列词汇：*simple / warmth / brings them closer / bonding experience / exciting / restaurant / KTV / fun activities / socialize with friends*。

Question: Are there many differences between family parties and parties given by friends?

Response: _____

_____

◎ 对立观点

除了解释、举例和比较，考生还可以通过引入一个**对立观点**来扩展回答。很多考生觉得"引入对立观点"与"做比较"是相似的，这是一种错误的观念，所谓"对立观点"是与之前的观点截然相反的观点，类似"一个硬币的两面"。一般来说，考生可以使用 "But, having said that""However" 或 "On the other hand" 来引出对立观点。请看以下例子：

Question: Do you often buy more than you expected?

Response: Not really, because I'm a student and I don't have that much money. I tend to buy only the things I need, like food and groceries. <u>But, having said that, sometimes I do overspend, especially if it's for an expensive thing like a smartphone that I want to replace.</u>

📝 **练习**

请回答下面这道题，试着在你的回答中加入比较，可尝试使用下列词汇：*career path / buying a house / wiser / more experienced / more knowledgeable / immature / decide their own future / personal happiness*。

Question: Should important choices be made by parents rather than by young adults?

Response: _____

_____

// 应急策略 //

当听到题目的一刹那不知道如何回答时，考生可以使用"I don't know"这种应急策略。需要特别说明的是，"I don't know"只能帮助考生缓解压力、拖延时间，避免在考官面前一言不发或者一直说"err..." "emm..."，考生还是需要尽快找到回答问题的方式和内容。具体操作请看以下例子：

Question: How has technology affected the kinds of music that young people listen to?

Response: To be honest, I don't really know the answer to that because I'm completely out of touch with what young people are listening to, and I'm not a fan of pop music. However, I suppose that technology must have affected the way music is made. Maybe young people are listening to music that's been made using computer software instead of real musical instruments like the piano or guitar.

📝 **练习**

请回答下面这道题，试着在你的回答中使用"I don't know"策略，可尝试使用以下词汇完成回答：*luxury brands / cars / mobile phones / food & drinks / restaurants / medicine*。

Question: What types of products are advertised most often on TV?

Response: _____

_____

> **注意：**
> 考生必须一直反复练习"I don't know"策略，以达到条件反射的程度。这样可以让你在遇到难题或者不熟悉的话题时，第一时间说出这个短语，而不是去想"我要说 I don't know 啦！"

📝 **特别提示**

以上所有答题要素并非必要的和顺序固定的。考生在**回答问题**之后，可根据题目和自己的语言储备随意挑选**解释**、**举例**、**比较**或**对立观点**来扩展回答。此外，如果回答的内容不够长，考生要强制自己说出类似"For example""In comparison"或"But, I also think that..."等引导词。这些词就像一个信号，可以帮助考生快速思考接下来要说的内容。

　　了解了以上这些答题要素之后，下一步需要学习的是 Part 3 的主要题目类型及对应的答题结构。所谓答题结构就是"按照一定顺序和逻辑将答题要素放在回答中"。

■ // 三大题目类型与答题结构 //

雅思口语 Part 3 的题型并不复杂，大致包含两类特殊题型（罗列观点型、比较与对立观点型）和一类普通题型。

◎ 罗列观点型

所谓罗列观点型，就是一些以 What，Which，Are there 等疑问词开头的问题。

【 例题 】

What problems can people have when they try new activities for the first time?

What types of things do young people in your country most want to own today?

Which groups of people generally need most support in a community?

Which skills should children learn at school?

Are there any important festivals in your country that celebrate a season or type of weather?

Are there any other jobs that you think should have high salaries?

【 推荐答题结构 】

虽然任何一种答题结构都可以回答此类题目，但使用**多种观点罗列**的答题结构来回答更合适，也更方便。所谓的观点是指一系列的**解释**或者**例子**。

答题结构：多种观点罗列（至少 2 个）

一种典型的答题框架为：

There are many different… / There are a variety of… / There are all kinds of situations…

+

Firstly, … (For example)

+

Also/Secondly, … (For example)

+

Finally, … (For example)

Tips：首先，在回答完题目之后，可以使用类似"Firstly"之类的连接词来展示观点的层次。当然，这不是必须的，这只是在提示自己和听者接下来要开始罗列观点了。其次，是不是需要使用举例来进一步说明是因人而异的，有例子就说，没有例子也可以不说。最后，如果觉得举例就可以解释清楚自己的观点，那也可以在回答问题之后直接举例。

【例题解析】

1. What problems can people have when they try new activities for the first time?

【回答问题】There are many different problems they might experience.【解释1】Firstly, they are unfamiliar with the activity, so they might make lots of mistakes.【举例】For example, when I played basketball for the first time, I didn't know how to shoot the ball or dribble.【解释2】Also, when you try activities for the first time, it can be a little dangerous, depending on the activity.【举例】For instance, the first time I went ice skating, I tripped a lot and hurt myself.

2. Which groups of people generally need most support in a community?

【回答问题】There are various groups of people who might need help.【举例1】For example, the elderly people need help because they're old and weak and might not be able to support themselves.【举例2】The same thing goes for people who are poor or homeless. They might not even be able to afford basic necessities like food, water, and shelter.【举例3】Finally, I think that single mothers need help because they not only have to take care of their children themselves, they also have to make money to support their family.

 练习

请回答下面这道题。在回答时，试着使用多种观点罗列的答题结构，可使用下列词汇：*luxury products / shoes / clothes / iPhones / mobile phones / cars / fashionable things / cool things*。

Question: What types of things do young people in your country most want to own today?

Response: _____

_____

◎ 比较与对立观点型

【例题】

Do you think that reading novels is more interesting than reading factual books?

Who tends to enjoy national celebrations more: young people or old people?

What is the difference between watching a film in the cinema and watching a film at home?

Do you think homes will look different in the future?

> **注意：**
> 任何与时间、年龄等有关的题目（过去和未来的对比，新旧对比，老少对比）都可以归类为比较与对立观点型题目。

推荐答题结构

针对这种类型的题目，回答时最简单的方法就是使用**比较**（"In comparison""By contrast"）和**对立观点**（"However""But"）这两种答题要素。当然，如果有自己熟悉的答题结构也可以使用。

答题结构：一个观点 + 另一个对比或比较的观点

一种典型的答题框架为：

It depends / It depends on the person / It depends on the situation / It depends on why… / I don't have a strong preference for either

+

but I think that …

+

比较：*By contrast/In comparison …*

对立：*However/But …*

> 注意：
>
> 在使用 "It depends…" 或 "I don't have a strong preference…" 回答问题之后，可以马上接上解释，"but I think that…" 是个不错的提出解释的方式；当然，如果不使用 "It depends…" 或 "I don't have a strong preference…" 也可以，那就将回答问题和解释合成一句话，使用 "I think that…" 直接引出解释。随后，如果有需要进一步说明的，可以使用 because 来引出说明；如果想举例，可以使用 For example/For instance；如果还需要添加解释，可以使用 Also。提出比较或者对立观点，可以使用 By contrast/In comparison 或 However/But。

例题解析

1. Who tends to enjoy national celebrations more: young people or old people?

【回答问题】It depends on the person, but I think that【解释 1】young people tend to enjoy national celebrations more because, first of all, they are usually extremely busy with school or work, so their only chance to relax is during national holidays.【解释 2】Also, national holidays provide them a chance to hang out with their friends or go to parties and events like that.【比较】By contrast, old people tend to just stay at home during national celebrations because they don't have as much energy.

2. What is the difference between watching a film in the cinema and watching a film at home?

【回答问题】Well, I think that watching a film in the cinema is more exciting【解释】because the screen is bigger and there are better sound effects.【举例】For example, I once saw a Marvel film on IMAX and it was an amazing experience.【比较】Compared to that, when you watch a movie at home, the sound effects and visual effects aren't as good, but at the same time it's also more convenient and comfortable and it's cheaper to watch a film at home.

📝 **练习**

请回答下面这道题。在回答时，试着使用比较或对立观点的答题结构，可使用下列词汇：

younger generation / older generation / fried chicken / burgers / convenient / cheap / delicious / lots of calories / become obese / healthier / are used to eating。

Question: Which are more popular in your country: fast food restaurants or traditional restaurants?

Response: _____

_____

◎ 普通题型

除以上两大类特殊题型，大部分的题目都属于普通题型。这些题目的问法各有不同，回答也比较自由随意，考生只需要使用**五大答题要素**中介绍的方法进行回答即可。

例题

Do you think it is a good thing to give prizes to children who do well at school?

Do you agree that schools should teach children how to manage money?

How important is it for people to do some regular physical exercise?

推荐答题结构

首先是回答问题，回答问题的方式随意，可以使用罗列观点型题目中的"there be"方式，也可以使用比较与对立观点型题目中的"It depends"。在回答问题之后，可以根据自己的喜好自由组合其他答题要素。

例题解析

1. How important is it for everyone to have a goal in their personal life?

【回答问题】I think it's pretty important【解释】because goals help you stay determined and focused.【举例】For example, when I tried to live a healthier lifestyle, it was hard for me to keep exercising every week, but I set a goal of doing 30 minutes of exercise every day, and that really helped me keep fit.【比较】Without a goal, you tend to lose focus and get lazy.

2. Why do you think some people like doing new things?

【回答问题】Well, it depends on the person, but I think【解释1】a lot of people like doing new things because they're bored and need something fresh or challenging.【举例】For example, I started playing a new mobile game recently because the other game I had been playing was getting too easy and boring.【解释 2】I guess people also try new things because they want to improve themselves.【举例】For instance, some people learn a new language because it might help their career.

📝 练习

请回答下面这道题。在回答时使用合理的答题结构，可使用下列词汇：*understand directions / communicate with local people / only a short visit / English is a global language / use hand signs and gestures*。

Question: How necessary is it for tourists to learn the language of the country they're visiting?

Response: _____

_____

▨ // 提升流利度的方法 //

在雅思口语考试的四项评分标准中，发音和流利度是很多考生的弱项。发音问题可以借助音标改善，流利度则相对较难训练。要提升流利度，除了熟悉题目、掌握答题思路和话题词汇，还可以借助一些特定的方法。

◎ 通用方法

▎适当放慢语速 ▎

部分中级到高级的考生往往语速过快，这导致他们频频犯错、重复用词或把多个单词连在一起说。语速太快会导致单词发音不清，单词与单词之间黏连，最终影响听者的理解。考生可以通过放慢语速并时不时地有意识地停顿来避免这种情况。这样考生能有更多的时间去思考要说什么以及选择正确的表达。

📝 练习

朗读以下问题的回答，记住在朗读时要放慢语速并适当添加停顿。

Question: On what occasions do people usually need to wait?

Response: Well, people need to wait when they're in a line—for example, when they're waiting for an elevator, or when they're waiting for a train to arrive. And I guess people might also wait when there's a special event that's about to happen. For example, a lot of people wait for the arrival of New Year by celebrating at a party, or going to a concert, or hanging out with friends, or something like that.

📝 停顿参考

Response: Well...people need to wait when they're in a line....for example...when they're waiting for an elevator...or when they're waiting for...a train to arrive....And I guess people might also wait when...there's a special event that's about to happen...For example...a lot of people wait for the arrival of New Year by...celebrating at a party...or going to a concert...or hanging out with friends...or...something like that.

使用填充词

很多考生容易在回答时出现明显的停顿。出现停顿的原因往往是他们需要从脑海中调取一些英文表达来继续他们的回答或者需要思考下一步该怎么说。这些明显的停顿会严重影响流利度及最后的评分。遇到这种情况，考生需要学会使用填充词（filler words）来填补这些停顿。

以下这些"万能"填充词可以用在各种场景中：*well, you know, I guess, I think, like*[①]。这些词在使用时不用考虑场景和语义，使用起来十分随意自由。请看以下例子：

【不含任何填充词】

Usually when people order Xiao Long Bao, it's eight at a time, because they're very small.

【添加填充词后】

Usually when people order Xiao Long Bao, it's, <u>like</u>, eight at a time, because they're, <u>like</u>, very small.

<u>Well, I think</u> usually when people order Xiao Long Bao, it's, <u>you know</u>, eight at a time, because they're, <u>I guess</u>, very small.

<u>Like</u>, usually when people, <u>you know</u>, order Xiao Long Bao, it's, <u>well</u>, eight at time, because they're very, <u>like</u>, small, <u>I think</u>.

注意，以上这些句子在填充词的使用上是十分自然和随意的。填充词可以出现在句子里的任何位置。当然，在回答问题时不必强行更换填充词，一段回答中使用 1～2 个不同的填充词即可。有些考生喜欢用类似"you know"这样的填充词，这对以英语为母语的听者来说是一个很好的填充词，但要避免过度使用。切记，使用填充词的目的只是为了避免长时间的停顿，减少说"Um/Uh"的频率。

---

① 此处"like"的意思不是"像"，该词没有任何实质上的含义。

接下来，考生来听一段以英语为母语的人的回答（扫描下方二维码），她在回答时并没有做准备，注意她所使用的填充词（她比较喜欢用"like"）。

最后，当考生不确定如何结束一个句子时，类似"something/stuff like that"的填充词可以起到很大的帮助，这些词的意思是"等等"，比如下面的两个例子：

A lot of people wait for New Year's to arrive by celebrating at a party, or going to a concert, or hanging out with friends, <u>or something like that</u>.

To get a job as a photographer, I suppose some kind of internship would be really helpful, especially if it were for a travel magazine <u>or something like that</u>.

📝 练习

请模拟在真实环境中说话的样子朗读以下问题的回答，注意语速不要过快，保持自然并伴有正常的停顿。

Question: Describe a popular product (e.g. food, handicraft...) made in your region.

Response: I'm going to describe a popular product in my region, and, well, the first one that comes to mind is Xiao Long Bao, otherwise known as, uh, small soup dumpling.

As for what the product is, well, like I said, it's, like, a soup dumpling, and generally there's some, you know, soup inside as well as meat—sometimes it could be, like, crab or pork or, I think, chicken or something like that, so it definitely varies, like, what's inside the Xiao Long Bao, but generally it's meat, I guess.

📝 停顿参考

Response: I'm going to describe a popular product in my region…and…well…the first one that comes to mind…is Xiao Long Bao…otherwise known as…uh…small soup dumpling.

…As for what the product is…well…like I said…it's…like…a soup dumpling…and generally there's some…you know…soup inside…as well as meat…sometimes it could be…like…crab or pork or…I think chicken…or something like that…so it definitely varies…like…what's inside the Xiao Long Bao…but generally…it's meat, I guess.

忽略语法或词汇错误

如果在回答的过程中发现自己犯了语法或者词汇方面的错误，请忽略这些错误，不要本能地去纠正。即使纠正了错误，考生也不会因此而获得额外的加分。纠正行为的唯一作用就是让考官知道考生的流利度有问题，考生在不断地修正英语上的错误。这无疑是一种暴露弱点的行为。此外，在考试的压力下，自我纠正会让考生更加慌乱，进而影响后续的流利度。因此，最好不做纠正并保持说话速度，以求在流利度上获得一个更好的分数。

◎ 遇到难题时的应对策略

以转述问题为开始

如果在考试时遇到一个很难的问题，考生可以通过转述问题来开始作答。用同义替换的方法重新说一遍题目可以为考生争取思考的时间，并将思维聚焦于如何回答问题上。请看以下例子：

Question: What would the world be like without the internet?

Response: If the world didn't have the internet, I think that…

Question: Should parents always let children choose the books they read?

Response: Letting children choose the books they read is not always a good thing because…

Question: What are the most difficult jobs that people do?

Response: I think that there are lots of different hard jobs that people do. For example…

练习

转述以下两个问题并做回答，回答时只需给出一个原因即可。

1. Question: Why has online shopping become so popular in many countries?

Response: _____

_____

2. Question: Do you think hotel work is a good career for life?

Response: _____

_____

学会说 "Let me think"

如果第一时间不确定该如何回答问题，可以使用 "Let me think" 表示自己需要一点时间来思考。但不能过度使用这个技能，如果在每次回答前都使用会显得极不自然。

示例

That's a hard question…let me think for a second…

That's an interesting question…let me think...

📝 **练习**

大声朗读示例中的表达，并尝试将这一技巧运用到以下题目中。

Question: In what ways might rich people use their money to help society?

Response: _____

_____

让考官重复问题

如果实在理解不了问题或者需要多一点时间思考，可以询问考官是否可以重复一下问题。当然，这种情况最多出现 1 ～ 2 次，多了肯定不行。

📝 **示例**

I'm sorry, could you repeat the question?

I'm sorry, do you mind saying that again?

Sorry, I didn't hear you clearly.

📝 **练习**

大声朗读示例中的句子，并尝试在不看文档的情况下说出这些句子。

用简单的答案回答难题

切记，雅思口语考试不是智力测试，答案没有对错。因此，遇到不熟悉的或者很难的问题，考生的回答可以尽量简单，使用任何已经掌握的词汇，哪怕像小孩子说出的答案也没关系。保持回答的连贯性才是最重要的。

📝 **示例**

Question: Should parents make plans for children?

复杂回答：I think that parents shouldn't always make plans for children because children will never grow that way and never become independent. Also, children need to feel like they have some control over their lives, or they will become unhappy. By contrast, if you give children more freedom, they will appreciate it and grow as a person.

简单回答：That's an interesting question... let me think for a second... well, I think parents shouldn't make plans for children because, you know, it's <u>boring</u> for children. It's more <u>exciting</u> when they can make plans for themselves. For example, when I was a child, my parents didn't make plans for me, so I was really <u>happy</u>.（注意有下画线的单词）

练习

请为以下问题准备一个简单甚至幼稚的回答。记住，优先考虑并关注流利度。

Question: What do you think it might be like to work in a customer service job?

Response: _____

_____

Part 3　核心话题及相关表达与素材

本部分按照话题分类，包括：教育；职业、个人目标、职业技能以及成功；商业与公司；朋友、家庭与邻居；科技；媒体与广告。

每个话题由若干小话题组成，每个小话题将按照以下 6 个部分进行讲解。

1. 话题解读：　　　介绍为何要选择这个话题、话题的出题频率等。

2. 口语题目展示：　展示与小话题相关的口语题目。

3. 答题思路分析：　挑选一道题目进行答题思路的分析。

4. 表达与素材罗列： 罗列与话题相关的表达与素材。

5. 表达与素材解读： 分析这些表达与素材。

6. 表达积累：　　　罗列重要的表达，并加上中文翻译。

由于 Part 3 的题目非常多且涉及的范围非常广泛，所以备考方法与 Part 2 不同。每一个大话题下面会包含若干小话题，而每个小话题下又包含 5 ～ 8 个相关问题。看到这些问题时，请不要惊慌，本书将提供一套非常直接且有效的方法帮助你解答这些问题。这里以小话题 Rewarding children（奖励孩子）为例，展示学习和训练过程。

◎步骤 1

首先，认真地读一下这个话题下的第一个题目（加粗的题目）。

Do you think parents should reward their children if they achieve something?

Should parents reward their children when they help others?

Should parents reward their children? Why and how?

What should parents do to teach their children good habits?

What rewards can children get from school?

◎步骤 2

读完题目之后，思考一下需要怎样回答。你的大脑活动可能是这样的：让我想想，"Do you think parents should reward their children if they achieve something?" 这个题目怎么回答呢？也许可以这样来说：这对孩子们来说是非常鼓舞人心的，但奖励的大小取决于孩子们获得了什么，是完成了一个小目标还是取得了很大的进步。

◎步骤 3

将你脑中的观点和想法与我们提供的表达与素材（每个话题下我们都会提供一些相关的表达与素材）进行比较。

Rewarding children for achievements or good behaviour is good because it encourages them to keep doing it. However, parents shouldn't reward their children for every small thing they do because if children are rewarded too often, they will get used to it and rewards will lose their meaning and effectiveness.

Children should be rewarded for good behaviour and big accomplishments, such as helping their parents with housework or getting excellent test scores.

Rewards can be a thing, like toys, food, or pocket money. It could also be a fun experience, like a trip to the zoo or amusement park.

Rewards can simply be vocal praise or encouragement. For example, parents could praise their children for accomplishing something.

通过快速思考，不难发现与题目相关的表达与素材如下：

Rewarding children for achievements or good behaviour is good because it encourages them to keep doing it. However, parents shouldn't reward their children for every small thing they do because if children are rewarded too often, they will get used to it and rewards will lose their meaning and effectiveness.

Children should be rewarded for good behaviour and big accomplishments, such as helping their parents with housework or getting excellent test scores.

◎步骤 4

将你的观点和想法与所提供的表达与素材结合起来就可以形成一个完整的回答。在这个过程中你可以结合所提供的表达与素材里的有用短语来组织自己的想法和观点，也可以将表达与素材里的大部分内容与自己的事例结合起来。

形成完整的回答之后，你必须大声练习。不要跳过这部分的口语练习，因为它可以帮助你记住这些表达与素材，达到融会贯通的效果。

◎步骤 5

转至本话题下的下一个问题（加粗部分），重复这个过程（先自己思考如何回答这个问题，然后与我们提供的表达与素材比对，最后得出自己的回答）。由于同一话题下的问题之间通常都有一定的关联或者相似性，这意味着在上一个问题中学到的表达与素材可以用来回答下一个问题，比如这里的 "Should parents reward their children when they help others?" 与第一个问题几乎是一致的，只是提问方式不同而已。

Do you think parents should reward their children if they achieve something?

Should parents reward their children when they help others?

Should parents reward their children? Why and how?

What should parents do to teach their children good habits?

What rewards can children get from school?

最后，再次提醒考生：在一个小话题中学到的素材与表达通常会在其他小话题中重复使用。掌握一些最实用的素材与表达并将它们运用到其他类似的题目中去，这是学习 Part 3 部分表达与素材的核心。

了解了本章的使用方法和规则之后，我们就可以正式进入口语题库及素材库的学习了。

话题 1　EDUCATION（教育）

教育是雅思口语 Part 3 中最常见的话题之一。教育的定义很宽泛，它不仅包括孩子们在学校接受的教育，还包括父母和长辈在家里对孩子的教育。在本章中，我们将学习如何回答与教育相关的问题。

1. Teaching children to help others（教孩子帮助他人）

◎ 话题解读

如何引导青少年帮助他人是教育类话题中很重要的一个组成部分。青少年除了需要学习学科知识、拥有强健的体魄和一定的审美观，还要学会关心他人、帮助他人。学会帮助他人及有帮助他人的意识是青少年人生课堂中非常重要的一课。以下这些口语题目都与帮助他人有关，请先通读题目，然后思考回答这些问题时该怎样组织信息和语言。

◎ 题目

Do you think children should be taught to help others?

What are the benefits of children helping their parents?

Are there any skills children should learn at home? What are they?

Can children provide any help to their parents?

What can parents do to cultivate children's quality of helping others?

How can we encourage children to help others?

Who should teach children to help others: parents or teachers?

How do students, such as high school students, help each other?

◎ 答题思路分析

这里以"Do you think children should be taught to help others?"为例，看看有哪些有用的英文素材可以用来回答这个问题。在学习这些素材之前，请先思考一下这个问题要从哪几个方面来回答。首先，需要做出一个肯定的回答，孩子们确实需要"be taught to help others"；其次，这种能力的培养需要家长和学校从不同方面共同努力（如果有例子，可以举例）。在掌握了回答的几个方面之后，我们来学习一些有用的表达与素材。

◎ 表达与素材

1. Children should learn how to help others because it teaches them useful skills and makes life more meaningful. They should begin learning how to help others at an early age.

2. To teach children to help others, parents must lead by example (in other words, be a role model). In addition, parents can teach children how to do basic housework, such as washing dishes and cleaning. Parents should also encourage, praise, or reward their children when they help others.

3. Students should be encouraged to help others at school. For example, students with good grades can help other students who have trouble with schoolwork. Schools can also organize field trips where students clean up the surrounding community or help at orphanages or elderly communities.

◎ 表达与素材解读

以上句子从回答题目、解释回答、举例说明三个方面展开。第一个句子非常简洁明了地回答了题目，告诉考官帮助别人是一种很好的品质，应该从小培养。第二个句子从家庭的角度阐述父母必须以身作则，要教孩子帮忙做家务，还要鼓励、表扬、奖励帮助了他人的孩子。第三个句子从学校的角度阐述学校应该鼓励学生去帮助他人，例如，成绩好的学生可以帮助做作业有困难的学生。学校也可以组织学生们打扫社区或为孤儿院、老年社区提供帮助。

这些句子不仅可以用于回答"Do you think children should be taught to help others?"，也可以用来回答其他问题，比如"parents must lead by example (be a role model)"可以用来回答题目"What can parents do to cultivate children's quality of helping others?"，后面的举例"teach children how to do housework, such as washing dishes and cleaning"可以用来回答"What can parents do to cultivate children's quality of helping others?""Can children provide any help to their parents?"及"Are there any skills children should learn at home? What are they?"。

◎ 表达积累

为了方便记忆和学习，我们将有用的表达罗列在以下表格中，考生可以尝试用这些表达的组合来回答之前罗列的相关题目。

学习要趁早	begin learning how to help others at an early age	从小开始学习怎样帮助他人
家长的教育	lead by example/be a role model	以身作则 / 成为榜样
	teach children how to do basic housework	教孩子如何做基础的家务
	wash dishes and clean	洗碗和清洁
	(parents should) encourage, praise, or reward their children when they help others	当孩子们帮助他人时，（家长应该）鼓励、表扬或奖励他们的孩子
	use punishments to discourage bad behaviour	用惩罚来阻止不良行为

	students should be encouraged to help others at school	在学校，学生应该被鼓励去帮助别人
学校的教育	students with good grades can help students who have problems with homework	成绩好的学生可以帮助写作业有困难的学生
	clean up the surrounding community	打扫周边社区
	help at orphanages or elderly communities	在孤儿院或老年社区提供帮助

2. Rewarding children（奖励孩子）

◎ 话题解读

给予奖励是鼓励和表扬孩子的常见手段。Part 3 的题目经常涉及"孩子们应该在什么情况下受到奖励"以及"怎样奖励孩子"。以下这些口语题目与奖励有关，请先通读题目，然后思考回答这些问题时该怎样组织信息和语言。

◎ 题目

Do you think parents should reward their children if they achieve something?

Should parents reward their children when they help others?

Should parents reward their children? Why and how?

What should parents do to teach their children good habits?

What rewards can children get from school?

◎ 答题思路分析

这里以"Should parents reward their children? Why and how?"为例，看看有哪些有用的英文句子可以用来回答这个问题。在学习这些英文句子之前，请先思考一下这个问题要从哪几个方面来回答。首先，你需要做出一个肯定的回答：当孩子们做成某些事情或达到某些目标时，父母确实应该给他们一点奖励。其次，你可以进一步说明奖励的内容，以及奖励的轻重程度。在掌握了回答的几个方面之后，一起来学习一些有用的表达与素材吧。

◎ 表达与素材

1. Rewarding children for achievements or good behaviour is good because it encourages them to keep doing it. However, parents shouldn't reward their children for every small thing they do because if children are rewarded too often, they will get used to it and rewards will lose their meaning and effectiveness.

2. Children should be rewarded for good behaviour and big accomplishments, such as helping their parents with housework or getting excellent test scores.

3. Rewards can be a thing, like toys, food, or pocket money. It could also be a fun experience, like a trip to the zoo or amusement park.

4. Rewards can simply be vocal praise or encouragement. For example, parents could praise their children for accomplishing something.

◎ 表达与素材解读

首先，需要肯定奖励对孩子是有效的，但奖励必须有限制，不是任何事情都能得到奖励。当孩子们达到了目标或行为良好时，家长应该给予一定的奖励。随后，对何为 "good behaviour and big accomplishments" 做进一步解释，比如帮助家长做家务或者考试成绩优异。其次，奖励的方式一般来说可以分为口头鼓励和物质奖励。口头鼓励即父母对孩子们的良好表现进行口头表扬。物质奖励则包括了很多内容，可以是玩具、食物、零花钱或者一次旅游。

这些句子及句子中的表达，不仅可以用来回答 "Should parents reward their children? Why and how?"，还可以回答其他题目，比如 "Do you think parents should reward their children if they achieve something?"。考生只需在使用表达与素材时稍加改动即可，比如素材里的第 2 个句子可以改成 "Children should be rewarded if they achieve something, for example getting excellent test scores." 奖励的两种形式也可以用来回答问题 "What rewards can children get from school?"，当然需要把 "parents" 改成 "teachers" 或 "school"，即 "Rewards can be in the form of encouragement. For example, teachers could praise their students' good behavior." 总之，要灵活运用这些短语和句子，切勿生搬硬套。

◎ 表达积累

为了方便记忆和学习，我们将有用的表达罗列在以下表格中，考生可以尝试用这些表达的组合来回答之前罗列的相关题目。

适度奖励	encourages them to keep doing it	鼓励他们继续做下去
	shouldn't reward their children for every small thing they do	不应该因为孩子做的每一件小事就奖励他们
	rewards will lose their meaning and effectiveness	奖励将失去其意义和有效性
好的行为	be rewarded for good behaviour and big accomplishments	因为良好的行为和巨大的成就而获得奖励
	help their parents with housework	帮助父母做家务
	get excellent test scores	获得优异的考试成绩
奖励的内容	toys, food, or pocket money	玩具、食物或者零花钱
	a trip to the zoo or amusement park	去动物园或游乐园的旅行
	vocal praise or encouragement	口头表扬或鼓励
	praise their children for accomplishing something	因为孩子完成了一些事情而表扬他们

3. Encouraging children（鼓励孩子）

◎话题解读

每个人都需要鼓励，尤其是孩子。Part 3 关于鼓励的话题通常会问"在什么情况下孩子需要鼓励"及"应该鼓励孩子做什么事情"。以下这些口语题目与鼓励孩子有关，请先通读题目，然后思考回答这些问题时该怎样组织信息和语言。

◎ 题目

On what occasions should children be encouraged? How should they be encouraged?

From a parent's perspective, is it useful to give children positive feedback?

What kind of encouragement should parents give?

Why should parents encourage children to have ambitions?

What will encourage children to learn more?

How can we encourage children to help others?

Do parents in your country encourage children to play games?

Do you think parents should encourage their children to share their toys with other kids?

What would happen if parents overly encourage their children?

◎ 答题思路分析

这里以 "On what occasions should children be encouraged? How should they be encouraged?" 为例，看看有哪些有用的英文句子可以用来回答这个问题。在学习这些英文句子之前，请先思考一下这个问题要从哪几个方面来回答。首先你需要回答孩子们需要被鼓励的场合，其次要回答怎样鼓励以及鼓励的内容，最后提一下鼓励不能太过。在掌握了答题的几个方面之后，就可以来学习一些有用的表达与素材了。

◎ 表达与素材

1. When children encounter difficulties, they need some encouragement. It helps cheer them up and motivates them to not give up.

2. Similarly, parents and teachers should encourage children to be ambitious and to have a learning mindset. It would be better for their future.

3. Parents should encourage their children to have good and kind behaviour. To do this, parents could praise their children for doing good things, such as helping others or sharing their toys.

4. However, parents shouldn't encourage their children too much. If children are encouraged for every little thing, they will get used to it and it will lose effectiveness.

◎表达与素材解读

根据以上内容，可以知道当孩子遇到困难时需要被鼓励。鼓励孩子什么呢？鼓励他们要有抱负并保持学习的心态，这对他们的未来有好处。此外，孩子们做好事或者行为良好（如帮助他人或者分享玩具）时，家长们更应该给予鼓励。最后，和奖励一样，鼓励也不要太过，不然孩子们会习惯鼓励，鼓励就变得没有效果了。

以上这些表达与素材也可以用于回答其他题目，比如"From a parent's perspective, is it useful to give children positive feedback?"，你可以说家长给孩子正面的反馈是有效的，这种正面反馈可以是鼓励，随后就可以使用与"鼓励孩子"相关的表达和素材来回答了。

◎表达积累

为了方便记忆和学习，我们将有用的表达罗列在以下表格中，考生可以尝试用这些表达的组合来回答之前罗列的相关题目。

encounter difficulties	遇到困难
need some encouragement	需要一些鼓励
encourage children to be ambitious and to have a learning mindset	鼓励孩子有抱负，保持学习的心态
encourage their children to have good and kind behaviour	鼓励他们的孩子有良好和善良的行为
praise their children for doing good things	表扬孩子做的好事
helps cheer them up and motivates them to not give up	帮助他们振作起来，激励他们不要放弃
be better for their future	对他们的未来更好
shouldn't encourage their children too much	不应该过多鼓励自己的孩子
get used to it and it will lose effectiveness	习惯了（鼓励）就会失去效力

4. Setting rules for children & students（制定规则）

◎ 话题解读

孩子们通常缺乏是非观和自制力，所以爸爸妈妈和学校会为其制定一些规则。Part 3 关于这个主题通常会问"这些规则的内容"以及"制定这些规则的好处"。以下这些口语题目与制定规则有关，请先通读题目，然后思考回答这些问题时该怎样组织信息和语言。

◎ 题目

What kinds of rules do Chinese families have?

What habits should children have?

What are the advantages and disadvantages of setting rules for children?

What kinds of rules do schools in China have?

Do you think strict rules are necessary for schools?

What do you think of students wearing uniforms in school?

Do you think students like to wear uniforms?

◎ 答题思路分析

这里以"What are the advantages and disadvantages of setting rules for children?"为例，看看有哪些有用的英文句子可以用来回答这个问题。在学习英文句子之前，请先思考一下这个问题要从哪几个方面来回答。首先你需要思考孩子们需要遵守哪些规则，其次挑选一种规则进行利弊讨论。现在，我们来学习一些有用的表达与素材。

◎ 表达与素材

1. Families may set rules such as requiring children to help with housework, not waste money, and to always tell the truth. Children may also be required to sleep earlier and spend time on schoolwork and studying. These kinds of rules are good for children's character development, physical development, and academics. What's more, following rules prepares children for the real world.

2. Schools may set rules such as requiring students to be on time, not cheat, not use their cellphones in class, and to dress properly. These rules promote a better learning environment.

3. Requiring school uniforms is not a bad thing because it helps reduce differences between the appearances of rich and poor students. This promotes equality and a sense of belonging among students. Also, school uniforms prevent students from wearing improper clothes.

4. On the other hand, setting rules can sometimes hurt a child's growth and development. For example, requiring school uniforms can limit children's creativity, freedom, and self-expression, preventing them from expressing themselves through their clothing.

◎ 表达与素材解读

家庭中给孩子设立的规则有帮助做家务、不浪费钱、说实话、早睡、好好学习、完成作业等。这些规则对孩子的性格发展、身体发育及学业有益，还能为其适应现实世界做好准备。学校的规则其实相对简单，除了按时上课、不作弊，还有课堂上不能使用手机、穿着得体等。然后选择了其中一条规则，即穿着得体来陈述其好处。关于穿着得体，这里提到了穿校服的规定。学校要求穿校服有什么好处呢？可以消除学生中的贫富差距、促进学生之间的平等和归属感以及防止学生穿着不合适的衣服。当然，这些规则也会带来一些负面的影响，比如影响孩子的发展，这其中包括创造力、自我表现等方面。

以上这些表达和素材同样也适用于其他题目，比如"What kinds of rules do schools in China have?"，考生可以使用学校规则中提到的内容，并加以解释或简单举例。

◎ 表达积累

为了方便记忆和学习，我们将有用的表达罗列在以下表格中，考生可以尝试用这些表达的组合来回答之前罗列的相关题目。

	require children to help with housework, not waste money, and to always tell the truth	（家长）要求孩子帮忙做家务，不浪费钱，而且永远讲真话
家中的规则	be required to sleep earlier and spend time on schoolwork and studying	要求早点睡觉，把时间花在作业和学习上
	good for children's character development, physical development, and academics	对孩子的性格发展、身体发育和学习都有好处
	following rules prepares children for the real world	遵守规则有助于帮助孩子适应现实世界
学校的规则	require students to be on time, not cheat, not use their cellphones in class, and to dress properly	（学校和老师）要求学生按时上课，不作弊，上课不使用手机，穿着得体
	promote a better learning environment	促进更好的学习环境
	reduce differences between the appearances of rich and poor students	（穿校服）减少贫富学生的外貌差异
	promotes equality and a sense of belonging among students	促进学生间的平等和归属感
规则带来的负面影响	hurt a child's growth and development	伤害孩子的成长和发展
	limit children's creativity, freedom, and self-expression	限制孩子的创造力、自由和自我表达
	prevent them from expressing themselves through their clothing	阻止他们通过服装来表达自己

5. Children's mistakes & Punishing children（犯错与惩罚）

◎ 话题解读

孩子们犯错误是很常见的。有的错误是偶然的、无意的，比如打碎了一个盘子；有的错误则比较严重，比如考试作弊。Part 3 关于这个话题通常会问"当孩子犯错时父母或老师应该做什么"或者"什么样的惩罚是合适的"。以下这些口语题目和犯错与惩罚有关，请先通读题目，然后思考回答这些问题时该怎样组织信息和语言。

◎ 题目

Do children make mistakes easily?

What should parents do if their children make mistakes?

Do parents and teachers punish children physically nowadays?

Are there teachers in China who punish students?

◎ 答题思路分析

这里以"What should parents do if their children make mistakes?"为例，看看有哪些英文句子可以用来回答这个问题。在学习这些英文句子之前，请先思考一下这个问题要从哪几个方面来回答。你需要思考两个方面：什么错误不需要被严格处罚及如何处罚；什么错误需要被严格处罚及如何处罚。在掌握了回答的几个方面之后，我们来学习一些有用的表达与素材。

◎ 表达与素材

1. Children should not be punished too harshly for making minor mistakes, because making mistakes is a natural part of growing up. Children are still learning about what's right and wrong, and they lack self-control. When a child makes a mistake, the parents should teach the child why the mistake is wrong and how to avoid it in the future.

2. Children should be punished for poor behaviour, such as lying, cheating, or breaking rules. However, children should not be punished with violence, as it could injure them and also teach them that violence is okay. Effective and non-abusive punishments include taking away a child's mobile phone or reducing the child's pocket money.

◎表达与素材解读

根据以上内容，可以知道当孩子们只是犯了一些小错误时，不需要被严厉处罚，因为犯错是成长的一部分，孩子们还在学习什么是对、什么是错，而且他们缺乏自制力。那么，家长应该做什么呢？应该让孩子知道为什么这是不对的，未来要如何避免这些错误。但当孩子们犯了严重的错误时，他们需要被处罚，严重的错误有哪些呢？包括说谎、作弊或违反规定。处罚的措施有哪些呢？可以是没收手机和减少零花钱，但不能使用暴力。

以上这些表达和素材同样适用于其他题目，比如"Are there teachers in China who punish students?"。回答这个问题可以从两个方面入手：如果是小错误，老师找学生谈话就好；如果错误比较严重，则可以使用一定的非暴力惩罚手段。

◎ 表达积累

为了方便记忆和学习，我们将有用的表达罗列在以下表格中，考生可以尝试用这些表达的组合来回答之前罗列的相关题目。

是否应该惩罚及惩罚的力度	should not be punished too harshly for making minor mistakes	小错误不应该受到太严厉的惩罚
	should not be punished with violence	不应该用暴力来惩罚
	should be punished for poor behaviour, such as lying, cheating, or breaking rules	撒谎、作弊或违反规则等不良行为应该受到惩罚
犯错的原因	making mistakes is a natural part of growing up	犯错是成长中很自然的一部分
	are still learning about what's right and wrong	还在学习什么是对、什么是错
	lack self-control	缺乏自控能力
惩罚的措施	teach the child why the mistake is wrong and how to avoid it in the future	教孩子为什么这是不对的，将来如何避免它
	Effective and non-abusive punishments include taking away a child's mobile phone or reducing the child's pocket money.	有效且非虐待性的惩罚包括拿走孩子的手机或减少孩子的零花钱。

6. Spending time with one's children（陪伴孩子）

◎ 话题解读

由于工作或其他原因，现代社会的许多父母并没有足够的时间来陪伴孩子。Part 3 关于这个话题通常会问"为什么父母应该花时间和孩子在一起，而不是让孩子自己玩玩具或让别人照顾他们"。以下这些口语题目与陪伴孩子有关，请先通读题目，然后思考回答这些问题时该怎样组织信息和语言。

◎ 题目

Do parents in your country spend a lot of time with their children?

What are the drawbacks if children are looked after by their grandparents?

How do grandparents take care of their grandchildren?

If you were a parent and you were busy at work, would you take care of your children on your own or hire a babysitter?

How much time should parents spend with their children every day?

Do you think parents should buy more toys for their kids or spend more time with them?

Do you think it's important for parents to read bedtime stories to their children?

◎ 答题思路分析

这里以"Do parents in your country spend a lot of time with their children?"为例，看看有哪些有用的英文句子可以用来回答这个问题。在学习英文句子之前，请先思考一下这个问题要从哪几个方面来回答。首先肯定要明确父母到底有没有花时间陪伴孩子，然后说明不陪伴孩子的坏处以及陪伴孩子的好处，最后可以给出一些陪伴孩子的建议，比如讲睡前故事。掌握了回答的几个方面之后，就可以来学习一些有用的表达与素材了。

◎ 表达与素材

1. Parents these days don't really spend a lot of time with their children because of work. Instead, grandparents or maids often take care of children. One drawback of this is that grandparents tend to spoil their grandchildren. Another drawback is that children become more distant from their parents.

2. Parents should try to spend more time with their children because it's important for children's social and emotional development, and it helps build a bond between parents and their children.

3. Reading bedtime stories is a fun and relaxing way for parents to get closer with their children. It also helps improve children's vocabulary, reading skills, and imagination.

◎ 表达与素材解读

根据以上内容，可以知道当今社会由于父母工作都很忙，没有很多时间去陪伴孩子，导致产生一些不好的后果，比如爷爷奶奶容易宠坏他们的孙子／孙女，孩子与父母疏离。因此，父母需要多留点时间陪伴孩子，这不仅对儿童的社交和情感发展很重要，还可以建立父母和孩子之间的纽带。在睡前给孩子读书、讲故事是一个非常好的增进父母与孩子感情的方式，同时还可以提高孩子的词汇量、阅读能力和想象力。

　　以上这些表达和素材同样也适用于其他题目，比如"How do grandparents take care of their grandchildren?"，考生可以说他们会溺爱孩子，缺乏对孩子的管教，如有可能还是建议父母多陪伴孩子。又比如题目"How much time should parents spend with their children every day?"，考生可以说父母一般很忙，没有很多时间陪伴，但为了孩子好还是要尽量多花一点时间和孩子在一起，然后就可以使用我们在表达与素材中列举的内容了。

◎ 表达积累

　　为了方便记忆和学习，我们将有用的表达罗列在以下表格中，考生可以尝试用这些表达的组合来回答之前罗列的相关题目。

缺乏父母陪伴带来的危害	grandparents tend to spoil their grandchildren	（外）祖父母往往会溺爱孙子/孙女
	children become more distant from their parents	孩子们和父母越来越疏远
父母陪伴带来的好处	it's important for children's social and emotional development	这对孩子的社交和情感发展很重要
	it helps build a bond between parents and their children	它有助于建立父母和孩子之间的纽带
陪伴的方式及好处	read bedtime stories	读睡前故事
	get closer with their children	和他们的孩子走得更近
	improve children's vocabulary, reading skills, and imagination	提高孩子的词汇量、阅读能力和想象力

7. Setting goals and making decisions for children（帮助孩子设定目标与做决定）

◎ 话题解读

　　成年人总是会为自己的学业、事业或个人生活设定目标，而孩子通常都是由父母替他们设定目标和做决定的。Part 3 关于这个话题通常会问"父母为孩子设定目标及做决定是否是一件好事"。以下这些口语题目和帮助孩子设定目标与做决定有关，请先通读题目，然后思考回答这些问题时该怎样组织信息和语言。

◎ 题目

Do parents in your country make decisions for their children?

Should parents set goals for children?

Do you think parents should make plans for their children?

Do you think parents should give kids challenges?

How can parents help their children achieve goals?

Can children make decisions on their own?

When do young children start to set goals for themselves?

Why is it important for teenagers to set goals?

◎ 答题思路分析

这里以 "Do parents in your country make decisions for their children?" 为例，看看有哪些英文句子可以用来回答这个问题。在学习英文句子之前，请先思考一下这个问题要从哪几个方面来回答。关于父母是否会替孩子设定目标、做决定，这取决于目标和决定的大小。如果是比较重要的决定和目标，还是需要家长和老师们来帮忙的，当然也需要提前与孩子沟通。等孩子长大些了，就应该慢慢培养他们独立设定目标和做决定的能力。在掌握了回答的几个方面之后，我们来学习一些有用的表达与素材。

◎ 表达与素材

1. Young children usually can't make big decisions for themselves because they don't know enough about the world and what's really important. They tend to not think about the big picture or the long-term consequences. That's why young children need adult guidance.

2. When a child is young, teachers and parents need to help set goals and plans for the child. Parents can also help their children achieve those goals by monitoring their progress, encouraging them, and rewarding them when they succeed.

3. Goals can be academic—for example, doing well on an exam or getting good grades. Goals should also not be too challenging or hard to achieve. Otherwise, it would discourage children.

4. When children become older, they should begin setting goals for themselves. It teaches them how to be more independent and responsible. It prepares them for university and their future jobs.

◎ 表达与素材解读

根据以上内容可知，孩子们不能独自做大的决定，这是因为他们不够了解世界，不知道什么是真正重要的东西，而且他们很难考虑大局或长期后果。因此，在孩子还小的时候，父母和师长应该帮助他们制定目标、做出决定，同时也要帮助他们实现这些目标。至于这些目标和决定的内容，可以是学习上的（在考试中表现良好、取得好成绩），也可以是生活上的。目标也不能太具有挑战性，不然孩子就不愿意尝试了。当孩子们长大成熟后，就要自己设定目标了，这对他们的未来有好处。

以上这些表达和素材同样也适用于其他题目，比如 "How can parents help their children achieve goals?"，这个题目的回答方式和 "Do parents in your country make decisions for their children?" 其实是一样的，"help children achieve goals" 就等同于 "make decisions for children"。

◎ 表达积累

为了方便记忆和学习，我们将有用的表达罗列在以下表格中，考生可以尝试用这些表达的组合来回答之前罗列的相关题目。

为何需要父母和师长帮助做决定及设定目标	they don't know enough about the world and what's really important	他们不够了解这个世界，也不知道什么才是真正重要的
	they tend to not think about the big picture or the long-term consequences	他们很难考虑大局或长期后果
	young children need adult guidance	小孩子需要大人的指导
父母、师长可以做的	help set goals and plans for the child	帮助孩子设定目标和计划
	help their children achieve those goals by monitoring their progress, encouraging them, and rewarding them when they succeed	通过监督他们的进步、鼓励他们，并在他们成功时奖励他们来帮助他们实现这些目标
什么时候该自己做决定、设定目标	they should begin setting goals for themselves	他们应该开始为自己设定目标
	how to be more independent and responsible	如何变得更独立和有责任心
	prepares them for university and their future job	为他们上大学和未来的工作做准备

8. Parent's advice for children（父母给孩子的建议）

◎ 话题解读

父母是孩子人生中的第一任导师，孩子经常会从父母那里得到建议。Part 3 关于建议的话题通常会问"父母会给你什么样的建议"及"来自父母的建议的优势"。以下这些口语题目与父母给孩子的建议有关，请先通读题目，然后思考回答这些问题时该怎样组织信息和语言。

◎ 题目

Should parents give children advice? Why?

Who do young people turn to for advice?

When young people are able to make decisions, should they still listen to some advice?

What general advice do parents give to children?

What kinds of advice should parents give to their children?

◎ 答题思路分析

这里以"Should parents give children advice? Why?"为例，看看有哪些英文句子可以用来回答这个问题。在学习英文句子之前，请先思考一下这个问题要从哪几个方面来回答。关于父母是否需要给孩子们建议，显而易见是需要给的。接下来可以具体谈一下父母应该给孩子什么样的建议以及父母给孩子建议的好处有哪些。在掌握了回答的几个方面之后，我们来学习一些有用的表达与素材。

◎ 表达与素材

1. Parents should give their children advice because it would help a lot. Children lack life experience, and they tend to not think about the long-term consequences of things.

2. Parents should give children advice about school and social relationships, as well as advice on their children's career and other future matters.

3. Parents can also give children advice about how to take care of themselves—for example, by teaching them how to do housework and how to cook, and emphasizing the importance of exercising, eating healthily, and sleeping early.

◎ 表达与素材解读

根据以上内容，可以知道由于缺乏生活经验并且倾向于不考虑事情的长期后果，父母需要给孩子们建议。这个理由其实在很多场景中都适用。至于父母需要给孩子怎样的建议，可分两方面展开回答，一是学习、工作方面，二是个人生活方面。

以上这些表达和素材同样也适用于其他题目，比如"When young people are able to make decisions, should they still listen to some advice?"，考生可以回答"他们确实需要听取父母的建议"，随后说明原因和该听取哪方面的建议。

◎ 表达积累

为了方便记忆和学习，我们将有用的表达罗列在以下表格中，考生可以尝试用这些表达的组合来回答之前罗列的相关题目。

需要听取建议的原因	lack life experience	缺乏生活经验
	tend to not think about the long-term consequences of things	往往不考虑事情的长期后果
父母应该给予哪些建议	advice about school and social relationships	关于学校和社会关系的建议
	advice on their children's career and other future matters	对孩子的事业和其他未来事务的建议
	advice about how to take care of themselves—for example, by teaching them how to do housework and how to cook, and emphasizing the importance of exercising, eating healthily, and sleeping early	关于如何照顾自己的建议——例如，教他们如何做家务、如何做饭，强调锻炼、健康饮食和早睡的重要性

9. Children's ability to be independent（孩子们独立自主的能力）

◎ 话题解读

在成长的过程中，孩子们从依赖父母变得越来越独立。Part 3 关于这个话题通常会问"孩子学习独立的好处"及"提高孩子独立能力的方法"。以下这些口语题目与孩子们的独立自主有关，请先通读题目，然后思考回答这些问题时该怎样组织信息和语言。

◎ 题目

Do you think children should be more independent or rely more on their parents?

Do you think children should go to school by themselves or be sent by parents? (What about teenagers, such as high school students?)

What are the effects if parents interfere with their children excessively?

How can we improve children's ability to be independent?

◎ 答题思路分析

这里以"Do you think children should be more independent or rely more on their parents?"为例，看看有哪些英文句子可以用来回答这个问题。在学习英文句子之前，请先思考一下这个问题要从哪几个方面来回答。回答这个问题可以有两种思路，一种是认为应该依靠父母，一种是认为应该更加独立。对于第一个思路，考生可以使用前面学过的表达和素材，比如孩子们还太小，缺少生活经验等。对于第二个思路，请看以下表达与素材。

◎ 表达与素材

1. As they grow older, children need to learn to become more independent because it will prepare them for the future when they're studying in university or working.

2. Parents can help children become more independent by encouraging them to explore and do things themselves, and by not interfering too much with their lives. Parents can also teach children to take care of themselves—for example, by teaching them how to do housework and cook.

◎ 表达与素材解读

根据以上内容可知，孩子们需要为未来做好准备，而学会独立是为未来做好准备的一部分。那么，家长在这个过程中能做什么呢？可以鼓励他们探索、自己做自己的事情、不过多地干涉他们的生活、教会孩子们如何照顾自己。

以上这些表达和素材同样也适用于其他题目，比如"How can we improve children's ability to be independent?"，考生完全可以使用第二个表达，当然，为了让回答更丰满，还可以举一个与自己有关的例子。

◎ 表达积累

为了方便记忆和学习，我们将有用的表达罗列在以下表格中，考生可以尝试用这些表达的组合来回答之前罗列的相关题目。

需要学会独立的原因	prepare them for the future	为他们的未来做好准备
家长们应该怎样做	encourage them to explore and do things themselves	鼓励他们去探索和自己做自己的事情
	not interfere too much with their lives	不要过多地干涉他们的生活
	teach children to take care of themselves—for example, by teaching them how to do housework and cook	教孩子照顾自己——例如，教他们做家务和做饭

10. Teaching children about money（培养孩子正确的金钱观）

◎ 话题解读

我们的生活离不开钱。对金钱有正确的态度及管理好金钱是每个人都需要学习的东西。关于这个话题，Part 3 通常会问"父母如何教孩子珍惜金钱"及"为什么对孩子来说学习金钱管理很重要"。以下这些口语题目与培养孩子正确的金钱观有关，请先通读题目，然后思考回答这些问题时该怎样组织信息和语言。

◎ 题目

Is it important for children to have the right attitude towards money?

Is it important to teach children how to manage their pocket money?

Do you think children should learn money management?

What should parents do when their children ask for things their friends have?

Some people think that children today have too many toys. What do you think?

Should parents spend a lot of money on their children's birthday parties?

Should parents buy expensive gifts for their children?

In your country, do parents give children money for doing housework?

◎ 答题思路分析

这里以 "Is it important for children to have the right attitude towards money?" 为例，看看有哪些英文句子可以用来回答这个问题。在学习英文句子之前，请先思考一下这个问题要从哪几个方面来回答。首先需要回答重要；接着要说明为何重要，例如，培养正确的金钱观与未来发展有关，如果花钱无度会产生很多问题；最后，如果有需要，还可以谈一下如何帮助孩子培养金钱观。在掌握了回答的几个方面之后，接下来我们来学习一些有用的表达与素材。

◎ 表达与素材

1. Children need to learn that money is valuable and that it shouldn't be wasted. Having the right attitude towards money and knowing how to manage money will help children become more independent and prepare them for the future when they're studying in university or working.

2. To help children develop awareness and money management skills, parents can give children pocket money and encourage them to save it or spend it wisely. Parents should also not give their children too much money, toys, or gifts. Otherwise, their children will get used to it and become spoiled. Money and gifts should only be given sometimes as a special reward, so that children are able to truly appreciate them.

◎ 表达与素材解读

首先孩子们需要了解钱是有价值的，它不应该被浪费。培养正确的金钱观的好处有哪些呢？

能帮助孩子变得更独立，并为他们将来上大学或工作做好准备。既然培养金钱观很重要，家长们应该怎么做呢？要帮助孩子们培养理财意识和管理金钱的技能，具体的做法是给孩子们零花钱，鼓励他们存起来或明智地使用，但不能给太多的钱、玩具或礼物。总之要适度，不然容易产生负面作用。

以上这些表达和素材同样也适用于其他题目，比如"In your country, do parents give children money for doing housework?"，考生可以说家长会给一些零用钱或者礼物作为奖励，但不能给太多，然后谈论给这些奖励的好处。

◎ 表达积累

为了方便记忆和学习，我们将有用的表达罗列在以下表格中，考生可以尝试用这些表达的组合来回答之前罗列的相关题目。

培养正确金钱观的好处	learn that money is valuable and that it shouldn't be wasted	要知道钱是有价值的，不应该被浪费
	help children become more independent and prepare them for the future when they're studying in university or working	帮助孩子们变得更加独立，并为他们将来上大学或工作做好准备
如何帮助孩子建立金钱观	help children develop awareness and money management skills	帮助孩子培养理财意识和管理金钱的技能
	give children pocket money and encourage them to save it or spend it wisely	给孩子们零花钱，鼓励他们存起来或明智地使用
	not give their children too much money, toys, or gifts	不要给孩子们太多的钱、玩具或礼物
	money and gifts should only be given sometimes as a special reward	金钱和礼物只应该在某些时候作为特殊奖励给到孩子

11. Benefits of children competing for prizes（参加比赛获奖的益处）

◎ 话题解读

在学校，成绩好的学生常常会得到奖励；在校外，家长们也会带孩子参加各种各样的比赛，这是很多孩子都会有的经历。Part 3 关于比赛和奖励的题目通常会问"奖励的目的"及"对学生的影响"。以下这些口语题目与参加比赛的益处有关，请先通读题目，然后思考回答这些问题时该如何组织信息和语言。

◎ 题目

Is it good for children to compete for prizes at school?

What are the benefits of giving prizes to children?

Should parents push their children to get prizes?

What are the problems if parents push their children to win the prizes?

When do parents feel proud of their children?

◎ 答题思路分析

这里以 "What are the problems if parents push their children to win the prizes?" 为例，看看有哪些有用的英文句子可以用来回答这个问题。在学习英文句子之前，请先思考一下这个问题要从哪几个方面来回答。首先要确认参加比赛并获得奖励是否合理，然后需要说明奖励的目的以及会对孩子产生怎样的影响。在掌握了回答的几个方面之后，我们来学习一些有用的表达与素材。

◎ 表达与素材

1. The chance to win a prize may encourage children to work harder. And if they win a prize, they feel a sense of accomplishment.

2. However, parents should not push their children too hard to win prizes because it would put too much pressure on them. Also, parents need to show pride when their children give a lot of effort, and encourage their children even if they fail.

◎ 表达与素材解读

根据以上内容可知，参加比赛获奖对孩子们来说很重要，因为这会鼓励孩子们更努力地学习，让他们有成就感。然而，无论是家长还是学校，都不应该逼迫孩子们去参加比赛并必须拿到奖。当孩子们参加比赛拿到奖之后，家长和学校应该为他们感到骄傲，如果没有拿到奖也要鼓励他们。

以上这些表达和素材同样也适用于其他题目，比如 "Should parents push their children to get prizes?"，考生可以回答不应该强迫孩子们去拿奖，但是可以鼓励他们去参加比赛，因为这对孩子们是有好处的，这时就可以用到以上罗列的表达和素材了。

◎ 表达积累

为了方便记忆和学习，我们将有用的表达罗列在以下表格中，考生可以尝试用这些表达的组合来回答之前罗列的相关题目。

参加比赛获奖的好处	encourage children to work harder	鼓励孩子们更加努力地学习
	feel a sense of accomplishment	有成就感
家长、学校的态度（如果是学校的话，需要将 children 换成 students）	not push their children too hard to win prizes	不要为了得奖把孩子逼得太紧
	show pride when their children give a lot of effort	当孩子们付出很多努力时要表现出（为他们）骄傲的样子
	encourage their children even if they fail	即使孩子们失败了，也要鼓励他们

12. The effect of age on learning（年龄对学习的影响）

◎ 话题解读

学习是陪伴我们终生的事情，活到老，学到老。Part 3 与这个话题相关的问题通常会问 "人们在不同的年龄阶段的学习状态" 及 "最佳的学习年龄"。以下这些口语题目和年龄对学习的影响有关，请先通读题目，然后思考回答这些问题时应该怎样组织信息和语言。

◎ 题目

Who do you think learns better: old people or young people?

Which age group is the best at learning?

Do you think childhood is the most important period in one's development?

Is it hard for old people to learn new skills?

What kinds of teaching methods are suitable for old people?

How to help old people learn?

◎ 答题思路分析

这里以"Who do you think learns better: old people or young people?"为例，看看有哪些有用的英文句子可以用来回答这个问题。在学习英文句子之前，请先思考一下这个问题要从哪几个方面来回答。年龄是雅思口语考试中经常提及的话题，年龄会影响到一些事情，但是对于学习，我们始终要抱着"活到老，学到老"的态度。在掌握新知识和新技能方面，年纪不同则学习的效率不同、学习的目的也不同。但只要愿意学习，任何年龄都可以。在掌握了回答的几个方面之后，我们来学习一些有用的表达与素材。

◎ 表达与素材

1. Young people tend to have an easier time learning new things than old people. Their brains are more suited to learning and they absorb new information better. Also, young people are more curious about the world, more open-minded, and more willing to explore than old people.

2. Old people can also learn new things, but they need extra motivation. They need to know that what they're learning is practical and useful for their daily lives. Old people's memories are also not as good, so they need to be taught at a slower pace with more repetition.

◎表达与素材解读

题目中提到了年轻人和老人，因此可以结合他们的特点来回答。根据以上内容可知，年轻人更容易学习新的东西，因为他们的大脑更适合学习，也能更好地吸收新信息，而且他们对世界更好奇，思想更开放，也更愿意去探索。相比之下，老年人如果要学习新的东西，则需要额外的动力，并且因为他们的记忆力没那么好了，会学得慢些。

以上这些表达和素材同样适用于其他题目，比如"Is it hard for old people to learn new skills?"这道题就可以直接使用表达与素材中关于老年人的那部分内容。如果觉得内容不够充实，还可以举一个身边人的例子，比如自己的爷爷去老年大学学习摄影。

◎ 表达积累

为了方便记忆和学习，我们将有用的表达罗列在以下表格中，考生可以尝试用这些表达的组合来回答之前罗列的相关题目。

年轻人与学习	Their brains are more suited to learning and they absorb new information better.	他们的大脑更适合学习，也能更好地吸收新信息。
	more curious about the world, more open-minded, and more willing to explore	对世界更好奇，思想更开放，更愿意探索
老年人与学习	need extra motivation	需要额外的动力
	need to know that what they're learning is practical and useful for their daily lives	需要知道他们所学的对他们的日常生活是实用的
	need to be taught at a slower pace with more repetition	需要以更慢的节奏来教授并重复更多次

13. Smartness & Intelligence（聪明与智商）

◎ 话题解读

有些人很聪明，但他们是天生聪明还是后天努力的结果？ Part 3 关于这个话题会问"为什么有些人很聪明"及"如何才能变得聪明"。以下这些口语题目和聪明与智商有关，请先通读题目，然后思考回答这些问题时该如何组织信息和语言。

◎ 题目

Why are some children more intelligent than others?

Do you think children are born smart or do they learn to become smart?

Which do you think is more important: nature or nurture?

How do you become a smart person?

◎ 答题思路分析

这里以"Do you think children are born smart or do they learn to become smart?"为例，看看有哪些有用的英文句子可以用来回答这个问题。在学习英文句子之前，请先思考一下这个问题要从哪几个方面来回答。首先，承认有些人的聪明是与生俱来的，但更多人需要后天的培养与努力，接着在回答中着重强调培养与努力的作用。在掌握了回答的几个方面之后，我们来学习一些有用的表达与素材。

◎ 表达与素材

1. Some people are naturally smart because of their genetics. Other people are smart because of their upbringing—for example, if they had a good learning environment and parents who set goals for them and encouraged them a lot.

2. A person can also become smarter by having the right attitude. It helps if they're curious about the world, open-minded, and willing to explore. It also helps if they make an effort to approach problems rationally, step by step.

◎ 表达与素材解读

有些人的聪明是天生的，有些人的聪明则是后天培养的。所谓天生的，就是人们常说的遗传基因好。但后天的努力也可以让人变聪明，比如良好的学习环境、父母会为孩子设立目标及不断地鼓励他们等。除此之外，正确的态度和个人的努力对变聪明也非常有用。

以上这些表达和素材同样适用于其他题目，比如"Which do you think is more important: nature or nurture?"这道题其实就是"Do you think children are born smart or do they learn to become smart?"的改写，"nature"等同于"born smart"，而"nurture"等同于"learn to become smart"。

◎ 表达积累

为了方便记忆和学习，我们将有用的表达罗列在以下表格中，考生可以尝试用这些表达的组合来回答之前罗列的相关题目。

天生拥有的	genetics	遗传
后天培养的	upbringing	教养，养育
	had a good learning environment	有良好的学习环境
	become smarter by having the right attitude	拥有正确的态度会变得更聪明
	are curious about the world, open-minded, and willing to explore	对世界充满好奇，思想开放，愿意探索
	make an effort to approach problems rationally, step by step	努力理性地处理问题，循序渐进

14. What good teachers do（优秀教师的品质）

◎ 话题解读

好的老师对学生的学习引导、品格培养及人生观和价值观塑造等有很大的帮助。Part 3 关于这个话题通常会问"教师应该具备的良好品质"及"教师的教学技能/方法"。以下这些口语题目和优秀教师的品质有关，请先通读题目，然后思考回答这些问题时该怎样组织信息和语言。

◎ 题目

What qualities do you think a good teacher should have?

What kind of teaching skills are important?

Is a good teacher very important for students' learning experience? Why?

How can teachers inspire students to have more ideas?

What kinds of teaching methods are not useful?

◎ 答题思路分析

这里以"What qualities do you think a good teacher should have?"为例，看看有哪些有用的英文句子可以用来回答这个问题。在学习英文句子之前，请先思考一下这个问题要从哪几个方面来回答。从品行上来说，优秀教师应该是一个正直、善良、关爱他人的人；从专业技能上来说，优秀教师必须学科知识扎实、授课思路清晰、语言组织能力强。在掌握了回答的几个方面之后，我们来学习一些有用的表达与素材。

◎ 表达与素材

1. Good teachers explain things clearly and patiently, and are able to make difficult concepts easier to understand.

2. Good teachers are able to make their classes interesting or fun so that students (especially younger ones) pay more attention.

3. Good teachers know how to encourage and motivate students. They help students understand the value of the things they're learning.

◎ 表达与素材解读

作为老师，最重要的职责就是传授知识，所以能够清楚、耐心地解释知识和将有难度的概念变得简单易懂是两个非常重要的能力。此外，为了让学生保持专注，教师要想办法让课堂变得有趣。最后，教师还要知道怎样鼓励和激励学生。以上这些表达与素材都与教师的职业能力息息相关，对于教师的品行，可以借鉴之前学过的描述人物优点的表达。

以上这些表达和素材同样适用于其他题目，比如"Is a good teacher very important for students' learning experience? Why?"这道题就可以使用以上内容来回答。如果是题目"What kinds of teaching methods are not useful?"，只需要将以上内容改成否定形式就可以了，比如将"explain things clearly and patiently"改成"not explain things clearly and patiently"。

◎ 表达积累

为了方便记忆和学习，我们将有用的表达罗列在以下表格中，考生可以尝试用这些表达的组合来回答之前罗列的相关题目。

explain things clearly and patiently	清楚且有耐心地解释
able to make difficult concepts easier to understand	能够使复杂的概念变得更容易理解
able to make their classes interesting or fun so that students pay more attention	能够使他们的课堂变得有趣，这样会让学生保持专注
know how to encourage and motivate students	知道如何鼓励和激励学生
help students understand the value of the things they're learning	帮助学生理解所学知识的价值

15. Popular and interesting teachers（受欢迎且有趣的教师）

◎ 话题解读

在学校，有些老师很受学生喜爱。他们通常都有自己的特点，或幽默风趣，或学识渊博，或充满爱心。学生喜欢这些老师，也喜欢上他们的课。Part 3 关于这个话题通常会问"什么样的老师最受欢迎"及"教师是否应该在课堂上表现得有趣"。以下这些口语题目和受欢迎且有趣的教师有关，请先通读题目，然后思考回答这些问题时该怎样组织信息和语言。

◎ 题目

What kinds of teachers are popular at school?

What methods can be applied to make math classes more interesting?

What makes a good foreign language teacher?

Do you think all teachers should have entertaining teaching styles?

Do you think teachers should be funny when they are teaching?

Should teachers tell jokes in class?

What kinds of primary school teachers will impress students?

Why do teachers need to be kind to students?

◎ 答题思路分析

这里以"What kinds of teachers are popular at school?"为例,看看有哪些有用的英文句子可以用来回答这个问题。在学习英文句子之前,请先思考一下这个问题要从哪几个方面来回答。首先可以谈谈什么样的性格会受欢迎,其次聊聊他们的教学方法,最后还可以说说老师对待学生的态度。在掌握了回答的几个方面之后,我们来学习一些有用的表达与素材。

◎ 表达与素材

1. Popular teachers usually have interesting classes and likeable personalities.

2. Teachers need to make their classes interesting or fun sometimes so that students (especially younger students) pay more attention. Teachers can accomplish this by using games, videos, competitions, and prizes. They can also joke around sometimes, as it makes class less boring and provides some relief.

3. Teachers should be kind, friendly, and encouraging to students. When students like and admire a teacher, they pay more attention to the teacher and it makes the class more enjoyable.

◎ 表达与素材解读

首先指出受欢迎的老师通常满足两个条件:interesting classes(有趣的课堂)和 likeable personalities(令人喜爱的性格)。接下来分别介绍这两个条件具体包含的内容。有趣的课堂可以让学生的注意力更集中,怎么做到有趣呢?可以通过游戏、视频、比赛和奖励来实现,也可以适当地开一些玩笑。就性格方面来说,体贴、友善、会鼓励学生的老师往往比较受学生喜欢。学生崇拜和喜欢自己的老师,会让课堂变得更享受。

以上这些表达和素材同样适用于其他题目,比如"Do you think teachers should be funny when they are teaching?"这个题目就可以使用以上罗列的部分内容来回答。可以说"funny"肯定是有优势的,老师有趣会让学生喜欢上这个老师的课,课堂有趣能让学生更好地集中注意力学习。

◎ 表达积累

为了方便记忆和学习,我们将有用的表达罗列在以下表格中,考生可以尝试用这些表达的组合来回答之前罗列的相关题目。

受欢迎的教师的特质	interesting classes and likeable personalities	有趣的课堂和令人喜欢的性格
有趣的课堂	need to make their classes interesting or fun sometimes so that students (especially younger students) pay more attention	有时需要使他们的课程变得有趣或愉快，这样能让学生（特别是年轻的学生）注意力更集中
	use games, videos, competitions, and prizes	使用游戏、视频、比赛和奖励
	joke around	开玩笑
令人喜欢的性格	be kind, friendly, and encouraging to students	对学生体贴、友善，会鼓励他们

16. Arts education（艺术教育）

◎ 话题解读

艺术的范畴很广，包括美术、音乐、戏剧、舞蹈等。学生在学校或多或少都会接触到不同类型的艺术。Part 3 关于这一话题通常会问"学习艺术的好处"及"学习某些类型的艺术的好处"。以下这些口语题目和艺术教育有关，请先通读题目，然后思考回答这些问题时该怎样组织信息和语言。

◎ 题目

Do you think art classes are necessary?

Are art classes important in schools?

Is it good for children to learn the arts?

How do you think art classes affect children's development?

What are the benefits of learning painting for children?

What benefits can you get from painting as a hobby?

Should children learn to play an instrument?

What are the advantages of learning music?

Is learning drama or dancing helpful for children?

◎答题思路分析

这里以"Do you think art classes are necessary?"为例，看看有哪些有用的英文句子可以用来回答这个问题。在学习英文句子之前，请先思考一下这个问题要从哪几个方面来回答。首先，可以说艺术教育是教育的一部分，当代学生需要做到德、智、体、美、劳全面发展；其次，艺术课程可以让学生在语、数、外等常规课程学习之余得到放松；最后，艺术教育可以帮助学生培养兴趣爱好。在掌握了回答的几个方面之后，我们一起来学习一些有用的表达与素材。

◎ 表达与素材

1. Art classes are important because they provide children with a well-rounded education. Art helps develop students' creativity and imagination, and gives them a chance to express

themselves.

2. Art classes give students a break from their regular classes, allowing them to relax. It can also be fun to do art, so it puts students in a better mood.

3. Learning the arts can help children discover a fun hobby. It may even help them discover that someday they want to become an artist.

◎ 表达与素材解读

根据以上内容可知，艺术教育的优势和重要性可以概括为三部分。首先，让孩子得到全面发展（well-rounded education），开发孩子们的创造力和想象力；其次，艺术课程让学生在学习常规课程之余得到休息和放松，让学生处于一个良好的情绪状态；最后，艺术课程可以帮助学生培养一个爱好，也许这对他们的职业规划也有帮助，比如成为一名艺术家。

以上这些表达和素材同样适用于其他题目，比如"What are the advantages of learning music?"这一题目就可以使用以上罗列的部分内容来回答，只需将表达与素材中的"art classes"换成"music"即可。

◎ 表达积累

为了方便记忆和学习，我们将有用的表达罗列在以下表格中，考生可以尝试用这些表达的组合来回答之前罗列的相关题目。

有助于全面发展	provide children with a well-rounded education	为孩子们提供全面的教育
	develop students' creativity and imagination	开发学生们的创造力和想象力
放松心情	give students a break from their regular classes	让学生们从常规课程中休息一下
	allow students to relax	让学生们放松
	put students in a better mood	让学生们拥有好心情
发掘爱好与未来发展	discover a fun hobby	发现一个有趣的爱好
	discover that someday they want to become an artist	发现有一天他们想成为一名艺术家

17. Physical education and activities（体育教育与体育活动）

◎ 话题解读

"全民健身"时代，人们越来越注重锻炼身体，增强体质。小学、中学都会开设各种体育课程，鼓励学生参加各种运动。Part 3 关于这个话题通常会问"体育教育和体育活动对学生的好处"。以下这些口语题目和体育教育与体育活动有关，请先通读题目，然后思考回答这些问题时该怎样组织信息和语言。

◎ 题目

Do you think physical education is necessary? Why?

Should children spend more time playing sports?

Do you think children should learn how to swim?

How do you think physical classes affect children's development?

How should schools teach students to live healthily?

What activities can schools organize for children to keep fit?

How can students balance their time spent on studying and sports?

What kinds of games do children play at school?

◎ 答题思路分析

这里以"Do you think physical education is necessary? Why?"为例，看看有哪些有用的英文句子可以用来回答这个问题。在学习英文句子之前，请先思考一下这个问题要从哪几个方面来回答。首先，要肯定体育课程的设置对孩子的成长有重要的作用；其次，体育运动对孩子的身体和心理都有好处。在掌握了回答的几个方面之后，我们来学习一些有用的表达与素材。

◎ 表达与素材

1. Physical education classes and activities are good for children's physical health. It helps them keep fit and stay in shape. It also provides them a good cardiovascular workout and helps them build strength and endurance.

2. Physical education classes and activities are good for children's mental health. It gives them a break from their regular classes, allowing them to relax and relieve stress. It can also be fun to play sports, so it puts students in a better mood. Finally, playing sports helps students clear their minds so that they're able to focus and concentrate better in the classroom afterwards.

3. Physical education classes and activities teach children social skills, as they will often be doing sports with fellow classmates. Sometimes, they will be divided into teams (for example, when playing basketball, soccer, dodge ball, or badminton), where they learn teamwork.

◎ 表达与素材解读

体育课程 / 体育运动给孩子的成长带来诸多好处。首先，毋庸置疑，对健康有益，其中包括让他们保持体型、对心血管好、增强力量和耐力等。其次，体育活动对心理健康有好处，能让孩子们从常规课程中得到休息和放松，缓解压力，拥有好心情，还可以帮助学生理清思路，让他们在课堂上更好地集中注意力。最后，参加体育活动对孩子们的社交和团队合作能力发展有好处。需要说明的是，这些优势不仅适用于体育课程，也适用于任何一项体育运动。

以上这些表达和素材同样适用于其他的题目，但在回答的时候需要稍加修改，比如回答"What kinds of games do children play at school?"时，考生首先需要说出一个可以在学校玩的游戏（如篮球），随后可以说一下它所带来的身体、心理和社交方面的好处。

◎ 表达积累

为了方便记忆和学习，我们将有用的表达罗列在以下表格中，考生可以尝试用这些表达的组合来回答之前罗列的相关题目。

对身体健康有益	good for children's physical health	对孩子的身体健康有好处
	keep fit and stay in shape	保持健康，保持身材
	a good cardiovascular workout	有益于心血管健康
	build strength and endurance	增强力量和耐力
对心理健康有益	good for children's mental health	对儿童的心理健康有好处
	gives them a break from their regular classes, allowing them to relax and relieve stress	让他们从常规课程中得到休息和放松，缓解压力
	be fun to play sports	做运动很有趣
	puts students in a better mood	让学生有更好的心情
	helps students clear their minds so that they're able to focus and concentrate better in the classroom afterwards	帮助学生理清思路，使他们能够在随后的课堂上更好地集中注意力
对培养社交技能有益	teach children social skills	教孩子社交技巧
	learn teamwork	学习团队合作

18. Benefits of learning a foreign language（学习一门外语的好处）

◎ 话题解读

语言是文化的载体，学习外语能让我们多一种角度看世界。现在的父母从小重视对孩子进行外语启蒙，而掌握一门外语，尤其是英语，对未来的学习深造、职业发展是非常有用的。Part 3 关于这个话题通常会问"掌握一门外语的好处"。以下这些口语题目和学习外语的好处有关，请先通读题目，然后思考回答这些问题时该怎样组织信息和语言。

◎ 题目

Why do we need to learn a foreign language?

Do Chinese people benefit a lot from learning English?

Is learning English popular in your country?

Do you think every part in language learning is more important (for instance, speaking)?

Do you think learning another language helps with creating ideas?

◎ 答题思路分析

这里以"Why do we need to learn a foreign language?"为例，看看有哪些有用的英文句子可以用来回答这个问题。在学习英文句子之前，请先思考一下这个问题要从哪几个方面来回答。

学习外语的好处很多，包括有利于升学考试、出国留学；有利于工作；有利于出国旅游、了解他国文化等。在掌握了回答的几个方面之后，我们来学习一些有用的表达与素材。

◎ 表达与素材

1. It's important to learn a foreign language, especially English. It helps us pass entrance examinations for schools. It also gives us more job opportunities, because many jobs require good English—for example, to communicate with foreign clients or exchange ideas with foreign co-workers if you work in an international company.

2. Learning another language improves our understanding of other cultures, including their literature and media. It makes us more open-minded and gives us new ideas, as we see things from different perspectives.

◎ 表达与素材解读

以上内容将学习外语的优势分为两大类，一类和工作、学习有关，一类和文化交流有关。学习外语有利于学习和工作，比如帮助我们通过学校入学考试，给我们提供更多的工作机会。此外，学习外语可以增强我们对其他文化的理解，使我们思想更开放，给我们提供新的想法。

以上这些表达和素材同样适用于其他题目，比如"Is learning English popular in your country?"这道题就可以完全使用表达与素材中提到的内容。

◎ 表达积累

为了方便记忆和学习，我们将有用的表达罗列在以下表格中，考生可以尝试用这些表达的组合来回答之前罗列的相关题目。

	helps us pass entrance examinations for schools	帮助我们通过入学考试
对学习与工作有益	gives us more job opportunities	给我们更多的就业机会
	communicate with foreign clients or exchange ideas with foreign co-workers	与外国客户沟通或与外国同事交流看法
	improves our understanding of other cultures	增强我们对其他文化的理解
对理解文化、拓展思路有益	makes us more open-minded and gives us new ideas	让我们的思想更开放，给我们提供新想法
	see things from different perspectives	从不同的角度看问题

19. Ways of learning a foreign language（学习一门外语的方法）

◎ 话题解读

虽然掌握一门外语很有用，但学习外语并不是一件容易的事情。Part 3 关于这个话题通常会问"学习一门外语的好方法""学习外语遇到的困难"及"什么时候开始学习外语"。以下这些口语题目和学习外语的方法有关，请先通读题目，然后思考回答这些问题时该怎样组织信息和语言。

◎ 题目

What's the best way to learn a new language?

What can people do to learn a second language?

Why do Chinese people have difficulties learning a foreign language? What can be done to improve this?

What are the difficulties of learning a foreign language?

When do people in your country start learning English?

At what age should children start learning a foreign language?

What do you think is the ideal age for learning a foreign language?

Do you think it takes a long time to learn a language?

◎ 答题思路分析

这里以"What's the best way to learn a new language?"为例，看看有哪些有用的英文句子可以用来回答这个问题。在学习英文句子之前，请先思考这个问题要从哪几个方面来回答。学习一门外语的最佳方法之一是参加课程学习，在专业的教师的指导下进行系统的学习相对来说是最有效的。在课程之外，可以多听、多看、多交流，比如看剧、听新闻和上论坛交流。关于何时开始学习外语，如果有条件，肯定是越早越好。在掌握了回答的几个方面之后，我们来学习一些有用的表达与素材。

◎ 表达与素材

1. People should learn a language by taking a class. Teachers can provide structured lessons and teach students proper grammar, vocabulary, and pronunciation. They can also answer questions, provide feedback, and offer words of encouragement. This is important because many language learners have difficulties staying motivated, as language learning is difficult and time-consuming. Taking a class basically forces students to stay on track.

2. Outside of class, people should try to consume lots of media (such as TV shows and books) in the language they're learning. It's an interesting and fun way to learn a language.

3. Ideally, people should start learning a foreign language when they are very young, like when they're in preschool. That's because young children absorb and learn languages the fastest. Also, becoming fluent in a language takes many years, so it's better to get started as soon as possible.

◎ 表达与素材解读

以上内容将学习外语的方法分为两类。一类是参加课程学习，由老师提供结构化的课程，教授学生正确的语法、词汇和发音，同时老师还会解答疑问，提供反馈，并给予学生鼓励，让其保持积极性和专注力。另一类是在日常生活中多听、多看、多交流，保持学习语言的环境和氛围。此外，学习语言多少和年龄有点关系，越早学越好。

以上这些表达和素材同样适用于其他题目，比如在回答"What are the difficulties of learning a foreign language?"时考生可以先说学习语言的困难是难以保持学习的动力（have difficulties staying motivated），随后可以提及解决方法，比如上语言课程。

◎ 表达积累

为了方便记忆和学习，我们将有用的表达罗列在以下表格中，考生可以尝试用这些表达的组合来回答之前罗列的相关题目。

	have difficulties staying motivated	难以保持动力
学习语言的困难	language learning is difficult and time-consuming	语言学习既困难又费时
	forces students to stay on track	迫使学生坚持正确的方向（保持学习语言的正确状态）
学习语言的方法——参加课程学习	learn a language by taking a class	通过上课来学习一门语言
	provide structured lessons and teach students proper grammar, vocabulary, and pronunciation	提供结构化的课程，教授学生正确的语法、词汇和发音
	answer questions, provide feedback, and offer words of encouragement	解答疑问，提供反馈，并给予鼓励
学习语言的方法——保持学习语言的氛围	try to consume lots of media (such as TV shows and books) in the language they're learning	尝试大量接触他们正在学习的语言的媒体（如电视节目和书籍）
学习语言的年龄	start learning a foreign language when they are very young	在他们很小的时候就开始学习外语
	young children absorb and learn languages the fastest	小孩子吸收和学习语言的速度最快
	becoming fluent in a language takes many years, so it's better to get started as soon as possible	说一口流利的语言需要很多年，所以最好尽早开始

20. Learning history（学习历史）

◎ 话题解读

历史是自然界和人类社会过去发生的活动和事件，学习历史有非常重大的意义。Part 3 关于这个话题通常会问"学习历史有何用""人们如何学习历史"及"历史的受欢迎程度"等。以下这些口语题目和学习历史有关，请先通读题目，然后思考回答这些问题时该怎样组织信息和语言。

◎ 题目

Do you think it's useful to learn history?

What are the advantages and disadvantages of learning history?

How do people learn history?

Do you think people spend a lot of time learning history?

Are students interested in history in your country?

Do people in your country like history?

Why do some people have no interest in history?

◎ 答题思路分析

这里以"How do people learn history?"为例，看看有哪些有用的英文句子可以用来回答这个问题。在学习英文句子之前，请先思考一下这个问题要从哪几个方面来回答。首先，学习历史不仅可以了解过去，而且会对当下和未来有所启示，所以学习历史是非常重要的。其次，人们通常通过历史课学习历史，很多人因为授课方式而对学习历史提不起兴趣，而如果将课堂变得更加有趣，历史课也会受到大家的欢迎。在课堂之外，读历史书、看纪录片也是学习历史的好方法。在掌握了回答的几个方面之后，我们来学习一些有用的表达与素材。

◎ 表达与素材

1. It's useful to learn history because it helps you understand your own country and other parts of the world. The past affects the present, so understanding the past is key to understanding the modern world.

2. People generally learn about history in history classes. Many people are not that interested in history because of the way it is taught in school (e.g. needing to memorize names, dates, and other facts). History classes can be made more interesting if there are more projects where students research subjects that interest them, or projects where they have to argue for a certain side.

3. Outside of the classroom, people can learn history by reading history books or watching history documentaries. Going on field trips can also be a fun way to learn about history—for example, when you visit ancient buildings or important cultural places.

◎ 表达与素材解读

首先，考生可以简单概括学习历史的重要性，即"helps you understand your own country and other parts of the world"（帮助你了解自己的国家和世界其他地方），此处可以举一个例子。随后进入正题，在课堂上学习历史可能会比较枯燥，因为"needing to memorize names, dates, and other facts"（需要记住名字、日期和其他事实）。但是，如果设置一些学生感兴趣的环节就不会那么无聊了。此外，还可以通过"reading history books or watching history documentaries"（阅读历史书籍和观看历史纪录片）或者"field trips"（实地考察）来学习历史知识。

以上这些表达和素材同样适用于其他题目，比如在回答"Why do some people have no interest in history?"时，考生可以先使用以上表达与素材中关于历史课为什么无聊的部分，随后说明学习历史是很重要的，需要找到一种有趣的方式来学习。

◎ 表达积累

为了方便记忆和学习，我们将有用的表达罗列在以下表格中，考生可以尝试用这些表达的组合来回答之前罗列的相关题目。

学习历史很重要	helps you understand your own country and other parts of the world	帮助你了解自己的国家和世界其他地方
	The past affects the present, so understanding the past is key to understanding the modern world.	过去影响现在，所以理解过去是理解现代世界的关键。
学习历史很无聊	because of the way it is taught in school (e.g. needing to memorize names, dates, and other facts)	因为学校的教授方式（例如，需要记住名字、日期和其他事实）
学习历史也可以很有趣	read history books or watch history documentaries	读历史书或看历史纪录片
	go on field trips	进行实地考察
	visit ancient buildings or important cultural places	参观古建筑或重要的文化场所

21. Learning math and science subjects（学习数学与科学）

◎ 话题解读

数学和科学都是很重要的科目，几乎每个人都学习过这些科目。Part 3 关于这个话题通常会问"数学和科学科目的重要性"及"学生如何从学习这些科目中受益"。以下这些口语题目和学习数学和科学有关，请先通读题目，然后思考回答这些问题时该怎样组织信息和语言。

◎ 题目

Is science an important subject in your school?

Should kids know more about stars and planets?

What is the importance of environmental education?

Is it important to teach students environmental protection at school?

Do you think everyone needs to learn math?

How do you use math in your daily life?

Some people say music is like math. Do you agree?

◎ 答题思路分析

这里以"Is science an important subject in your school?"为例，看看有哪些有用的英文句子可以用来回答这个问题。在学习英文句子之前，请先思考这个问题要从哪几个方面来回答。首先，无论是数学、物理、化学还是生物，这些学科的实用性都是非常高的，有助于人们认知世界；其次，这些学科可以帮助人们培养逻辑思维能力和研究能力。在掌握了回答的几个方面之后，我们来学习一些有用的表达与素材。

◎ 表达与素材

1. Science subjects (such as biology, chemistry, physics, astronomy, and environmental science) are very important to learn. They help students learn more about the world around them, which broadens their horizons. Science courses also teach students critical-thinking and research skills.

2. Environmental science is important because it teaches children to care about important environmental issues, such as climate change and pollution. It encourages children to have environmentally friendly habits, such as recycling and saving electricity. It also inspires them to be more engaged with their communities.

3. Mathematics is very important because it teaches students logical-thinking skills, which is important for making good decisions. Math is also required in the daily work of many fields, such as engineering, accounting, physics, and finance.

◎ 表达与素材解读

首先肯定科学学科是非常重要的，其优势非常明显，可以"help students learn more about the world around them"（帮助学生更多地了解他们周围的世界）及"teach students critical-thinking and research skills"（教授学生批判性思维和研究方法）。然后详细阐述环境科学和数学这两个科目的重要性。环境科学可以"teaches children to care about important environmental issues"（教会孩子关心重要的环境问题），或"encourages children to have environmentally friendly habits"（鼓励孩子养成环保的习惯）。数学可以"teaches students logical-thinking skills"（教授学生逻辑思维技能），而且数学是其他科学类学科的基础，学好数学对其他学科也是有利的。

以上这些表达和素材同样适用于其他题目，比如在回答"Do you think everyone needs to learn math?"时，考生就可以选择以上表达中关于数学的那一部分来回答。

◎ 表达积累

为了方便记忆和学习，我们将有用的表达罗列在以下表格中，考生可以尝试用这些表达的组合来回答之前罗列的相关题目。

科学学科的重要性	help students learn more about the world around them	帮助学生更多地了解他们周围的世界
	teach students critical-thinking and research skills	教授学生批判性思维和研究技能
环境科学的重要性	teaches children to care about important environmental issues, such as climate change and pollution	教会孩子关心重要的环境问题，如气候变化和污染
	encourages children to have environmentally friendly habits, such as recycling and saving electricity	鼓励孩子养成环保习惯，如循环利用、节约用电
	inspires them to be more engaged with their communities	激励他们更多地参与到社区中去
数学的重要性	teaches students logical-thinking skills	教授学生逻辑思维技巧
	important for making good decisions	对做出正确的决定很重要
	be required in the daily work of many fields	在许多领域的日常工作中都需要

22. The usefulness of knowing different subjects（学习不同学科的有用之处）

◎ 话题解读

一直以来都有一种争论，即我们应该把重点放在实用的学科上还是注重各学科的全面发展。Part 3 关于这个话题通常会问"哪些科目被认为是实用的或不实用的"及"学习各种各样的科目是否有用，即使是那些被认为不太实用的科目"。以下这些口语题目和学习不同的学科有关，请先通读题目，然后思考回答这些问题时该怎样组织信息和语言。

◎ 题目

What subjects are practical in everyday life?

What subjects are more practical to learn nowadays?

What subjects are less practical in everyday life?

Do you think what you've learnt in university is going to help in your future job?

Do you think learning many subjects is beneficial to your work?

Do you think it's better to learn many subjects at a time or to learn one subject?

Do you think art subjects are less useful than science subjects?

What can schools do for students' intellectual development?

What suggestions would you give to schools to develop the potential of students?

Why are some people well-rounded, while others are only good at one thing?

◎ 答题思路分析

这里以"What subjects are practical in everyday life?"为例，看看有哪些有用的英文句子可以用来回答这个问题。在学习英文句子之前，请先思考这个问题要从哪几个方面来回答。首先，需要回答哪些学科被认为是实用的，哪些是不实用的，也可以说各学科一样实用；其次，可以结合自身经验分别介绍这些学科的特征与优势；最后，如果觉得某些学科非常重要，则可以在回答中单独提及。在掌握了回答的几个方面之后，我们来学习一些有用的表达与素材。

◎ 表达与素材

1. Math and science subjects are normally considered more practical in everyday life, while art subjects are considered less practical. However, all subjects are actually practical and useful in their own ways. Math and science subjects develop your logical thinking and critical thinking skills, while art subjects develop your creativity and imagination. This may help you not only in school but also in your future career.

2. Schools are responsible for helping student become well-rounded by exposing them to a wide variety of subjects. This also helps them find a passion or direction in their lives.

◎ 表达与素材解读

根据以上内容可知，所有学科实际上都有其自身的实用性和用途（all subjects are actually practical and useful in their own ways）。随后，分别说明它们的优势和实用性，这部分内容可以参考前文有关语言、历史、数学、科学等话题中的素材。最后，学校提倡全面发展，让学生接触各种各样的学科（helping student become well-rounded by exposing them to a wide variety of subjects）。

以上这些表达和素材同样适用于其他题目，比如"Do you think art subjects are less useful than science subjects?"这一题目就可以使用本题的表达与素材。

◎ 表达积累

为了方便记忆和学习，我们将有用的表达罗列在以下表格中，考生可以尝试用这些表达的组合来回答之前罗列的相关题目。

所有学科都很实用	All subjects are actually practical and useful in their own way.	事实上，所有学科都有各自的实用性。
	Math and science subjects develop your logical thinking and critical thinking skills, while art subjects develop your creativity and imagination.	数学和科学学科开发你的逻辑思维和批判性思维技能，而艺术学科开发你的创造力和想象力。
学校的责任	be responsible for helping student become well-rounded by exposing them to a wide variety of subjects	负责通过让学生接触各种各样的学科来帮助他们全面发展

 话题 2 CAREER, PERSONAL GOALS, WORK-RELATED SKILLS, AND SUCCESS（职业、个人目标、职业技能及成功）

很多人从大学毕业后就开始工作，一直工作到退休，工作占据了我们生活的很大一部分时间。与职业相关的话题在 Part 3 中经常出现。影响职业成功和职业满意度的因素有很多，比如个人目标和技能、工作类型、行业、公司的规模、公司性质等。下面我们将学习如何回答与这些话题相关的问题。

1. What is considered a good job?（什么是令人满意的工作）

◎ 话题解读

工作的种类很多，工作的内容也是千差万别。Part 3 关于这个话题通常会问"什么样的工作是受欢迎的"及"什么样的工作是好工作"。以下这些口语题目和什么是令人满意的工作有关，请先通读题目，然后思考回答这些问题时该怎样组织信息和语言。

◎ 题目

What kind of job would you like?

How would you define "a good job"?

What factors should people take into consideration when choosing jobs?

What kinds of jobs do children want to do?

What kinds of jobs do young people prefer?

What kinds of professions are popular in your country?

◎ 答题思路分析

这里以"What kind of job would you like?"为例，看看有哪些有用的英文句子可以用来回答这个问题。在学习英文句子之前，请先思考这个问题要从哪几个方面来回答。关于喜欢的工作，大部分人的回答里会提到薪酬待遇好、工作时间合理、工作稳定且有挑战、公司地理位置好、公司环境好、领导同事好相处等。在掌握了回答的几个方面之后，我们来学习一些有用的表达与素材。

◎ 表达与素材

Qualities of a good job:

Has a good salary.

Has reasonable working hours.

Is stable and secure. Is unlikely to lay off employees.

Is in a good location, so that you don't spend too much time commuting to work.

Is interesting. Doesn't make you feel bored.

Jobs that have some of these qualities: businessman, accountant, doctor, software engineer.

◎ 表达与素材解读

好工作的特点是非常明确的，商人、会计、医生、软件工程师都是人们心目中的好职业。将这些内容自由组合就可以回答以上罗列的题目，当然在回答时最好能举个例子，这样能让你的回答更饱满。

◎ 表达积累

为了方便记忆和学习，我们将有用的表达罗列在以下表格中，考生可以尝试用这些表达的组合来回答之前罗列的相关题目。

好工作的特点	has a good salary	薪水不错
	has reasonable working hours	有合理的工作时间
	is stable and secure/is unlikely to lay off employees	稳定和安全／不太可能裁员
	is in a good location, so that you don't spend too much time commuting to work	位置好，这样你就不会在通勤上花太多时间
	is interesting/doesn't make you feel bored	有趣／不会让你感到无聊
好工作有哪些	businessman, accountant, doctor, software engineer	商人，会计，医生，软件工程师

2. Working in big vs. small companies (including family businesses)
（在大公司工作与在小公司工作的区别）

◎ 话题解读

大公司对很多人有吸引力，但小公司也有自己的优势。这里需要说明的是，小公司除了指那些规模小的公司，还包括家庭作坊等。关于这个话题，Part 3 通常会问"在大公司和小公司工作的优势和劣势"。以下这些口语题目与在大公司工作和小公司工作的区别有关，请先通读题目，然后思考回答这些问题时该怎样组织信息和语言。

◎ 题目

Would you prefer working in a big company or small company in the future?

What are the differences between big companies and small companies?

Do people in your country prefer to work for big companies or small companies?

What are the advantages of working in a big company?

Is it difficult to get a promotion in a large company?

What are the advantages and disadvantages of working in a family business?

◎ 答题思路分析

这里以"Would you prefer working in a big company or small company in the future?"为例，看看有哪些有用的英文句子可以用来回答这个问题。在学习英文句子之前，请先思考一下这个问题要从哪几个方面来回答。其实，无论考生选择哪一个，都需要把优势说清楚。如果选择大公司，则优势往往跟稳定、福利待遇好等有关。如果选择小公司，则优势往往和满足感、有利于成长等有关。在掌握了回答的几个方面之后，我们来学习一些有用的表达与素材。

◎ 表达与素材

Advantages of working in big companies:

1. Big companies are more stable. They are less likely to go bankrupt or lay off employees.

2. They usually offer better salaries.

3. They offer better benefits, like better healthcare, insurance, and training.

Advantages of work in small companies / family businesses:

1. Having fewer employees means that you take on a bigger role in the company and can make a bigger impact, which can be satisfying.

2. There's more room for you to grow, especially into leadership and management roles.

3. Companies with fewer people feel more like a family. You'll develop stronger friendships with your co-workers.

◎ 表达与素材解读

大公司和小公司各有优势，在回答问题时，考生需要挑选适合的内容进行回答，例如，如果更喜欢在大公司工作，则可以选取大公司工作的优势的相关表达。当考生需要回答类似"What are the advantages and disadvantages of working in a family business?"的题目时，优势部分可以直接选取上述表达与素材，而劣势部分则可以将大公司的优势改成否定形式，就是小公司的劣势了。

◎ 表达积累

为了方便记忆和学习，我们将有用的表达罗列在以下表格中，考生可以尝试用这些表达的组合来回答之前罗列的相关题目。

大公司的优势	are more stable	更稳定
	are less likely to go bankrupt or lay off employees	不太可能破产或解雇员工
	offer better salaries	提供更好的工资
	offer better benefits, like better healthcare, insurance, and training	提供更好的福利，比如更好的医疗、保险和培训
小公司的优势	take on a bigger role in the company	在公司里扮演更重要的角色
	make a bigger impact	创造更大的影响
	there's more room for you to grow, especially into leadership and management roles	有更多的成长空间，尤其是在领导力和管理角色上
	feel more like a family	感觉更像一家人
	develop stronger friendships with your co-workers	和同事建立更牢固的友谊

3. Customer service & Sales-related jobs（客服及销售相关的工作）

◎ 话题解读

有些工作需要经常与人打交道，尤其是与客服和销售相关的工作。Part 3 关于这个话题通常会问"什么样的工作需要员工与他人互动"及"这些员工应该拥有什么样的技能和态度"。以下这些口语题目和客服及销售相关的工作有关，请先通读题目，然后思考回答这些问题时该怎样组织信息和语言。

◎ 题目

What kinds of jobs involve dealing with the public?

What jobs require staff to be in touch with many people?

What jobs need employees to be talkative?

What kinds of jobs require people to be confident?

In what kinds of professions do people help others more?

What kinds of professions are related to giving information to others?

Would you like to work in the service industry in the future?

◎ 答题思路分析

这里以 "What jobs require staff to be in touch with many people?" 为例，看看有哪些有用的英文句子可以用来回答这个问题。在学习英文句子之前，请先思考一下这个问题要从哪几个方面来回答。首先，考生需要回答销售或客服一类的工作需要员工与不同的人打交道；其次，考生可以说明这些工作需要的基本技能和性格特征。在掌握了回答的几个方面之后，我们来学习一些有用的表达与素材。

◎ 表达与素材

1. Customer service representatives and salesmen need good communication skills because they're constantly interacting with customers and other members of the public.

2. Having good communication skills means that they're good at listening, can communicate clearly, and are polite. They also need to be patient, confident, and (for salesmen) talkative and persuasive.

◎ 表达与素材解读

众所周知，客服和销售类的工作经常需要与人交流，除了专业知识，他们需要有良好的沟通技能，包括擅长倾听、表达清晰、礼貌谦虚。在性格特征方面，他们需要有耐心、有自信、健谈、有说服力。

以上这些表达和素材同样适用于其他题目，比如在回答 "What kinds of jobs require people to be confident?" 时，考生可以先回答客服和销售类的工作需要人们有自信，除此之外，还需要有耐心、健谈和有说服力。随后，考生可以具体描述这类职业的特征，灵活使用上述表达与素材里的内容。

◎ 表达积累

为了方便记忆和学习，我们将有用的表达罗列在以下表格中，考生可以尝试用这些表达的组合来回答之前罗列的相关题目。

	need good communication skills	需要良好的沟通技巧
客服和销售类工作需要的技能及性格特征	are good at listening	善于倾听
	can communicate clearly	可以清楚地沟通
	are polite	有礼貌
	need to be patient, confident, and talkative and persuasive	需要有耐心、自信、健谈、有说服力

4. Interesting, creative, or artistic jobs（有趣的、有创意的或与艺术有关的工作）

◎ 话题解读

工作的种类有很多，有的工作内容比较单一，只需按部就班地去做即可，有的工作则比较灵活、有意思，需要发挥员工的创意，比如一些与艺术有关的工作。Part 3 关于这个话题通常会问"这些类型的工作有哪些"以及"以这些工作为生的好处"。以下这些口语题目和有趣的、有创意的或与艺术有关的工作有关，请先通读题目，然后思考回答这些问题时该怎样组织信息和语言。

◎ 题目

What kinds of professions require imagination?

How would you define an interesting job?

What are the benefits of working as a writer?

What are the benefits of being a singer?

Why do so many young people choose communication and media studies as their major?

Is it hard to find an interesting job in China?

Are there many Chinese people who want to work as an actor?

◎ 答题思路分析

这里以"How would you define an interesting job?"为例，看看有哪些有用的英文句子可以用来回答这个问题。在学习英文句子之前，请先思考一下这个问题要从哪几个方面来回答。首先肯定要正面回答问题，说明什么工作是有趣的工作，比如与艺术有关的工作就比较有趣。随后可以举具体的例子，比如当歌手或者舞者。为了让回答更完整，接下来可以说明这个工作的优势在哪里。在掌握了回答的几个方面之后，我们来学习一些有用的表达与素材。

◎ 表达与素材

1. Jobs in the arts are generally considered more interesting and creative than other fields—for example, a job as a singer, writer, artist, dancer, or actor.

2. These jobs allow you to explore new ideas and express yourself more. They might also allow you to travel more and do a wider variety of things.

◎ 表达与素材解读

首先直接回答问题，认为艺术领域的工作通常被认为比其他领域的工作更有趣、更有创造力，随后列举具体的工作例子。仅仅说艺术领域的工作有趣是不够的，还需要添加一些关于这类工作的优势的描述，比如"探索新的想法""更多地表达自己"及"到处旅行并做更多不同的事情"。

以上这些表达和素材同样适用于其他题目，比如在回答"Are there many Chinese people who want to work as an actor?"时，考生可以先回答"yes"，随后说明为何大家愿意选择这个职业，这其中的原因可以选取表达与素材中的部分内容，此外，还可以说明收入不错（offer better salaries）等。

◎ 表达积累

为了方便记忆和学习，我们将有用的表达罗列在以下表格中，考生可以尝试用这些表达的组合来回答之前罗列的相关题目。

有趣的、有创意的或与艺术有关的工作	jobs in the arts	艺术领域的工作
	a job as a singer, writer, artist, dancer, or actor	歌手、作家、艺术家、舞蹈家或演员的工作
这些工作的优势	allow you to explore new ideas and express yourself more	让你探索新的想法，更多地表达自己
	allow you to travel more and do a wider variety of things	让你有更多旅行的机会，做更多不同的事情

5. Moving for a career & The importance of location（为了工作搬家以及地理位置的重要性）

◎ 话题解读

近年来，人们从农村向城市迁移的趋势日益增长。Part 3 关于这个话题通常会问"为什么人们会搬到城市"。以下这些口语题目和人们为了工作搬家有关，请先通读题目，然后思考回答这些问题时该怎么组织信息和语言。

◎ 题目

Do people nowadays like to leave their hometown to work in other cities?

Will more people move to cities in the future?

Why do people sometimes move to a new home?

What are some factors that attract people to settle down in certain places?

What are the differences between young and old people when choosing where to live?

◎ 答题思路分析

这里以"Do people nowadays like to leave their hometown to work in other cities?"为例，看看有哪些有用的英文句子可以用来回答这个问题。在学习英文句子之前，请先思考这个问题要从哪几个方面来回答。首先，考生需要给出一个肯定的回答，现在的人确实会离开家乡到大城市学习、工作或者生活。然后，针对这一现象分析背后的原因，比如工作机会多、高薪和发展前景好。在掌握了回答的几个方面之后，我们来学习一些有用的表达与素材。

◎ 表达与素材

1. Many people—especially young people—leave their hometown for big cities in order to find better job opportunities. There are more jobs in cities, and it's where all the big companies and offices are located.

2. For example, a lot of Chinese people move to tier one cities like Beijing, Shanghai,

Guangzhou or Shenzhen in order to find jobs. They are likely to make more money in these places and achieve more career success.

◎ 表达与素材解读

在回答这类问题时，首先要做出正面回应，直接回答人们确实会 "leave their hometown for big cities in order to find better job opportunities"（离开家乡到大城市去寻找更好的工作机会）。随后可以具体说明为何大城市的工作机会多，因为大公司都在城市里。除了更好的工作机会，在大城市还可以 "make more money"（赚更多的钱）、"achieve more career success"（获得更多的职业成就）。

以上这些表达和素材同样适用于其他题目，比如 "What are some factors that attract people to settle down in certain places?" 这个题目就可以用以上的表达与素材来回答，即工作机会、薪酬福利和发展前景都会影响人们在某地定居。

◎ 表达积累

为了方便记忆和学习，我们将有用的表达罗列在以下表格中，考生可以尝试用这些表达的组合来回答之前罗列的相关题目。

	move to tier one cities	搬到一线城市
在大城市工作的原因	leave their hometown for big cities in order to find better job opportunities	离开家乡去大城市是为了得到更好的工作机会
	There are more jobs in cities, and it's where all the big companies and offices are located.	城市有更多的工作机会，所有的大公司和办公室都设在城市。
	are likely to make more money in these places and achieve more career success	有可能在这些地方赚到更多的钱，获得更多的职业成就

6. Working in foreign countries（在海外工作）

◎ 话题解读

越来越多的人选择出国学习和工作。Part 3 关于这个话题通常会问 "国外工作的优点和缺点"。以下这些口语题目和在海外工作有关，请先通读题目，然后思考回答这些问题时该怎样组织信息和语言。

◎ 题目

What are the advantages and disadvantages of working in a foreign country?

Is it good for young people to have the experience of living in other countries?

Do people like working in a foreign country?

What's the difference between working in an international company and working in a local one?

What do you think is the biggest problem with working in a foreign country?

Why are some people unwilling to work in other countries?

What are the disadvantages of working in an international company?

◎ 答题思路分析

这里以 "What are the advantages and disadvantages of working in a foreign country?" 为例，看看有哪些有用的英文句子可以用来回答这个问题。在学习英文句子之前，请先思考一下这个问题要从哪几个方面来回答。首先，可以罗列在国外工作的优点，比如全新的体验、独立的生活、与不同文化的人交流、拓展视野和有助于个人发展等；其次，在海外工作的缺点也比较明显，比如孤独以及由文化差异带来的不便与冲击。在掌握了回答的几个方面之后，我们来学习一些有用的表达与素材。

◎ 表达与素材

Advantages of working in a foreign country:

1. It's exciting to be in a foreign country. It's something new and different.

2. You learn to become more independent.

3. You gain exposure to different ideas, people, and culture. You learn to think and work differently. It broadens your horizons and makes you a more well-rounded person.

4. Sometimes, there are better job opportunities in a foreign country, with higher salaries.

Disadvantages of working in a foreign country:

1. You'll be far from family and friends, which might make you lonely and homesick.

2. If you're not familiar with the language and culture, it can make your life difficult and uncomfortable. You might experience culture shock and not adapt well.

3. You might experience conflicts or miscommunication with others (including co-workers) because of cultural differences.

◎ 表达与素材解读

在海外工作的优势很明显，比如心情感受上的 "new and different"、生活上的 "learn to become more independent" 以及工作中的 "gain exposure to different ideas, people, and culture" "think and work differently" 及 "sometimes better job opportunities"。当然，在海外工作也有很多弊端，比如 "far from family and friends" "not familiar with the language and culture" 及 "experience conflicts or miscommunication with other"。

以上这些表达和素材同样适用于其他题目，比如 "What's the difference between working in an international company and working in a local one?" 这一题目就可以借鉴在海外工作的表达和素材，考生可以回答在跨国公司工作可以接触到不同的思想、人和文化，有更广阔的发展，而在本土公司工作会有熟悉的环境，与他人交流不会有很大的文化冲突。

◎ 表达积累

为了方便记忆和学习，我们将有用的表达罗列在以下表格中，考生可以尝试用这些表达的组合来回答之前罗列的相关题目。

	exciting to be in a foreign country	身处异国他乡令人感到兴奋
海外工作的优势	something new and different	一些新的和不同的东西
	learn to become more independent	学会变得更加独立
	gain exposure to different ideas, people, and culture	接触不同的思想、人和文化
	learn to think and work differently	学会用不同的方式思考和工作
	It broadens your horizons and makes you a more well-rounded person.	它开阔了你的视野，让你成为一个更全面的人。
	there are better job opportunities in a foreign country, with higher salaries	在国外有更好的工作机会，薪水更高
海外工作的弊端	far from family and friends	远离家人和朋友
	make you lonely and homesick	让你感到孤独和想家
	not familiar with the language and culture	不熟悉语言和文化
	make your life difficult and uncomfortable	让你的生活变得困难和不舒服
	experience culture shock and not adapt well	经历文化冲击，不适应
	experience conflicts or miscommunication with others (including co-workers) because of cultural differences	因为文化差异而与他人（包括同事）发生冲突或沟通不畅

7. Work-life balance（工作与生活的平衡）

◎ 话题解读

现代社会，人们面临着很大的压力，工作占据了人们生活的很大部分，有时让人无暇顾及家庭。Part 3 关于这个话题通常会问"保持工作与生活的平衡的重要性"。以下这些口语题目和工作与生活的平衡有关，请先通读题目，然后思考回答这些问题时该怎样组织信息和语言。

◎ 题目

Do you think it is important to have a work and life balance?

Do you think it's important to take some time off work or studying and do some leisure activities?

Do you think relaxing is a waste of time?

What do you think of a job that has a low salary but lots of holidays?

What do better working conditions mean?

What are the disadvantages of working overtime?

◎ 答题思路分析

这里以"Do you think it is important to have a work and life balance?"为例，看看有哪些有

用的英文句子可以用来回答这个问题。在学习英文句子之前，请先思考这个问题要从哪几个方面来回答。首先，保持生活和工作的平衡很重要，这对身心健康有很大帮助；其次，工作之余有时间享受生活是很重要的，你可以陪伴自己的家人、和朋友聚会、发展自己的爱好等。在掌握了回答的几个方面之后，我们来学习一些有用的表达与素材。

◎ 表达与素材

1. A good work-life balance is important because it helps reduce stress and prevent burnout in the workplace. People who work a lot of overtime are more likely to have physical health issues (like heart problems) and mental health issues (such as depression).

2. Having a good work-life balance is also important for our relationships. It allows us to spend more time with our friends and family, which is important for our happiness.

◎ 表达与素材解读

工作和生活得以平衡对身体和心理健康的好处体现在 "helps reduce stress and prevent burnout in the workplace"（帮助缓解压力，防止对工作产生倦怠）。如果长时间工作，没有休息，就容易出现身体上或心理上的健康问题。除此之外，在工作和生活中找到平衡会对我们的人际关系产生正面影响，让我们有更多时间陪伴家人和朋友。

以上这些表达和素材同样适用于其他题目，比如在回答 "Do you think relaxing is a waste of time?" 时，考生可以说放松当然不是浪费时间，劳逸结合才是最佳状态。随后，考生可以使用表达与素材中的内容进行补充，说明放松是很有必要的。

◎表达积累

为了方便记忆和学习，我们将有用的表达罗列在以下表格中，考生可以尝试用这些表达的组合来回答之前罗列的相关题目。

超时工作的坏处	are more likely to have physical health issues (like heart problems) and mental health issues (such as depression)	更容易出现身体问题（如心脏问题）和心理问题（如抑郁症）
平衡工作与生活的好处	helps reduce stress and prevent burnout in the workplace	帮助减轻工作压力，防止对工作产生倦怠
	is also important for our relationships	对我们的人际关系也很重要
	allows us to spend more time with our friends and family	让我们有更多的时间和家人、朋友在一起

8. Goals and plans（目标与计划）

◎ 话题解读

学习需要有目标和计划，工作也不例外。Part 3 关于这个话题通常会问"设定目标和计划的好处"及"我们应该设定什么样的目标和计划"。以下这些口语题目和目标与计划有关，请先通读题目，然后思考回答这些问题时该怎样组织信息和语言。

◎ 题目

Why is setting goals important in the workplace?

Do you think it's important for people to set goals?

Is time management important?

Do you think successful people have better time management skills than others?

Do people usually set long-term goals or short-term ones?

Is it important to have a daily plan?

What kind of things do people need to plan carefully?

What kinds of plans are practical?

What kinds of goals are not realistic?

◎ 答题思路分析

这里以 "Why is setting goals important in the workplace?" 为例，看看有哪些有用的英文句子可以用来回答这个问题。在学习英文句子之前，请先思考这个问题要从哪几个方面来回答。在工作中设定目标和做计划的主要目的是帮助自己在规定的时间内完成一定的任务。目标和计划分为短期和长期两种，各有用处。此外，人们设定的目标和计划要实际、便于执行。在掌握了回答的几个方面之后，我们来学习一些有用的表达与素材。

◎ 表达与素材

1. Goals and plans help you complete things on time, allowing you to meet important deadlines from school or work.

2. Long term goals help you think about the big picture, and motivate you to achieve those goals.

3. Short term goals help you understand what you need to work on every day, and help you focus on your daily work.

4. People should make goals for school, work, or even for exercise. Academic, career, and fitness goals are important to a person's well-being. Goals also need to be practical. They should not be too challenging or impossible to do. For example, a practical and achievable goal is to exercise for 30 minutes every day, while a less practical one is to exercise for 3 hours daily.

◎表达与素材解读

设定目标与计划的主要目的是 "help you complete things on time"（帮助你按时完成事情）。为了进一步说明，考生可以将目标分成长期和短期两种，长期目标让你考虑大局，并激励你实现这些目标，短期目标让你知道每天需要做什么，并帮助你专注于每天的工作。

以上这些表达和素材同样适用于其他题目，比如 "Is it important to have a daily plan?" 这个题目，"daily plan" 就相当于 "short term goal"，那么考生就可以使用相关的表达来回答了。当然，这些内容肯定是不够的，考生还需要举一个例子，比如什么样的 "daily plan" 是好执行的，每天坚持锻炼 30 分钟就是一个非常不错的范例。

◎ 表达积累

为了方便记忆和学习，我们将有用的表达罗列在以下表格中，考生可以尝试用这些表达的组合来回答之前罗列的相关题目。

设定目标与计划的好处	help you complete things on time, allowing you to meet important deadlines from school or work	帮助你按时完成任务，让你在学校或工作要求的重要截止日期前完成任务
设定长期目标与计划的好处	help you think about the big picture	帮助你考虑大局
	motivate you to achieve those goals	激励你去实现这些目标
设定短期目标与计划的好处	help understand what you need to work on every day	帮助你了解你每天需要做什么
	help you focus on your daily work	帮助你专注于日常工作
为哪些事情设定目标	make goals for school, work, or even for exercise	为学习、工作甚至锻炼制定目标
	Academic, career, and fitness goals are important to a person's well-being.	学业、事业和健身目标对一个人的幸福安康很重要。
	a practical and achievable goal is to exercise for 30 minutes every day	一个切实可行的目标是每天锻炼 30 分钟

9. Communication and teamwork skills（沟通及团队合作的技巧）

◎ 话题解读

无论是在学校还是在职场，我们都经常需要与他人交流或者协作。Part 3 关于这个话题通常会问"为什么团队合作和沟通技巧是重要的"及"良好的沟通和团队合作技巧包括什么"。以下这些口语题目和沟通及团队合作的技巧有关，请先通读题目，然后思考回答这些问题时该怎样组织信息和语言。

◎ 题目

Do you think teamwork and communication skills are important?

Do you think interpersonal skills are more important than studying?

Do you think it is a good thing to have disagreements within a team?

What communication skills are important?

What problem is better solved through group work?

How can a person become a good member of a team in the workplace?

◎ 答题思路分析

这里以"Do you think teamwork and communication skills are important?"为例，看看有哪些有用的英文句子可以用来回答这个问题。在学习英文句子之前，请先思考这个问题要从哪几个方面来回答。首先，考生肯定需要说明团队合作和沟通技能是非常重要的；其次，应解释说明为何它们很重要；最后，提及好的沟通及团队合作技能包括什么。在掌握了回答的几个方面之后，我们来学习一些有用的表达与素材。

◎ 表达与素材

1. Teamwork and communication skills are very important in the workplace because we often need to work together with others.

2. Additionally, poor communication or interpersonal skills leads to conflicts or miscommunication with co-workers, which can hurt productivity and team spirit.

3. Good communication within a team involves openly exchanging ideas—even if they're different—and closely cooperating with each other. This allows a team to complete big, complex projects more efficiently and produce things with better quality. Good teamwork also makes it more enjoyable for people to work together, which improves team spirit.

◎ 表达与素材解读

团队合作和沟通技能很重要，一是因为我们经常与其他人一起工作，二是因为如果缺乏这种技能会导致与同事的冲突或沟通不畅，从而影响生产力和团队精神。考生在描述团队合作和沟通技能的重要性时可以从正反两个方面来阐述。好的团队合作和沟通技能包括哪些呢？由上述表达与素材可知，包括开放地交流想法和密切地合作，这会使你的团队更有效地完成大型的、复杂的项目，并生产出更高质量的产品，同样也会使参与其中的人更愉快，从而促进团队合作。

以上这些表达和素材同样适用于其他题目，比如在回答"What communication skills are important?"时，考生可以使用表达与素材中的第 3 点内容。

◎ 表达积累

为了方便记忆和学习，我们将有用的表达罗列在以下表格中，考生可以尝试用这些表达的组合来回答之前罗列的相关题目。

	often need to work together with others	经常需要与他人一起工作
团队合作与沟通技能的重要性	poor communication or interpersonal skills leads to conflicts or miscommunication with co-workers, which can hurt productivity and team spirit	糟糕的沟通或人际交往技能会导致与同事发生冲突或沟通错误，这可能会损害生产力和团队精神
优秀的团队合作与沟通技能及优势	involves openly exchanging ideas and closely cooperating with each other	包括公开交换意见和彼此密切合作
	allows a team to complete big, complex projects more efficiently and produce things with better quality	让团队更有效地完成大而复杂的项目，并生产出更高质量的产品
	makes it more enjoyable for people to work together, which improves team spirit	让人们在一起工作更愉快，这提高了团队士气

10. Management/leader/business skills（管理 / 领导 / 商业技能）

◎ 话题解读

每个企业都需要领导者，他们对公司的成功起着至关重要的作用。Part 3 关于这个话题通常会问"领导者应该具备哪些技能和素质"。以下这些口语题目和领导者所需技能有关，请先通读题目，然后思考回答这些问题时该怎样组织信息和语言。

◎ 题目

What skill set should a manager have?

What qualities should a team leader have?

What are the key skills for managing a business?

What kinds of qualities do people need to run their own business?

What kinds of qualities should a successful businessman have?

What kind of personality should a good leader have?

Do you think managers can be friends with their subordinates?

Can everyone become a leader?

◎ 答题思路分析

这里以"What qualities should a team leader have?"为例，看看有哪些有用的英文句子可以用来回答这个问题。在学习英文句子之前，请先思考这个问题要从哪几个方面来回答。对于一个领导者来说，决策力、组织能力、沟通能力、人格魅力都是非常重要的品质。在掌握了回答的几个方面之后，我们来学习一些有用的表达与素材吧。

◎ 表达与素材

1. Decision-making skills: the success of your team depends on you making good decisions.

2. Organisation skills: you need to be able to schedule goals properly, as well as divide work effectively.

3. Communication skills: you need to be able to communicate clearly to subordinates so that they understand what you need and expect from them.

4. People skills: you need to be friendly with subordinates and build trust with them, so that they will be more loyal to you and work harder for you.

◎ 表达与素材解读

首先，"Decision-making skills"（决策能力）是非常重要的，因为整个团队的成功取决于领导做出正确的决定；其次，"Organisation skills"（组织能力）也不可缺少，好的领导者需要合理安排目标及有效地分配工作；再者，作为领导，"Communication skills"（沟通技能）也很重要，这样才能让下属明白自己需要什么，对他们的期待是怎样的；最后，性格也是非常重要的，人们都喜欢有人格魅力的领导，所以领导需要与下属友好相处、与他们建立信任。

以上这些表达和素材同样适用于其他题目，比如在回答"Can everyone become a leader?"

时，考生可以先回答"并不是每个人都适合做领导"，随后列举适合当领导的人都有哪些特征，这时就可以使用表达与素材中的内容了。

◎ 表达积累

为了方便记忆和学习，我们将有用的表达罗列在以下表格中，考生可以尝试用这些表达的组合来回答之前罗列的相关题目。

Decision-making skills（决策能力）	the success of your team depends on you making good decisions	你的团队的成功取决于你做出正确的决定
Organisation skills（组织能力）	be able to schedule goals properly, as well as divide work effectively	能够合理安排目标，有效地分配工作
Communication skills（沟通技能）	be able to communicate clearly to subordinates so that they understand what you need and expect from them	能够清楚地与下属沟通，以便他们了解你的需求和对他们的期望
People skills（人际交往技能）	be friendly with subordinates and build trust with them, so that they will be more loyal to you and work harder for you.	与下属友好相处，建立信任，这样他们会对你更忠诚，为你更努力地工作

11. Special or practical skills in modern society（现代社会特殊的或实用的技能）

◎ 话题解读

近年来，新技术突飞猛进，世界变得更加全球化，市场竞争日益激烈，对人才的需求也越来越高。要想在竞争中立于不败之地，就得有一些技能。Part 3 关于这个话题通常会问"在现代社会哪些技能是必要的或有用的"。以下这些口语题目和现代社会特殊的或实用的技能有关，请先通读题目，然后思考回答这些问题时该怎样组织信息和语言。

◎ 题目

What is the difference between required skills in the past and in the present?

What is the most important practical skill in modern society?

What skills and abilities do people most want to learn today?

What are some special skills that people can learn?

What skills do adults need to have?

Which skills do you think will be important in the future?

◎ 答题思路分析

这里以"What skills and abilities do people most want to learn today?"为例，看看有哪些有用的英文句子可以用来回答这个问题。在学习英文句子之前，请先思考这个问题要从哪几个方面来回答。在现代社会，掌握一门外语和一些计算机相关的技能非常有用。除此之外，一些生存技能，比如开车、做饭、游泳、急救也是非常必要的。在掌握了回答的几个方面之后，我们来学习一些有用的表达与素材。

◎ 表达与素材

1. Basic computer skills (e.g. knowing how to use Microsoft Word, Excel, and PowerPoint), online research skills, and programming skills.

2. Foreign language skills are useful because the world is becoming more connected every day. Foreign languages such as English allow us to communicate with foreign clients or co-workers.

3. Other useful skills include cooking, driving, swimming, and rescue skills like CPR and first aid.

◎表达与素材解读

以上表达与素材将当今社会需要学习的技能分为三类：计算机技能、外语技能及其他有用的技能。首先，计算机技能包括基本的计算机操作能力（如使用一些办公软件）、"online research skills"（在线搜索研究能力）及 "programming skills"（编程技能）；外语能力能够帮助人们与外国客户或同事沟通。此外，人们还需要具备一些有用的技能，比如烹饪、驾驶、游泳及心肺复苏和急救等救援技能。

以上这些表达和素材同样适用于其他题目，比如在回答"What is the difference between required skills in the past and in the present?"时，考生既可以直接对比过去与现在的差别，也可以说现在比过去有更多的要求，比如计算机技能、外语技能和某些有用的技能等都是当今社会需要的。

◎ 表达积累

为了方便记忆和学习，我们将有用的表达罗列在以下表格中，考生可以尝试用这些表达的组合来回答之前罗列的相关题目。

计算机技能	basic computer skills (e.g. knowing how to use Microsoft Word, Excel, and PowerPoint)	基本的计算机操作技能（例如学会使用 Microsoft Word、Excel 和 PowerPoint）
	online research skills	在线搜索研究技能
	programming skills	编程技能
外语技能	allow us to communicate with foreign clients or co-workers	让我们能够与外国客户或同事交流
其他有用的技能	cooking, driving, swimming, and rescue skills like CPR and first aid	烹饪、驾驶、游泳以及心肺复苏和急救等救援技能

12. How to become successful（如何获得成功）

◎ 话题解读

成功人士通常具有一些优秀的品质和卓越的技能。Part 3 关于这个话题通常会问"什么样的技能和品质能让一个人成功"。以下这些口语题目和如何获得成功有关，请先通读题目，然后思考回答这些问题时该怎样组织信息和语言。

◎ 题目

What does it take to become successful?

What kinds of skills should successful people have?

Which do you think is more important for people to become successful: hard work or opportunities?

What qualities do you think are the most important for work?

What kinds of employees should be rewarded?

How can people improve their job performance?

Do you think a university degree would guarantee one's career success?

What are the reasons for failure?

◎ 答题思路分析

这里以"What does it take to become successful?"为例，看看有哪些有用的英文句子可以用来回答这个问题。在学习英文句子之前，请先思考一下这个问题要从哪几个方面来回答。成功这个话题十分宽泛，但无论哪一类人想要在职场中获得成功都必须做到以下几点：有坚定的目标、有顽强的毅力，以及与他人共事的能力。在掌握了回答的几个方面之后，我们来学习一些有用的表达与素材。

◎ 表达与素材

1. In order to be successful, you should set both long-term and short-term goals.

2. You need to work hard and stay focused. Whenever you experience hardships or failure, learn from it and keep going. Take responsibility for all of your actions and never blame anyone for your mistakes.

3. You need to develop good people skills so that you gain more connections and so that you get along with your co-workers. Both of these things are important for career success.

◎ 表达与素材解读

首先，想要成功肯定需要有目标，根据前面"目标"话题的内容可知，目标包括长期目标与短期目标；其次，成功的路上总是充满了困难，所以"work hard and stay focused"（努力工作与保持专注）是十分重要的；最后，工作中总是要与人打交道的，这就离不开"good people skills"（良好的人际交往技能）。

以上这些表达和素材同样适用于其他题目，比如"How can people improve their job performance?"，这里的"improve job performance"就等同于在工作中获得成功，考生可以这样回答：为了能够提升工作中的表现，人们应该有工作目标，遇到困难能够坚持，并且要学会和同事们共事。

◎ 表达积累

为了方便记忆和学习，我们将有用的表达罗列在以下表格中，考生可以尝试用这些表达的组合来回答之前罗列的相关题目。

制定目标	set both long-term and short-term goals	同时设定长期和短期目标
努力与专注	work hard and stay focused	努力工作，保持专注
	learn from hardships or failure and keep going	从困难和失败中学习，然后继续前进
	Take responsibility for all of your actions and never blame anyone for your mistakes.	为自己所有的行为负责，不要因为自己的错误责怪任何人。
良好的人际交往技能	develop good people skills	培养良好的人际交往能力
	gain more connections	获得更多人脉
	get along with your co-workers	和你的同事好好相处

 ## 话题 3　BUSINESSES & COMPANIES（商业与公司）

不同于与职业相关的问题，商业和公司相关的问题更多地围绕商业运营展开，比如企业应该做什么来获得商业成功，企业应该如何对待他们的员工。下面我们将学习如何回答这些问题。

1. Customer service（客户服务）

◎ 话题解读

客户服务是公司在顾客购买公司产品或服务之前和之后提供的服务和支持。Part 3 关于这个话题通常会问"为什么需要客户服务"及"好的客户服务意味着什么"。以下这些口语题目和客户服务有关，请先通读题目，然后思考回答这些问题时该怎样组织信息和语言。

◎ 题目

Is it necessary for companies to set up customer service?

Are there any disadvantages to setting up customer service?

Why should companies react quickly when customers have difficulties?

How can companies improve their customer service?

As a boss, what would you do to prevent bad service?

What kinds of service are bad services?

◎ 答题思路分析

这里以"Is it necessary for companies to set up customer service?"为例，看看有哪些有用的英文句子可以用来回答这个问题。在学习英文句子之前，请先思考这个问题要从哪几个方面来回答。人们在日常购物时，除了看中产品本身，通常也会关注与产品相关的售前和售后服务。比如，当我们在网上浏览一款商品时，除了查看产品介绍，还会向客服询问一些问题，客服的工作态度和专业性在促进订单成交的过程中起到了十分重要的作用。完成购买之后，如果在使用中遇到问题，售后能否及时解决问题也很重要。在掌握了回答的几个方面之后，我们来学习一些有用的表达与素材。

◎ 表达与素材

1. Good customer service is important because it keeps the customers happy, satisfied, and loyal to the company. This is good for business and helps improve the company's reputation.

2. If a company wants to improve its customer service, it must train its employees properly, and make sure that they are responsive and respectful to customers, quickly addressing any complaints, questions, or feedback.

3. Poor customer service means ignoring customers and not responding to their complaints, questions, or feedback. Poor customer service harms a company's reputation.

◎ 表达与素材解读

好的客户服务是非常重要的，它能让客户感到高兴、满意并且忠诚于公司，同时对公司本身有好处，有助于提高公司的声誉。为了提高客户服务水平，公司需要适当地培训员工，确保员工积极响应和尊重客户，迅速处理任何投诉、问题或反馈。如果一个公司忽视客户和客户服务，就会损害公司的声誉。

以上这些表达和素材同样适用于其他题目，比如在回答"As a boss, what would you do to prevent bad service?"这个题目时，考生可以说杜绝糟糕的服务很重要，随后使用上述表达与素材中关于客户服务的重要性及如何培训员工的内容。

◎ 表达积累

为了方便记忆和学习，我们将有用的表达罗列在以下表格中，考生可以尝试用这些表达的组合来回答之前罗列的相关题目。

良好的客户服务对公司的重要性	keeps the customers happy, satisfied, and loyal to the company	使客户高兴、满意，对公司忠诚
	This is good for business and helps improve the company's reputation.	这对生意有好处，也有助于提高公司的声誉。
如何提供良好的客户服务	must train its employees properly	必须对员工进行适当的培训
	make sure that employees are responsive and respectful to customers, quickly addressing any complaints, questions, or feedback	确保员工对客户积极反应和尊重，迅速处理任何投诉、问题或反馈
糟糕的客户服务带来的危害	Poor customer service means ignoring customers and not responding to their complaints, questions, or feedback.	糟糕的客户服务意味着忽视客户，不回应他们的投诉、问题或反馈。
	Poor customer service harms a company's reputation.	糟糕的客户服务会损害公司的声誉。

2. Business success（商业成功）

◎ 话题解读

影响商业成功的因素很多。Part 3 关于这个话题通常会问"什么因素驱动商业成功"。以下这些口语题目和商业成功有关，请先通读题目，然后思考回答这些问题时该怎样组织信息和语言。

◎ 题目

What are important factors in making a company successful?

What do you think are the key factors that contribute to the success of a business?

What skills are important for the success of business?

Why do most businesses fail in the first year?

◎ 答题思路分析

这里以"What are important factors in making a company successful?"为例，看看有哪些有用的英文句子可以用来回答这个问题。在学习英文句子之前，请先思考这个问题要从哪几个方面来回答。这个问题看似很空泛，但仔细想想回答起来并不难。首先，公司需要有好的产品和服务；其次，需要注重售前、售后的客户服务；最后，公司需要有优秀的领导者和员工。在掌握了回答的几个方面之后，我们来学习一些有用的表达与素材。

◎ 表达与素材

1. Having good products and services.

2. Having good customer service, which raises customer satisfaction.

3. Having great leaders and managers with good organization, communication, and decision-making skills.

4. Having talented employees, as well as a good working environment.

◎表达与素材解读

上述表达与素材将商业成功归纳为四个方面：产品与服务、客户服务（售前与售后）、领导者、员工。考生在回答问题时可以罗列这些内容，也可以专门就其中的某一项内容进行详细解说。

以上这些表达和素材同样适用于其他题目，比如"Why do most business fail in the first year?"，回答这个问题时考生可以说因为产品与服务、客户服务、领导者与员工方面存在问题，所以导致很多企业在开业的第一年便失败了。

◎ 表达积累

为了方便记忆和学习，我们将有用的表达罗列在以下表格中，考生可以尝试用这些表达的组合来回答之前罗列的相关题目。

产品与服务	having good products and services	有良好的产品和服务
客户服务（售前与售后）	having good customer service, which raises customer satisfaction	有良好的客户服务，提高客户满意度
领导者	having great leaders and managers with good organization, communication, and decision-making skills	有优秀的领导者和管理者，具有良好的组织、沟通和决策能力
员工	having talented employees, as well as a good working environment	拥有优秀的员工，以及良好的工作环境

3. Company-employee relationships（公司与员工的关系）

◎ 话题解读

人才对于公司的发展至关重要。公司与员工之间的关系好坏会影响员工的生产力和忠诚度。Part 3 关于这个话题通常会问"公司应该如何对待他们的员工"。以下这些口语题目和公司与员工的关系有关，请先通读题目，然后思考回答这些问题时该怎样组织信息和语言。

◎ 题目

What should a good employer do?

What kinds of employees should be rewarded?

What kinds of rewards should companies give to employees who work hard?

Should people be allowed to rest during work hours?

What can employers do to help employees concentrate?

What does it mean to have better working conditions?

Should companies have rules?

◎ 答题思路分析

这里以"What should a good employer do?"为例，看看有哪些有用的英文句子可以用来回答这个问题。在学习英文句子之前，请先思考一下这个问题要从哪几个方面来回答。从员工的角度出发，他们肯定希望公司提供良好的职位、优厚的薪资和较多的晋升机会，此外，公司要有良好的管理制度、宽松舒适的工作环境。在掌握了回答的几个方面之后，我们来学习一些有用的表达与素材。

◎ 表达与素材

1. Companies should reward good employees by giving them raises, promotions, and special rewards (such as bonuses, gift cards, tickets, or extra vacation time).

2. Companies should not require employees to work too much overtime, as it's bad for a person's physical and mental health. Instead, companies need to allow employees to have a healthy work-life balance. Companies should also allow employees to take regular breaks during work. Breaks help employees relax and focus better afterwards.

3. Companies should not be too controlling or have too many strict rules. It would create a stressful and unpleasant work environment.

◎ 表达与素材解读

首先，优秀的公司应该给优秀的员工奖励，比如加薪（raises）、升职（promotions）、特殊奖励（special rewards）等；其次，员工们都不喜欢加班太多的公司，他们希望有自己的生活；最后，公司不应该有太多管控措施（too controlling）和严格规定（strict rules），这会让员工感到压抑和不快。

以上这些表达和素材同样适用于其他题目，比如在回答"What does it mean to have better working conditions?"这个题目时，考生可以使用表达与素材中的部分内容，比如第 2 点"不要加班太多"。

◎ 表达积累

为了方便记忆和学习，我们将有用的表达罗列在以下表格中，考生可以尝试用这些表达的组合来回答之前罗列的相关题目。

加薪、升职与奖励	should reward good employees by giving them raises, promotions, and special rewards	应该通过加薪、升职和特殊奖励来奖励优秀员工
减少加班	should not require employees to work too much overtime, as it's bad for a person's physical and mental health	不应该要求员工加班太多，因为这对一个人的身心健康有害
	need to allow employees to have a healthy work-life balance	需要让员工拥有健康的工作与生活的平衡
	allow employees to take regular breaks during work	允许员工在工作期间定期休息
人性化管理	should not be too controlling or have too many strict rules	不应该有太多的管控措施或有太多严格的规定

4. Types of businesses & opening a business（企业类型及创业）

◎ 话题解读

很多人都有创业的梦想，尤其是一些热门的或者新兴的行业非常受人追捧。Part 3 关于这个话题通常会问"主要的企业类型"及"人们喜欢创建什么样的企业"。以下这些口语题目和企业类型及创业有关，请先通读题目，然后思考回答这些问题时该怎样组织信息和语言。

◎ 题目

What kinds of businesses are popular in your country?

What emerging industries do you know?

What kinds of companies will help the development of a place?

If you had the opportunity to have your own business, what business would it be?

Do people want to open an online business or a more traditional business?

◎ 答题思路分析

这里以"What kinds of businesses are popular in your country?"为例，看看有哪些有用的英文句子可以用来回答这个问题。在学习英文句子之前，请先思考这个问题要从哪几个方面来回答。一般来说，餐饮、互联网、科技等行业既符合题目要求，又为人熟悉且比较容易描述。在掌握了回答的几个方面之后，我们来学习一些有用的表达与素材。

◎ 表达与素材

China has many thriving businesses:

The food industry, including cafés, bars, teashops, and restaurants.

E-commerce or online businesses, where people sell things over the internet.

Other technology-related businesses, like ones where people develop an app or mobile game.

Real-estate businesses, where people rent houses to others through online platforms like Airbnb.

◎ 表达与素材解读

有些行业在国内比较受欢迎，比如食品行业（food industry）、互联网（E-commerce or online businesses）、高科技公司（technology-related businesses）及房地产业（real-estate businesses）。这些行业与我们的衣食住行息息相关。考生可以罗列这些行业，也可以深入分析某一个行业，分析时最好使用例子。

◎ 表达积累

为了方便记忆和学习，我们将有用的表达罗列在以下表格中，考生可以尝试用这些表达的组合来回答之前罗列的相关题目。

餐饮	the food industry, including cafés, bars, teashops, and restaurants	食品行业，包括咖啡店、酒吧、茶馆和餐馆
互联网	e-commerce or online businesses, where people sell things over the internet	电子商务或在线业务，人们在互联网上出售自己的商品
其他高科技企业	other technology-related businesses, like ones where people develop an app or mobile game	其他与技术相关的业务，比如开发应用程序或手机游戏的业务
房地产	real-estate businesses, where people rent houses to others through online platforms like Airbnb	房地产业务，你可以通过 Airbnb 等在线平台把房子租给别人

话题 4 FRIENDS, FAMILY, AND NEIGHBOURS （朋友、家庭与邻居）

社会关系对个体的幸福感有着直接影响。每个人都处在一个社会关系网中，包括朋友、家人、同事、邻居等。下面我们将学习如何回答与社会关系相关的问题。

1. Making friends（交朋友）

◎ 话题解读

交朋友是生活的重要组成部分，朋友使我们的生活变得更加开心、快乐。Part 3 关于这个话题通常会问"人们如何交朋友"及"人们喜欢和什么样的人交朋友"。以下这些口语题目和交朋友有关，请先通读题目，然后思考回答这些问题时该怎样组织信息和语言。

◎ 题目

How do Chinese people make new friends?

Do you think people can make more friends if they often attend parties?

Do you think it's strange to make friends online?

What kind of people do you like to be friends with?

Do you prefer to make friends with young people or old people?

◎答题思路分析

这里以"How do Chinese people make new friends?"为例，看看有哪些有用的英文句子可以用来回答这个问题。在学习英文句子之前，请先思考一下这个问题要从哪几个方面来回答。大部分人是在工作和学习中交朋友的，也有很多人通过社交活动或者社交媒体认识新朋友。能成为朋友的原因有很多，但一般而言可以归纳为有共同的爱好、年龄相仿、可以互相交流想法和理解对方等。在掌握了回答的几个方面之后，我们来学习一些有用的表达与素材。

◎ 表达与素材

1. Usually, people normally make friends through school or work. When you spend a lot of time with someone, you naturally become friends. However, it's also quite common for people to make friends through social events such as parties, as well as in communities where people share a common interest, like in clubs or online communities.

2. People tend to prefer making friends with those who are similar to them. Usually, this means people around their age. There are just more things to talk about, and they are able to understand each other better.

◎ 表达与素材解读

上述表达与素材总结了交朋友的两种途径：school or work 和 social events。两个人能成为好朋友是有原因的，人们都倾向于和志趣相投的人交朋友，他们年龄相仿、性格相似、有共同的话题、能够理解对方。

以上这些表达和素材同样适用于其他题目，比如在回答"What kind of people do you like to be friends with?"这个题目时，考生就可以使用上述表达与素材中的第 2 点内容。

◎ 表达积累

为了方便记忆和学习，我们将有用的表达罗列在以下表格中，考生可以尝试用这些表达的组合来回答之前罗列的相关题目。

	make friends through school or work	通过学习或工作交朋友
交朋友的途径	make friends through social events such as parties, as well as in communities where people share a common interest, like in clubs or online communities	通过聚会等社交活动结交朋友，也可以在有共同兴趣的社区结交朋友，比如俱乐部或在线社区
什么样的人能成为朋友	prefer making friends with those who are similar to them	喜欢和与自己相似的人交朋友
	people around their age	和他们年龄相仿的人
	There are just more things to talk about, and they are able to understand each other better.	有更多的事情可以谈论，他们能够更好地理解彼此。

2. Maintaining friendships（保持友谊）

◎ 话题解读

有些友谊会因时间和距离而变淡；还有些友谊是一辈子不变的。Part 3 关于这个话题通常会问"友谊的重要性"和"如何保持友谊"。以下这些口语题目和保持友谊有关，请先通读题目，然后思考回答这些问题时该怎样组织信息和语言。

◎ 题目

Which is more important: new friendships or old ones?

Is it important to stay together longer with friends?

Why do people still remember many of their friends from primary school?

Do you still keep in touch with your childhood friends?

Why do people lose contact with their friends after graduation?

Do you prefer to expand your social circle or be friends with a small group of people?

◎ 答题思路分析

这里以"Which is more important: new friendships or old ones?"为例，看看有哪些有用的英文句子可以用来回答这个问题。在学习英文句子之前，请先思考一下这个问题要从哪几个方面来回答。人们通常认为新朋友与老朋友一样重要，我们会维护从小到大的友谊，也会在生活、学习和工作中认识新的朋友。老朋友可能因为距离等原因不常见面，维系友情有一定的困难，但他们陪我们度过了很多快乐和艰难的时光，所有对我们来说仍然很重要。新朋友是我们社交生活中重要的存在，对我们的身心健康有好处。在掌握了回答的几个方面之后，我们来学习一些有用的表达与素材。

◎ 表达与素材

1. Old friendships, including childhood friendships, are important because you've known each other for many years and share lots of experiences. They've been with you through happy and tough times.

2. However, it can be hard to stay in touch with old friends if you no longer see each other often—for example, if you attend different schools or live far from each other.

3. It's important to make new friends if you're in a new environment—for example, if you're going to a new school or working at a new company. That's because having an active social life is good for your physical and mental health.

◎表达与素材解读

"old friendship"是非常重要的，因为彼此相识多年，有过很多共同的经历，一起度过了很多快乐和艰难的时光。然而，要维系这样的友谊也是很难的，因为不在同一个学校上学了，或者不在一块住了。同样，认识新朋友也很有必要，因为积极的社交生活对人的身心健康有好处。

以上这些表达和素材同样适用于其他题目，比如在回答"Why do people lose contact with

their friends after graduation?"这个题目时，考生可以说因为毕业后大家各奔东西，离得很远，所以疏于联系了。

◎ 表达积累

为了方便记忆和学习，我们将有用的表达罗列在以下表格中，考生可以尝试用这些表达的组合来回答之前罗列的相关题目。

老朋友的重要性	you've known each other for many years and share lots of experiences	你们相识多年，有过很多共同的经历
	They've been with you through happy and tough times.	他们陪你度过了快乐和艰难的时光。
保持友谊有难度的原因	if you no longer see each other often—for example, if you attend different schools or live far from each other	如果你们不再经常见面——例如，你们上不同的学校，或者住得很远
结识新朋友的重要性	It's important to make new friends if you're in a new environment	如果你在一个新的环境中，结交新朋友是很重要的。
	having an active social life is good for your physical and mental health	积极的社交生活对你的身心健康有好处

3. Activities with friends（和朋友们一起进行的活动）

◎ 话题解读

朋友们在一起可以做各种各样的事情。针对这个话题 Part 3 通常会问"这些活动是什么"及"活动的重要性"。以下这些口语题目与和朋友们一起活动有关，请先通读题目，然后思考回答这些问题时该怎样组织信息和语言。

◎ 题目

What are the benefits of going out with friends?

Do you like to hang out with your friends?

In general, do people like going out alone or with friends?

What do you usually do when you hang out with your friends?

What do young people like to do together?

Do you think having meals together is a very common social activity?

◎ 答题思路分析

这里以"In general, do people like going out alone or with friends?"为例，看看有哪些有用的英文句子可以用来回答这个问题。在学习英文句子之前，请先思考这个问题要从哪几个方面来回答。跟朋友一起出去玩，既可以培养感情、增进友谊，又可以获得乐趣。朋友们可以一起做的事情非常多，比如室内活动、户外运动、休闲娱乐等。在掌握了回答的几个方面之后，我们来学习一些有用的表达与素材。

◎ 表达与素材

You can do a lot of fun and relaxing things with your friends:

Hang out at coffee shops, go shopping, or have meals together.

Go to the movies or go sing karaoke together.

Play sports with each other, like basketball or badminton.

Play card games, board games, or video games together.

Go on trips together during holidays.

◎表达与素材解读

可以与朋友们一起进行的活动有很多，比如一起逛街、喝咖啡、吃美食，一起看电影、唱歌，一起做运动、锻炼身体，一起打牌、打游戏，还可以一起结伴旅行。和朋友们一起活动的好处很多，可以使用前文学过的表达，比如 "good for your physical and mental health" 及 "build a bond"。

以上这些表达和素材同样适用于其他题目，比如在回答 "Do you like to hang out with your friends?" 这个题目时，考生可以说很喜欢和朋友出去，然后说明出去都玩些什么，随后可以选择一种活动进行介绍，或者罗列多种不同的活动。

◎ 表达积累

为了方便记忆和学习，我们将有用的表达罗列在以下表格中，考生可以尝试用这些表达的组合来回答之前罗列的相关题目。

逛街、购物、吃美食	hang out at coffee shops, go shopping, or have meals together	光顾咖啡店，购物，或者一起吃饭
休闲娱乐	go to the movies or go sing karaoke together	一起去看电影或唱歌
体育运动	play sports with each other, like basketball or badminton	一起做运动，比如打篮球或羽毛球
室内活动	play card games, board games, or video games together	一起玩纸牌游戏、桌游或电子游戏
旅行	go on trips together during holidays	节假日一起去旅行

4. Friends vs. Family（朋友与家人）

◎ 话题解读

朋友和家人都是我们人生中比较重要的人。Part 3 关于这个话题通常会要求你比较朋友和家人的影响和重要性。以下这些口语题目与朋友和家人的影响及重要性有关，请先通读题目，然后思考回答这些问题时该怎样组织信息和语言。

◎ 题目

Are people influenced more by their friends or their parents?

Whose influence on children is more important: friends' or parents'?

Whose advice is more helpful: parents' or friends'?

Is the advice given by family the same as the advice given by friends?

Which do you prefer, support from family members or friends?

What have you learned from your friends?

Who should people spend more time with: family or friends?

What's the difference between spending time with friends and spending time with family?

◎ 答题思路分析

这里以 "Are people influenced more by their friends or their parents?" 为例，看看有哪些有用的英文句子可以用来回答这个问题。在学习英文句子之前，请先思考一下这个问题要从哪几个方面来回答。其实，很难笼统地说我们是受家人影响更大还是受朋友影响更大。这个问题需要分年龄讨论。在我们很小的时候，肯定是来自家庭的影响更大，但当我们进入学校和步入社会后，来自朋友、同学的影响可能会更大。然而，在做一些大的决定时，比如选择专业和工作方向，父母的影响则会大于朋友的影响。在掌握了回答的几个方面之后，我们来学习一些有用的表达与素材。

◎ 表达与素材

1. Most people are more influenced by their family than their friends. The reason is that people usually spend more time with their family, especially during early childhood. Also, friendships can fade over time, while family lasts forever.

2. Friends can give advice about other friends or schoolwork. Parents can give advice for almost everything, including school, social relationships, health, and their children's career. Parents are able to do that because they are older, wiser, and more experienced with life. They also always have their children's best interests in mind. Because of that, usually it's better to take advice from parents more seriously.

3. It's important to spend time with your friends. It's fun to talk with friends and do things together. They are closer to you in age, so there are just more things to talk about, and you are able to understand each other better. Friends can also give you emotional support whenever you are unhappy or experiencing difficulties in life.

◎ 表达与素材解读

首先，当我们还小的时候，大多数人受家庭的影响比朋友的影响更大，因为我们与家人相处的时间更长，友谊可能会随着时间的推移而变淡，但家庭关系则是永恒的。其次，朋友可以给你关于其他朋友或功课的建议，父母则几乎可以为所有事情提供建议，因为他们年龄更大、更有智慧、对生活更有经验，而且总是把孩子的最大利益放在心上。尽管如此，也不能忽视朋友的影响，由于年龄比较接近，当我们在生活中遇到困难或者不开心的事时，朋友可以给予情感上的支持。

以上这些表达和素材同样适用于其他题目，比如 "Who should people spend more time with: family or friends?"。

◎ 表达积累

为了方便记忆和学习，我们将有用的表达罗列在以下表格中，考生可以尝试用这些表达的组合来回答之前罗列的相关题目。

父母的影响力与重要性	people usually spend more time with their family, especially during early childhood	人们通常会花更多的时间和家人在一起，尤其是在幼儿时期
	friendships can fade over time, while family lasts forever	友谊会随着时间的推移而变淡，而家庭关系则是永恒的
	give advice for almost everything, including school, social relationships, health, and their children's career	几乎可以给所有事情提供建议，包括学校、社会关系、健康和孩子的职业
	Parents are able to do that because they are older, wiser, and more experienced with life. They also always have their children's best interests in mind.	父母之所以能够这样做，是因为他们年龄更大，更有智慧，对生活更有经验。他们也总是把孩子的最大利益放在心上。
朋友的影响力与重要性	give advice about other friends or schoolwork	对其他朋友或学业提出建议
	It's fun to talk with friends and do things together.	和朋友一起聊天、一起做事情是很有趣的。
	They are closer to you in age, so there are just more things to talk about, and you are able to understand each other better.	他们在年龄上与你更接近，所以有更多的事情可以谈论，而且你们能够更好地理解对方。
	Friends can also give you emotional support whenever you are unhappy or experiencing difficulties in life.	当你在生活中感到不开心或遇到困难时，朋友也可以给你情感上的支持。

5. Old family members（家中的长辈）

◎ 话题解读

每个家庭都会有一些年老的家庭成员，比如祖父母。尊老爱幼是我们的优良传统。Part 3 关于这个话题通常会问"照顾和陪伴家人的重要性"。以下这些口语题目与家中的长辈有关，请先通读题目，然后思考回答这些问题时该怎样组织信息和语言。

◎ 题目

How much do you think people should be responsible for (the welfare of) their own parents?

Do you think old people should live with their family?

Do you think that old people should be taken care of at home?

These days, people from different generations live together. Do you think this is a problem?

Is it important to visit family members?

Do you think family relationships are important?

◎ 答题思路分析

这里以"Do you think old people should live with their family?"为例，看看有哪些有用的英文句子可以用来回答这个问题。在学习英文句子之前，请先思考这个问题要从哪几个方面来回答。首先，无论是从肯定的角度还是否定的角度来回答这个问题，考生都要谈及照顾和陪伴家中老人是我们应尽的义务。其次，要说明原因，可以说为了报答养育之恩，也可以说这是社会的一种约定俗成的做法，对我们自己和老人都有不少好处。在掌握了回答的几个方面之后，我们来学习一些有用的表达与素材。

◎ 表达与素材

1. We should take care of old people in our family, either by living with them or visiting them regularly. Old people made sacrifices for us and took care of us when we were younger, so it's only fair that we repay them. Also, old people are weaker and get sick more easily, so they actually need people around to take care of them.

2. Young people should spend time with old people because it's good for both of them. Young people can help and take care of old people, while old people can pass wisdom and advice to young people.

◎ 表达与素材解读

照顾老人可以跟他们住在一起，也可以定期去看望他们。这其中的原因包括：其一，老人在我们小的时候照顾我们，当他们老了，我们理应回报他们；其二，人老了之后身体会变得虚弱，容易生病，所以需要人照顾他们。照顾老人不仅对老人有好处，对于年轻人也有好处，老人可以传递一些智慧和建议给年轻人。

以上这些表达和素材同样适用于其他题目，比如在回答"Is it important to visit family members?"这个题目时，考生可以说经常去访问家庭成员，尤其是祖父母、外祖父母，是很重要的，然后就可以使用上述表达和素材了。

◎ 表达积累

为了方便记忆和学习，我们将有用的表达罗列在以下表格中，考生可以尝试用这些表达的组合来回答之前罗列的相关题目。

照顾家中长辈的方法	either by living with them or visiting them regularly	要么和他们住在一起，要么定期去看望他们
为何要照顾长辈	Old people made sacrifices for us and took care of us when we were younger, so it's only fair that we repay them.	老人们在我们年轻的时候为我们做出了牺牲，照顾我们，所以我们要回报他们才公平。
	Old people are weaker and get sick more easily, so they actually need people around to take care of them.	老年人身体较弱，更容易生病，所以他们实际上需要身边有人照顾他们。
照顾长辈对大家都好	Young people can help and take care of old people, while old people can pass wisdom and advice to young people.	年轻人可以帮助和照顾老人，而老人可以传递智慧和建议给年轻人。

6. Importance of neighbours and communities（邻居和社区的重要性）

◎ 话题解读

无论是住在自己的房子里还是公寓里，人们通常都住在一个社区里，会有很多邻居。Part 3 关于这个话题通常会问"邻居的重要性"及"生活在一个社区的重要性"。以下这些口语题目与邻居和社区的重要性有关，请先通读题目，然后思考回答这些问题时该怎样组织信息和语言。

◎ 题目

Do you think neighbours are important?

Do you think it's important to have a good relationship with one's neighbours?

What are the benefits of belonging to a community?

Why do people living in a community act friendly with each other?

Do people like living in a community?

Where do people in a community usually have social gatherings?

Do you have many friends in your community?

◎ 答题思路分析

这里以"Do you think neighbours are important?"为例，看看有哪些有用的英文句子可以用来回答这个问题。在学习英文句子之前，请先思考这个问题要从哪几个方面来回答。俗话说"远亲不如近邻"，邻居和社区对我们的生活是十分重要的。邻居可以提供各种帮助，比如代收快递、借东西、交换食物等，还可以一起聊天、出去玩。至于社区，一个干净整洁、治安良好的社区对于居住者来说非常重要。在掌握了回答的几个方面之后，我们来学习一些有用的表达与素材。

◎ 表达与素材

1. Living in a community and having neighbours is good for your safety. They can alert you to dangerous situations, like a burglar or a fire.

2. Living in a community and having neighbours can help you in times of trouble—for example, if you need to borrow something, or if you have an emergency.

3. Neighbours and members of your community can provide social and emotional support. It can be fun and relaxing to chat with your neighbours, and even visit their homes.

◎ 表达与素材解读

住在社区并有好邻居的好处是具有安全性（提醒危险情况）和便利性（借东西、紧急救助）。有的邻居很亲切，相处起来像家人一样，可以跟他们聊天，串门，遇到不开心的事情时还可以得到社交和情感上的支持。

以上这些表达和素材同样适用于其他题目，比如在回答"Do people like living in a community?"时，考生可以说住在一个好的社区里是一种非常棒的经历，随后使用上述表达与素材中的内容进行回答。

◎ 表达积累

为了方便记忆和学习，我们将有用的表达罗列在以下表格中，考生可以尝试用这些表达的组合来回答之前罗列的相关题目。

社区与邻居的重要性之生活与安全	good for your safety	对你的安全有好处
	alert you to dangerous situations, like a burglar or a fire	提醒你危险的情况，比如窃贼或火灾
	help you in times of trouble—for example, if you need to borrow something, or if you have an emergency	在你有困难的时候帮助你——例如，如果你需要借东西，或者有紧急情况
社区与邻居的重要性之情感与社交	provide social and emotional support	提供社交和情感上的支持
	can be fun and relaxing to chat with your neighbours and even visit their homes	和邻居聊天能够让你感到有趣和放松，甚至还可以拜访他们的家

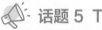 话题 5 TECHNOLOGY（科技）

科技进步对人类社会产生了巨大的影响。Part 3 关于科技的问题大多与最具影响力的技术有关，比如互联网和手机。考生通常会被问到这些科技是如何影响我们生活的各个方面的，比如教育、工作、沟通和人际关系等。下面我们将学习如何回答与科技相关的问题。

1. The Internet（互联网）

◎ 话题解读

互联网是 20 世纪最伟大的技术发明之一，它极大地改变了我们的生活，但同时也带来了一些不好的影响。Part 3 关于这个话题通常会问"人们使用互联网的原因"及"互联网的有害影响"。以下这些口语题目与互联网有关，请先通读题目，然后思考回答这些问题时该怎样组织信息和语言。

◎ 题目

What are the different reasons why people use the internet?

What do people usually do with the Internet?

What do people do online in their free time?

Do many people waste their time on the Internet?

What influence can the internet have on children?

Do you think parents should control what websites their children visit on the internet?

◎ 答题思路分析

这里以 "What influence can the internet have on children?" 为例，看看有哪些有用的英文句子可以用来回答这个问题。在学习英文句子之前，请先思考一下这个问题要从哪几个方面来回答。首先，需要回答孩子们在互联网上会做些什么事情；其次，需要谈论这些事情带来的后果，正面的和负面的都可以。在掌握了回答的几个方面之后，我们来学习一些有用的表达与素材。

◎ 表达与素材

People use the internet to:

1. Access social media, or chat with friends.

2. Play games, watch online videos/streams, or listen to music.

3. Get news.

4. Find information.

Downsides of the internet:

1. People can become addicted to it, and waste lots of time, which is bad for their body and studies/work.

2. Children can get exposed to violent or sexual content. They can also get influenced by fake information or news.

3. It can hurt people's self-esteem when they compare themselves to others on social media, such as celebrities, influencers, or even friends.

◎ 表达与素材解读

人们可以在互联网上做很多事情，比如 "chat with friends" "play games" "get news" 及 "find information"，这些事情不仅成年人可以做，青少年也可以做。以上是互联网好的一面。那么坏处又有哪些呢？比如容易 "addicted to"（上瘾）和 "waste lots of time"，孩子们容易 "get exposed to violent or sexual content"（接触到暴力或色情内容），而且与名人、网络红人甚至朋友等比较时，会 "hurt people's self-esteem"（伤害他们的自尊）。

以上这些表达和素材同样适用于其他题目，比如在回答 "What do people do online in their free time?" 这个题目时，考生可以使用 "人们在互联网上做什么" 中提到的表达与素材。

◎ 表达积累

为了方便记忆和学习，我们将有用的表达罗列在以下表格中，考生可以尝试用这些表达的组合来回答之前罗列的相关题目。

	access social media, or chat with friends	访问社交媒体，或与朋友聊天
人们通过互联网可以做的事	play games, watch online videos/streams, or listen to music	玩游戏、看在线视频或听音乐
	get news	获取新闻
	find information	查找信息

	become addicted to it, and waste lots of time	沉迷其中，浪费大量时间
沉迷上网的危害（尤其是青少年）	bad for their body and studies/work	对他们的身体和学习 / 工作不好
	get exposed to violent or sexual content	接触暴力或色情内容
	get influenced by fake information or news	受虚假信息或新闻影响
	hurt people's self-esteem when they compare themselves to others on social media, such as celebrities, influencers, or even friends	当他们在社交媒体上与名人、网络红人甚至朋友等比较时，会伤害他们的自尊

2. Social media（社交媒体）

◎ 话题解读

社交媒体拥有数以亿计的网络用户，它改变了人们发现和分享信息的方式。Part 3 关于这个话题通常会问"社交媒体的优点和缺点"及"人们使用社交媒体的原因"。以下这些口语题目与社交媒体有关，请先通读题目，然后思考回答这些问题时该怎样组织信息和语言。

◎ 题目

Why do people like to use social media?

What kinds of things are popular on social media?

What do you think of making friends on social media?

What do you think of the news on social media?

Why do some people like to share news on social media?

What are the advantages and disadvantages of using social media?

◎ 答题思路分析

这里以"Why do people like to use social media?"为例，看看有哪些有用的英文句子可以用来回答这个问题。在学习英文句子之前，请先思考一下这个问题要从哪几个方面来回答。首先，社交媒体是互联网的一部分，人们喜欢它的原因肯定与互联网的优势有关；其次，社交媒体带来的问题在很大程度上也和互联网有关。在掌握了回答的几个方面之后，我们来学习一些有用的表达与素材。

◎ 表达与素材

1. People usually use social media to keep in touch with their friends and family, or to read news stories. It's fast, easy, and convenient to use social media.

2. Sometimes people share interesting news on social media. It allows them to discuss it with friends and family.

3. The disadvantages of social media are:

News on social media is not as reliable and can be fake, because anyone can post anything.

News from newspapers or news channels is usually more reliable and trustworthy.

People can become addicted to social media, and waste lots of time, which is bad for their body and studies/work.

It can hurt people's self-esteem when they compare themselves to others on social media, such as celebrities, influencers, or even friends.

◎ 表达与素材解读

社交媒体的好处是人们可以与朋友和家人保持联系、了解新闻故事、分享有趣的新闻。当然，凡事过犹不及，如果沉迷于社交媒体，也会带来很多危害，这些危害和沉迷于网络所带来的危害大致相同，比如接触到虚假新闻、浪费时间、影响学习 / 工作，以及因为与他人比较导致伤害自尊。

以上这些表达和素材同样适用于其他题目，比如在回答 "What are the advantages and disadvantages of using social media?" 这个话题时，考生可以选取以上表达和素材中的内容进行回答。

◎ 表达积累

为了方便记忆和学习，我们将有用的表达罗列在以下表格中，考生可以尝试用这些表达的组合来回答之前罗列的相关题目。

通过社交媒体可以做的事情	keep in touch with their friends and family	与他们的朋友和家人保持联系
	read news stories	读新闻
	share interesting news on social media	在社交媒体上分享有趣的新闻
沉迷社交媒体的坏处	News on social media is not as reliable and can be fake, because anyone can post anything.	社交媒体上的新闻不那么可靠，有可能是假的，因为任何人都可以发布任何东西。
	become addicted to it, and waste lots of time	沉迷其中，浪费大量时间
	bad for their body and studies/work	对他们的身体和学习 / 工作都不好
	hurt people's self-esteem when they compare themselves to others on social media, such as celebrities, influencers, or even friends	当人们在社交媒体上与名人、网络红人甚至朋友等比较时，会伤害他们的自尊

3. Technology's effects on games & toys（科技对于游戏或玩具的影响）

◎ 话题解读

科技的影响无处不在，孩子们玩的游戏和玩具也深受科技的影响。Part 3 关于这个话题通常会问 "当代儿童的游戏和玩具" 及 "它们的优点和缺点"。以下这些口语题目与科技对于游戏或玩具的影响有关，请先通读题目，然后思考回答这些问题时该怎样组织信息和语言。

◎ 题目

What's the difference between children's games nowadays and in the past?

What's the difference between the toys that kids play with now and in the past?

What indoor games do children like to play nowadays?

What are the advantages of children's games nowadays?

What toys are popular with kids in China today?

Do children like to play with toys or computer games nowadays?

Do you think playing with electronic toys has a good influence on kids?

◎ 答题思路分析

这里以"What's the difference between children's games nowadays and in the past?"为例，看看有哪些有用的英文句子可以用来回答这个问题。在学习英文句子之前，请先思考一下这个问题要从哪几个方面来回答。过去和现在的一些区别通常与互联网的诞生及普及有关。过去的游戏和玩具往往是看得见、摸得着的实物，而现在的游戏多半是线上的，玩具则多为电子产品。在掌握了回答的几个方面之后，我们来学习一些有用的表达与素材。

◎ 表达与素材

1. Children in the past often played games like card games or board games (e.g. Chinese chess). They also played with physical toys, like action figures, Barbie dolls, and teddy bears. Physical toys help train children's imagination because children can create stories with these toys.

2. These days, kids still play with physical toys, but many children also play with electronic toys, like video games, mobile games, or computer games. It's very fast, easy, and convenient to play electronic games. Electronic toys also help children become familiar with technology. However, playing with electronic toys too much can be unhealthy for children. It's bad for their eyes, body, and social development.

◎ 表达与素材解读

过去孩子们玩的游戏有哪些呢？有"card games or board games"（纸牌游戏或者棋盘游戏），玩具也是"physical toys"（实物玩具），比如人偶、芭比娃娃、泰迪熊等。这些玩具有诸多好处，其中之一是有助于培养孩子们的想象力。而现在的孩子们的玩具大多是一些电子产品，并且他们经常在网上玩游戏，这可以帮助孩子们熟悉科技，但如果玩太久，也会对他们的眼睛、身体和社会发展不利。

以上这些表达和素材同样适用于其他题目，比如在回答"What toys are popular with kids in China today?"时，考生可以选取以上表达和素材中的内容进行回答。

◎ 表达积累

为了方便记忆和学习，我们将有用的表达罗列在以下表格中，考生可以尝试用这些表达的组合来回答之前罗列的相关题目。

以前的玩具与游戏	played games like card games or board games (e.g. Chinese chess)	玩纸牌游戏或棋类游戏（如中国象棋）
	played with physical toys, like action figures, Barbie dolls, and teddy bears	玩实物玩具，比如人偶、芭比娃娃和泰迪熊
	Physical toys help train children's imagination because children can create stories with these toys.	实物玩具有助于培养孩子们的想象力，因为孩子们可以用这些玩具创造故事。
现在的玩具与游戏	still play with physical toys, but many children also play with electronic toys	仍然玩实物玩具，但许多孩子也玩电子玩具
	video games, mobile games, or computer games	电子游戏、手机游戏或电脑游戏
	Electronic toys also help children become familiar with technology.	电子玩具也能帮助孩子们熟悉科技。
	playing with electronic toys too much can be unhealthy for children	过多地玩电子玩具对孩子们是不健康的
	bad for their eyes, body, and social development	对他们的眼睛、身体和社会发展都不利

4. Books vs. Online information（书本信息与网上信息）

◎ 话题解读

互联网上充斥着各种各样的信息，作为获取信息的途径，互联网无疑是便捷的。然而，纸质书籍仍然在发挥它的作用。Part 3 关于这个话题通常会问"网上的信息与书本的信息相比有何优点与缺点"。以下这些口语题目与书本信息和网上信息的对比有关，请先通读题目，然后思考回答这些问题时该怎样组织信息和语言。

◎ 题目

Do people trust the information online?

Is it good to ask advice from strangers online?

How can you tell whether a website is reliable or not?

How can people find reliable information on the internet?

If it is just about gaining information, why is it necessary for books to exist?

Which can provide helpful learning materials, internet or books?

◎答题思路分析

这里以"Do people trust the information online?"为例，看看有哪些有用的英文句子可以用来回答这个问题。在学习英文句子之前，请先思考这个问题要从哪几个方面来回答。首先，肯定不能完全相信互联网上的信息，因为人人都可以在互联网上发布信息。那些有来源的、由官方机构提供的信息才是可靠的。其次，相对而言，纸质书籍提供的信息可信度更高，因为国家对出版物的要求更高。在掌握了回答的几个方面之后，我们来学习一些有用的表达与素材。

◎ 表达与素材

1. Information on the internet is not always reliable because anyone can post anything. There's a lot of fake information and news.

2. Online information can be trusted if it includes sources and references, like in online encyclopedias. Online information can also be trusted if it's written by professionals or is from a major news website.

3. The publishing process for books can be quite strict, so books tend to have more reliable information. However, it's harder and takes more time to find information from books than from the internet.

◎表达与素材解读

互联网上的信息不是完全可信的，因为任何人都可以在互联网上发布任何信息。当然，不是所有信息都不可靠，如果标明了信息的来源和参考，或者由专业人士撰写，或者来自主流新闻网站，那通常也是可信的。对比网上的信息，出版物的可信度肯定更高，因为书籍的出版过程相当严格，但人们需要花费较长的时间从书本中找到需要的信息。

以上这些表达和素材同样适用于其他题目，比如在回答"How can people find reliable information on the internet?"这个问题时，考生可以选取以上表达和素材中的第 2 点进行回答。

◎ 表达积累

为了方便记忆和学习，我们将有用的表达罗列在以下表格中，考生可以尝试用这些表达的组合来回答之前罗列的相关题目。

网上信息的缺点	is not always reliable because anyone can post anything	并不总是可靠的，因为任何人都可以发布任何信息
	There's a lot of fake information and news.	有很多虚假的信息和新闻。
哪一类网上信息比较可靠	if it includes sources and references, like in online encyclopedias	如果它包括来源和参考书目，比如在线百科全书
	if it's written by professionals or is from a major news website	如果它是由专业人士编写的，或者来自一个主流的新闻网站
书本信息的优点与缺点	The publishing process for books can be quite strict, so books tend to have more reliable information.	书籍的出版过程相当严格，所以书籍往往有更可靠的信息。
	It's harder and takes more time to find information from books than from the internet.	从书上找信息比从网上找信息更困难，也需要更多的时间。

5. E-books vs. Paper books（电子书与纸质书）

◎ 话题解读

由于方便携带，很多人都喜欢阅读电子书而不是纸质书。Part 3 关于这个话题通常会问"电子书和纸质书相比有何优点与缺点"。以下这些口语题目与电子书和纸质书的对比有关，请先通读题目，然后思考回答这些问题时该怎样组织信息和语言。

◎ 题目

Do you prefer paper books or E-books?

What's the difference between paper books and e-books?

Do you think printed books will continue to exist?

What's the difference between the reading habits of old people and young people?

◎ 答题思路分析

这里以"Do you prefer paper books or E-books?"为例，看看有哪些有用的英文句子可以用来回答这个问题。在学习英文句子之前，请先思考这个问题要从哪几个方面来回答。如果选择电子书，其优势可以是便于携带，只需要一个 kindle 或者一部手机即可。如果选择纸质书，其优势可以是对眼睛好、不容易分心等。在掌握了回答的几个方面之后，我们来学习一些有用的表达与素材。

◎ 表达与素材

1. E-books are easier and more convenient to carry around with you. You can read them on your cellphone.

2. Paper books are better for your eyes.

3. You're not as likely to get distracted while reading a paper book.

4. Paper books allow you to underline phrases or sentences and to take notes on the page.

◎ 表达与素材解读

电子书的优势是方便、易携带。纸质书的优势是对眼睛好，不容易分心，并且方便做笔记。值得注意的是，电子书的优点往往是纸质书的缺点，反之亦然。因此，如果是问电子书的缺点，考生只需将纸质书的优点反过来表述即可。

以上这些表达和素材同样适用于其他题目，比如在回答"Do you think printed books will continue to exist?"这个题目时，考生可以说因为纸质书有一定的优势，所以它还会继续存在。

◎ 表达积累

为了方便记忆和学习，我们将有用的表达罗列在以下表格中，考生可以尝试用这些表达的组合来回答之前罗列的相关题目。

电子书的优势	are easier and more convenient to carry around with you	更容易、更方便随身携带
	read them on your cellphone	在手机上阅读
纸质书的优势	are better for your eyes	对眼睛更好
	are not as likely to get distracted	不容易分心
	allow you to underline phrases or sentences and to take notes on the page	让你可以在短语或句子下画下画线，并在页面上做笔记

6. Effects of technology on education（科技对教育的影响）

◎ 话题解读

过去的上课方式是学生坐在教室里听老师讲课，但现代技术已经改变了传统的学习方式，课堂不再局限于固定的地点，网络课堂也是人们学习的途径。Part 3 关于这个话题通常会问"在线学习和在学校学习相比有何优点和缺点"。以下这些口语题目与科技对教育的影响有关，请先通读题目，然后思考回答这些问题时该怎样组织信息和语言。

◎ 题目

Is the internet good for learning new skills?

What impacts does the Internet have on schools?

Should students be allowed to use computers at school?

How is online help different from help in real life?

What's the difference between being taught by teachers and by AI?

Do you think there will be no teachers to teach in schools in the future?

◎ 答题思路分析

这里以"Is the internet good for learning new skills?"为例，看看有哪些有用的英文句子可以用来回答这个问题。在学习英文句子之前，请先思考这个问题要从哪几个方面来回答。互联网是有利于学习新技能和新知识的，因为它的便捷性及丰富的资源。但如果只依靠互联网来学习，那是远远不够的，因为互联网自带一些弊端，并且缺乏互动性。在掌握了回答的几个方面之后，我们来学习一些有用的表达与素材。

◎ 表达与素材

Advantages of learning from the internet:

1. It's fast, easy, and convenient to learn from the internet.

2. It's flexible. You can learn from any place at any time.

3. It saves time. You don't have to dress up and travel to another place, like school or the library.

Disadvantages of learning from the internet:

1. While using the internet, you might by get distracted by social media, news/gossip, games, or videos/streams.

2. Not having face-to-face interactions can be physically, mentally, and socially unhealthy.

3. Information on the internet is not always reliable because anyone can post anything. There's a lot of fake news and information.

4. Teachers are usually a more reliable source of information, and they can also answer questions, provide feedback, and offer words of encouragement.

◎ 表达与素材解读

首先，互联网在学习新知识和新技能方面具有很多优势：快速、简单、方便，随时随地都能学，并且节约时间。但是，互联网也有一些弊端，在前面的话题中也有涉及这些内容，比如容易分心，对身体、精神和社交不利，以及信息不一定可靠等。因此，在学习新知识、新技能的时候，教师是非常重要的存在，他们更可靠，能回答学生的问题，提供反馈，给学生鼓励。

以上这些表达和素材同样适用于其他题目，比如在回答"What's the difference between being taught by teachers and by AI?"这个题目时，考生可以选取以上表达与素材进行回答，"being taught by AI"就相当于"learn from internet"。

◎ 表达积累

为了方便记忆和学习，我们将有用的表达罗列在以下表格中，考生可以尝试用这些表达的组合来回答之前罗列的相关题目。

网上学习的优点	fast, easy, and convenient to learn from the internet	快速、简单、方便地从互联网上学习
	flexible	灵活
	You can learn from any place at any time.	你可以在任何时间、任何地点学习。
	it saves time	节省时间
	You don't have to dress up and travel to another place, like school or the library.	你不需要穿戴整齐去另一个地方（上课），比如学校或图书馆。
网上学习的缺点	get distracted by social media, news/gossip, games, or videos/streams	被社交媒体、新闻/八卦、游戏或视频/流媒体分散注意力
	Not having face-to-face interactions can be physically, mentally, and socially unhealthy.	没有面对面的互动对身体、精神和社交都不利。
	Information on the internet is not always reliable because anyone can post anything. There's a lot of fake news and information.	互联网上的信息并不总是可靠的，因为任何人都可以发布任何信息。互联网上有很多假新闻和假信息。
线下教师授课的优势（该部分内容还可以参考教育类话题中关于教师的部分）	Teachers are usually a more reliable source of information, and they can also answer questions, provide feedback, and offer words of encouragement.	老师通常是更可靠的信息来源，他们也可以回答问题，提供反馈，并给予鼓励。

7. General advantages and disadvantages of mobile phones（手机的优势与弊端）

◎ 话题解读

如今，手机的功能已经不仅仅是打电话、发消息了，它更像是一台小型电脑，可以办公、学习、娱乐等。与互联网一样，手机给人类提供便利，也带来了一些危害。Part 3 关于这个话题通常会问"人们用手机做什么"及"使用手机的优点和缺点"。以下这些口语题目与手机的优势与弊端有关，请先通读题目，然后思考回答这些问题时该怎样组织信息和语言。

◎ 题目

What do people use cellphones for?

What can smart phones do these days?

Which phone app is the most popular in your country?

What are the advantages of having a mobile phone?

What are the advantages and disadvantages of using cell phones?

Do you think people depend on phone apps too much?

What positive and negative impacts do mobile phones have on friendships?

Which do you think is better for communication, face to face conversations or phone calls?

◎ 答题思路分析

这里以"What are the advantages and disadvantages of using cell phones?"为例，看看有哪些有用的英文句子可以用来回答这个问题。在学习英文句子之前，请先思考这个问题要从哪几个方面来回答。首先要说明使用手机带来的好处，比如方便沟通、为生活和工作提供便利、提供各种娱乐等。其次要说明使用手机带来的坏处，比如对身体不好、使得人与人之间的关系变得冷漠等。在掌握了回答的几个方面之后，我们来学习一些有用的表达与素材。

◎ 表达与素材

Advantages of using mobile phones:

1. Mobile phones can be used from anywhere to instantly communicate with other people. It's fast, easy, and convenient.

2. Mobile phones can be used for entertainment—for example, to play games, watch videos, listen to music, and browse social media.

3. There are many useful mobile apps for daily life, including food delivery apps, taxi apps, and payment apps.

Disadvantages of using mobile phones:

1. People can become addicted to social media, and waste lots of time, which is bad for their body and studies/work.

2. Mobile phones can be very distracting, preventing people from focusing on their surroundings. This can be bad for social interactions, like when you're with your friends or family.

◎ 表达与素材解读

在学习某个话题的相关表达与素材时，有时会发现该部分的内容与前面的某个话题非常接近，甚至是一样的。这是因为这两个话题的本质其实是一样的，比如手机是高科技产品，也带有互联网的属性，所以手机对青少年的影响跟高科技和互联网对青少年的影响其实是一样的。在回答相关问题时，考生可以灵活使用各种表达与素材，并结合适当的例子。上述表达与素材中提到的手机的优点（沟通便捷、娱乐功能、方便生活）和缺点（容易沉迷、浪费时间、让人分心、不利于社交）等其实在前面的话题中都有提到过。

◎ 表达积累

为了方便记忆和学习，我们将有用的表达罗列在以下表格中，考生可以尝试用这些表达的组合来回答之前罗列的相关题目。

手机的优点	fast, easy, and convenient	快速、简单、方便
	can be used from anywhere to instantly communicate with other people	可以在任何地方与他人即时交流
	can be used for entertainment	可以用来娱乐
	There are many useful mobile apps for daily life.	日常生活中有许多有用的移动应用程序。
手机的缺点	can become addicted to social media	会对社交媒体上瘾
	waste lots of time	浪费大量的时间
	is bad for their body and studies/work	对他们的身体和学习 / 工作有害
	can be very distracting, preventing you from focusing on your surroundings	会非常分散注意力，让你无法专注于周围的环境
	can be bad for social interactions	会不利于社交

8. Children's use of mobile phones（儿童使用手机的问题）

◎ 话题解读

孩子们到了一定年龄后，通常会有自己的手机，但由于青少年的一些特点，父母往往会对他们使用手机进行一定的约束。Part 3 关于这个问题通常会问"使用手机如何影响孩子"及"父母应该在多大程度上限制他们的使用"。以下这些口语题目与儿童使用手机的问题有关，请先通读题目，然后思考回答这些问题时该怎样组织信息和语言。

◎ 题目

Are children allowed to use mobile phones in your country?

Is it popular for children to use cell phones in your country?

What do teenagers in your country use cell phones for?

Is it harmful for children to use mobile phones?

Do you think parents should limit the time that their children spend on phones?

For children, what age do you think is suitable for allowing them to use cell phones?

◎ 答题思路分析

这里以"Are children allowed to use mobile phones in your country?"为例，看看有哪些有用的英文句子可以用来回答这个问题。在学习英文句子之前，请先思考一下这个问题要从哪几个方面来回答。首先，到了一定的年龄，孩子们肯定是可以使用手机的，但因为他们的心智还不太成熟，所以需要父母监督和限制。其次，手机会给孩子们带来不少好处，同时也会带来危害，这些内容可以参考前面几个话题中罗列的表达与素材。在掌握了回答的几个方面之后，我们来学习一些有用的表达与素材。

◎ 表达与素材

1. Many parents limit the time their children can spend on their phones. Children often aren't even allowed to have their own phones until they are older.

2. Mobile phones can be bad for children in many ways:

Children can become addicted to social media, and waste lots of time, which is bad for their body and studies;

Children can be exposed to violent or sexual content;

Children can be exposed to fake or harmful information.

3. However, mobile phones can also be useful for children:

Children can use it to communicate with family members;

It helps children relax (e.g. through mobile games, videos, and music);

It can be useful for their daily life (e.g. food delivery apps, taxi apps, and payment apps).

◎ 表达与素材解读

在孩子使用手机这件事上，父母需要考虑是否需要给孩子买手机及如何监督和限制孩子玩手机。孩子们使用手机的好处颇多，比如与家人交流、有助于放松、对日常生活有帮助。然而，过度地使用手机也会带来很多问题，比如沉迷于社交网络、接触暴力或者色情内容、接触虚假或者有害的信息。这些内容在前面的话题中都有所提及。

以上这些表达和素材同样适用于其他题目，比如"Is it harmful for children to use mobile phones?"。

◎ 表达积累

为了方便记忆和学习，我们将有用的表达罗列在以下表格中，考生可以尝试用这些表达的组合来回答之前罗列的相关题目。

家长需要做什么	limit the time their children can spend on their phones	限制孩子们玩手机的时间
	Children often aren't even allowed to have their own phones until they are older.	孩子们在长大之前甚至都不被允许拥有自己的手机。

续表

过度使用手机的坏处	become addicted to social media, and waste lots of time, which is bad for their body and studies	沉迷于社交媒体，浪费了大量的时间，这对他们的身体和学习都不好
	be exposed to violent or sexual content	接触暴力或色情内容
	be exposed to fake or harmful information	接触虚假或有害的信息
使用手机的好处	use it to communicate with family	用它和家人交流
	helps children relax (e.g. through mobile games, videos, and music)	帮助孩子放松（如通过手机游戏、视频和音乐）
	be useful for their daily life (e.g. food delivery apps, taxi apps, and payment apps)	对他们的日常生活有帮助（如外卖、出租车和支付软件）

9. Using mobile phones in public（在公共场所使用手机）

◎ 话题解读

人们经常在公共场所使用手机，这在大多数情况下是没问题的，但某些行为可能会导致问题。Part 3 关于这个话题通常会问"公共场所使用手机不当所带来的负面影响"。以下这些口语题目与在公共场所使用手机有关，请先通读题目，然后思考回答这些问题时该怎样组织信息和语言。

◎ 题目

What is your attitude towards people using mobile phones in public places?

What are the effects of people making lots of noise with their mobile phones in a public place?

Does the use of mobile phones cause any problems for others?

Should people be banned from talking loudly in public places?

◎ 答题思路分析

这里以"What is your attitude towards people using mobile phones in public places?"为例，看看有哪些有用的英文句子可以用来回答这个问题。在学习英文句子之前，请先思考一下这个问题要从哪几个方面来回答。一般情况下，人们在公共场所使用手机是没问题的。但如果在公共场所大声讲电话，或大声播放音乐、视频，则会对别人产生影响。此外，如果在过马路或者开车时使用电话，则会造成危险。在掌握了回答的几个方面之后，我们来学习一些有用的表达与素材。

◎ 表达与素材

1. When people use mobile phones in public places, it disturbs the peace and can be very distracting if they speak loudly or watch a video with the speakers on.

2. When people use their phones in public, it can be dangerous to themselves and others if they're not paying attention to their surroundings—for example, when they're driving or crossing the street.

◎ 表达与素材解读

在公共场所大声打电话或者开启音频、视频外放功能会扰乱平静，让人分心。如果是在过马路或者开车时使用手机，那就更危险了，这样会容易分心、注意不到周围环境，给自己和他人带来危险。

以上这些表达和素材同样适用于其他题目，比如 "Should people be banned from talking loudly in public places?"。

◎ 表达积累

为了方便记忆和学习，我们将有用的表达罗列在以下表格中，考生可以尝试用这些表达的组合来回答之前罗列的相关题目。

在公共场所大声打电话或者打开外放	it disturbs the peace and can be very distracting if they speak loudly or watch a video with the speakers on	如果他们大声说话或开着扬声器看视频，就会扰乱平静，分散注意力
开车或走路时打电话或看手机	it can be dangerous to themselves and others if they're not paying attention to their surroundings—for example, when they're driving or crossing the street	如果他们不注意周围的环境——例如，开车或过马路时，这可能对他们自己和他人都是危险的

10. Effects of technology on communication（科技对于沟通的影响）

◎ 话题解读

科技已经彻底改变了人们的沟通方式，人们不再依赖信件或见面来沟通和联系。Part 3 关于这个话题通常会问"现代通信的各种方式（比如电话和短信）"及"它们的优缺点"。以下这些口语题目与科技对于沟通的影响有关，请先通读题目，然后思考回答这些问题时该怎样组织信息和语言。

◎ 题目

What are the differences between giving information by using mobile phone and email?

Are there any disadvantages of face-to-face conversations?

Does technological development have a negative impact on communication among people?

What are the differences between communicating with customers face to face and through phone calls?

Why do people make phone calls instead of sending messages when there is something important?

Is it more polite to make phone calls than to send text messages?

◎ 答题思路分析

这里以 "What are the differences between giving information by using mobile phone and email?" 为例，看看有哪些有用的英文句子可以用来回答这个问题。在学习英文句子之前，请先

思考一下这个问题要从哪几个方面来回答。首先，邮件是可以在深思熟虑后编辑的，可以附上一些资料、文件，同时可以发送很多人，往往用于发送工作通知或一些重要文件。其次，打电话简便快捷，有利于保证沟通的及时性和互动性。在掌握了回答的几个方面之后，我们来学习一些有用的表达与素材。

◎ 表达与素材

Benefits of sending text messages or emails:

1. Sending text messages or emails is fast, easy, and convenient, especially text messages because you usually carry your phone around with you.

2. It allows you to send information to a large group of people all at once.

3. It also allows people to reply later if they are busy.

Benefits of making a phone call or talking face-to-face:

1. When talking to someone face-to-face, you can see the person's body language and expressions. This helps you communicate better.

2. For important things, it's often better to call someone or talk face-to-face. It's more personal and polite, and also helps you avoid misunderstandings.

◎ 表达与素材解读

上述表达与素材把当下的沟通方式分为两类：一类是发送短信或电子邮件，它们都是便捷的沟通方式，可以同时发送给一大群人，这类信息通常不需要及时回复，在回复时间上比较灵活；另一类是打电话或者面对面交流，它们共同的优势是交流沟通更顺畅，可以避免产生误解。

以上这些表达和素材同样适用于其他题目，比如在回答"What are the differences between communicating with customers face to face and through phone calls?"这个题目时，考生可以使用面对面交流的好处中的第 1 点。

◎ 表达积累

为了方便记忆和学习，我们将有用的表达罗列在以下表格中，考生可以尝试用这些表达的组合来回答之前罗列的相关题目。

发短信或电子邮件的好处	fast, easy, and convenient	快速、简单、方便
	allows you to send information to a large group of people all at once	允许你同时向一大群人发送信息
	allows people to reply later if they are busy	如果人们很忙，可以稍后回复
打电话或面对面交谈的好处	When talking to someone face-to-face, you can see the person's body language and expressions. This helps you communicate better.	当和某人面对面交谈时，你可以看到对方的肢体语言和表情。这有助于你更好地沟通。
	It's more personal and polite, and also helps you avoid misunderstandings.	这样更有针对性、更有礼貌，也能帮你避免误解。

11. Effects of technology on relationships and friendships（科技对于人际关系和友谊的影响）

◎ 话题解读

许多人依赖科技产物（比如手机、电脑）来维持关系，殊不知科技有时也会伤害关系。Part 3 关于这个话题通常会问"科技对人际关系和友谊的积极和消极影响"。以下这些口语题目与科技对于人际关系和友谊的影响有关，请先通读题目，然后思考回答这些问题时该怎样组织信息和语言。

◎ 题目

How does technology help the relationship between people?

Does science and technology improve the relationships between people?

What are the positive and negative impacts mobile phones have on friendships?

What's the influence of social media on friendships?

What do you think of making friends on social networks?

Why do some people like to share news on social media?

Do you think people nowadays visit other people more or less?

◎ 答题思路分析

这里以"What are the positive and negative impacts mobile phones have on friendships?"为例，看看有哪些有用的英文句子可以用来回答这个问题。在学习英文句子之前，请先思考这个问题要从哪几个方面来回答。手机属于一种科技产品，手机对于友谊的影响就等同于科技对友谊的影响。从积极的方面来看，使用手机可以让我们随时随地与朋友们联系，分享各种心情和感受，有利于增进友谊。从消极的方面来说，用手机交流不如面对面交流来得真切。在掌握了回答的几个方面之后，我们来学习一些有用的表达与素材。

◎ 表达与素材

Positive effects of technology on relationships/friendships：

1. Technology allows you to keep in touch with friends and family who live far from you.

2. Social media allows you to share things with your friends and family, such as details about your personal life, gossip, or news. This provides interesting topics to talk about.

3. Online communities allow you to make friends with people who share interests with you (e.g. a community for cat owners or a community for a certain game).

Harmful effects of technology on relationships/friendships：

1. Technology such as games and TV can be very addictive, so they can isolate people from their friends and family if they stay home all day.

2. It is easier to have misunderstandings when sending text messages or talking over the phone because you can't see the other person's body language and expressions.

247

◎ 表达与素材解读

科技对于友谊的正面影响包括让人们与远方的朋友和家人保持联系，可以与朋友和家人分享身边的事情，以及与有共同兴趣的人交朋友。科技对于友谊的负面影响包括使人容易沉迷于游戏和电视剧，使人们与朋友和家人疏远，以及因看不到对方的肢体语言或面部表情而导致误解。

以上这些表达和素材同样适用于其他题目，比如在回答"Why do some people like to share news on social media?"这个题目时，考生可以说人们通过分享新闻与家人和朋友保持联系，甚至可以因此交到新朋友。

◎ 表达积累

为了方便记忆和学习，我们将有用的表达罗列在以下表格中，考生可以尝试用这些表达的组合来回答之前罗列的相关题目。

科技对人际关系 / 友谊的积极影响	allows you to keep in touch with friends and family who live far from you	让你与远方的朋友和家人保持联系
	allows you to share things with your friends and family, such as details about your personal life, gossip, or news	让你能够与朋友和家人分享事情，例如关于你的个人生活的细节、八卦或新闻
	allow you to make friends with people who share interests with you	让你和与你有共同兴趣的人交朋友
科技对人际关系 / 友谊的消极影响	can be very addictive	很容易上瘾
	can isolate people from their friends and family if they stay home all day	如果人们整天呆在家里，会与朋友和家人疏远
	It is easier to have misunderstandings when sending text messages or talking over the phone because you can't see the other person's body language and expressions.	发短信或打电话时，因为看不见对方的肢体语言和表情，容易产生误解。

12. Technology and machines at home（家里的高科技产品）

◎ 话题解读

得益于一些高科技的产品，比如洗衣机、扫地机、冰箱、空调等，人们的生活变得更轻松、更舒适。Part 3 关于这个话题通常会问"家里的各种技术和机器及其用途"。以下这些口语题目与家里的高科技产品有关，请先通读题目，然后思考回答这些问题时该怎样组织信息和语言。

◎ 题目

Which is the most important technology you use at home?

What kinds of machines are there in people's homes?

Which invention do you think is the most useful at home?

What do think are the advantages and disadvantages of inventions at home?

Do you think entertainment methods will be home-based in the future?

◎答题思路分析

这里以"Which is the most important technology you use at home?"为例，看看有哪些有用的英文句子可以用来回答这个问题。在学习英文句子之前，请先思考一下这个问题要从哪几个方面来回答。说起家里的高科技产品，人们通常会想到电脑、电视、冰箱、洗衣机等，它们确实改变了人们的生活，使人们的生活变得更便捷、舒适。但是有些娱乐性的高科技产品会影响人们的学习和工作，需要加以克制。在掌握了回答的几个方面之后，我们来学习一些有用的表达与素材。

◎ 表达与素材

1. Useful and important technology/machines at home include the computer, TV, refrigerator, washing machine, and air conditioner.

2. Machines such as the TV or computer provide entertainment, while other machines such as the fan or air conditioner provide comfort.

3. The disadvantages of machines are that they can be expensive, and some of them (such as computers & TV) can be very distracting when you're trying to study or work.

◎ 表达与素材解读

家里有用且重要的高科技产品有电脑、电视、冰箱、洗衣机和空调。它们给人们的生活带来了很多好处，比如电视或电脑这类机器为人们提供了娱乐，而风扇或空调这类机器则为人们提供了舒适。当然，它们也会有一些缺点，比如价格比较高，有些家电（如电脑、电视）会在你学习或工作时分散你的注意力。

以上这些表达和素材同样适用于其他题目，比如"What do think are the advantages and disadvantages of inventions at home?"。

◎ 表达积累

为了方便记忆和学习，我们将有用的表达罗列在以下表格中，考生可以尝试用这些表达的组合来回答之前罗列的相关题目。

家中有用的高科技产品与机器	computer, TV, refrigerator, washing machine, and air conditioner	电脑、电视、冰箱、洗衣机和空调
高科技产品与机器带来的好处	provide entertainment	提供娱乐
	provide comfort	提供舒适
高科技产品与机器带来的坏处	can be expensive	会很贵
	can be very distracting when you're trying to study or work	会让你在学习或工作时分心

13. Effects of technology on work（科技对于工作的影响）

◎ 话题解读

科技使工作变得更容易，但同时有些人也在担心有一天它会威胁到我们的工作，比如人工智能的出现。Part 3 关于这个话题通常会问 "科技如何影响人们的工作" 以及 "机器和机器人在未来是否会取代人类"。以下这些口语题目与科技对于工作的影响有关，请先通读题目，然后思考回答这些问题时该怎样组织信息和语言。

◎ 题目

Do you think people's work in the future will be heavily affected by technology?

How does technology influence our work?

What kinds of professions require people to use machines?

Do you think it's a good thing to use more technology at work?

Will many people's work be done by robots in the future?

Do you think robots will replace human workers in the future?

Do you think machines could replace human workers in the future?

Are all the boring jobs going to be done by robots in the future?

Do you think some practical skills will be replaced by computers?

◎ 答题思路分析

这里以 "Do you think people's work in the future will be heavily affected by technology?" 为例，看看有哪些有用的英文句子可以用来回答这个问题。在学习英文句子之前，请先思考这个问题要从哪几个方面来回答。首先，科技已经开始影响人们的工作了，未来只会越来越多地改变人们工作的方式和内容。其次，互联网的普及让很多事情可以在网上完成，科技的发展使得机器取代了很多人类工作。在掌握了回答的几个方面之后，我们来学习一些有用的表达与素材。

◎ 表达与素材

How technology affects work:

1. Computers make work more efficient and increases productivity. Lots of computer programs are used for work all the time, such as Microsoft Word, Excel, and PowerPoint.

2. The internet makes it easy to search for information that you need for work, and it allows us to communicate with each other for work—for example, through instant messaging apps or video meetings apps.

Will robots/machines replace human workers in the future?

1. Robots/machines might replace some human workers—such as factory workers and translators—but robots/machines can't replace everything.

2. We will always need humans for work that requires creativity, imagination, and a sense of

beauty. For example, there probably always be human artists, musicians, and novelists.

◎ 表达与素材解读

以上表达与素材将科技对于工作的影响分为两点：一是电脑使工作更有效率，提高了生产力；二是互联网使信息检索变得容易，一些即时通讯软件让人们在工作中可以相互交流。机器人的诞生和发展正在影响人们的工作与生活，在一些行业，机器可以替代人类，但有关创造力的行业还是依赖人类本身。

以上这些表达和素材同样适用于其他题目，比如在回答 "Will many people's work be done by robots in the future?" 这个题目时，考生可以使用以上表达与素材中关于未来机器人是否会取代人类工人中的内容来回答。

◎ 表达积累

为了方便记忆和学习，我们将有用的表达罗列在以下表格中，考生可以尝试用这些表达的组合来回答之前罗列的相关题目。

科技如何影响工作	Computers make work more efficient and increases productivity.	电脑使工作更有效率并提高了生产力。
	Lots of computer programs are used for work all the time, such as Microsoft Word, Excel, and PowerPoint.	许多计算机程序一直被用于工作，如 Word、Excel 和 PowerPoint。
	The internet makes it easy to search for information that you need for work, and it allows for us to communicate with each other for work—for example, through instant messaging apps or video meetings apps.	互联网使你能够很容易地搜索到所需的工作信息，通过诸如即时通讯或视频会议之类的应用程序，我们得以在工作中相互交流。
机器人将来是否会取代人类工人	might replace some human workers	可能会取代一些人类工人
	We will always need humans for work that requires creativity, imagination, and a sense of beauty.	对于那些需要创造力、想象力和美感的工作，我们总是需要人类的。

话题 6 MEDIA & ADVERTISING（媒体与广告）

我们每天都会接触到各种媒体，包括新闻、电影和广告。Part 3 有不少题目会涉及媒体与广告，下面我们就来学习如何回答这些问题 [①] 。

---

① 与电视相关的话题会在之后的 "LEISURE（休闲娱乐）" 话题中学习，与社交媒体相关的话题已经在之前的 "TECHNOLOGY（科技）" 话题中做了介绍。

1. Popular types of news（受欢迎的新闻种类）

◎ 话题解读

每个人所处的环境不同，关注的新闻类型也不尽相同。然而，某些类型的新闻出现在报纸、电视和社交媒体上的频率往往比较高。Part 3 关于这个话题通常会问"人们通常感兴趣的新闻类型"及"你经常在新闻中看到的人的类型"。以下这些口语题目与受欢迎的新闻种类有关，请先通读题目，然后思考回答这些问题时该怎样组织信息和语言。

◎ 题目

Which kind of news is more popular: domestic news or international news?

What kind of news do people like to read?

What kind of people do you usually see in the news?

Is news often about famous people?

Do you think the media puts too much attention on famous people?

◎ 答题思路分析

这里以"Which kind of news is more popular:domestic news or international news?"为例，看看有哪些有用的英文句子可以用来回答这个问题。在学习英文句子之前，请先思考这个问题要从哪几个方面来回答。新闻可以分为国内新闻和国际新闻，国内新闻与人们的生活更贴近，国际新闻让人们知道其他国家发生了什么，这也可能对本国产生影响。新闻有重大和非重大之分，奥运会、世界杯、战争、自然灾害之类的重大新闻自然关注度更高。新闻也可以按照对象来划分，有的新闻是关于一些有名的人物的，而另一些新闻是关于普通老百姓的。在掌握了回答的几个方面之后，我们来学习一些有用的表达与素材。

◎ 表达与素材

1. People are more interested in local news than international news because they are more affected by local events. However, many people are also interested in international news because the world is closely connected and foreign events may affect their country.

2. People are more interested in big news, such as news about a war or a natural disaster. People are also more interested in news about sports or the entertainment industry—for example, news about the World Cup.

3. News is often about famous people, such as politicians, businessmen, sports stars, pop stars, actors, and other celebrities.

4. It's bad to have too much news on celebrities because people will become obsessed with celebrities. Also, celebrities can be a negative influence if they promote something harmful or behave poorly.

◎ 表达与素材解读

新闻的种类有很多，按照地域来分，可以分为国内新闻和国际新闻。关注国内新闻是因为人们更容易受到当地事件的影响，而关注国际新闻是因为世界是紧密相连的，国外事件可能会影响他们的国家。按照新闻的影响来分，有大新闻和小新闻，像战争、自然灾害、体育与娱乐行业这些新闻影响群体比较广，自然比较受关注。除此之外，大众也喜欢关注名人的新闻，比如政治家、商人、体育明星、流行歌手、演员等。值得注意的是，新闻只是人们生活的一部分，不能过分沉迷其中。

以上这些表达和素材同样适用于其他题目，比如在回答"Is news often about famous people?"这个题目时，考生可以使用以上表达与素材中的部分内容来回答。比如，可以首先承认"现在的新闻的确过分关注名人了"，随后补充道"我认为这一现象会带来很多危害"，然后使用表达与素材里的第 4 点内容来展开回答。

◎ 表达积累

为了方便记忆和学习，我们将有用的表达罗列在以下表格中，考生可以尝试用这些表达的组合来回答之前罗列的相关题目。

人们感兴趣的新闻	more interested in local news than international news because they are more affected by local events	对当地新闻比对国际新闻更感兴趣，因为他们更容易受到当地事件的影响
	interested in international news because the world is closely connected and foreign events may affect their country	对国际新闻感兴趣，因为世界是紧密相连的，外国事件可能会影响他们的国家
	more interested in big news, such as news about a war or a natural disaster	对大新闻更感兴趣，比如关于战争或自然灾害的新闻
	more interested in news about sports or the entertainment industry	对体育或娱乐行业的新闻更感兴趣
	News is often about famous people, such as politicians, businessmen, sports stars, pop stars, actors, and other celebrities.	新闻经常是关于名人的，如政治家、商人、体育明星、流行歌星、演员和其他名人。
过度关注名人新闻的坏处	It's bad to have too much news on celebrities because people will become obsessed with celebrities.	有太多关于名人的新闻是不好的，因为人们会对名人着迷。
	Celebrities can be a negative influence if they promote something harmful or behave poorly.	如果名人宣传有害的东西或行为不当，他们可能会产生负面影响。

2. Ways to get news（获取新闻的方式）

◎ 话题解读

新闻是人们了解世界和周围发生的事情的重要途径，人们通过各种方式获取新闻。Part 3 关于这个话题通常会问"现在人们获取新闻和信息的常见方式"。以下这些口语题目与获取新闻的方式有关，请先通读题目，然后思考回答这些问题时该怎样组织信息和语言。

◎ 题目

How do Chinese people usually get news?

Where do people get news?

What ways can people get information these days?

How is the news media changing recently?

Do people read the newspaper where you live?

◎ 答题思路分析

这里以"How do Chinese people usually get news?"为例,看看有哪些有用的英文句子可以用来回答这个问题。在学习英文句子之前,请先思考这个问题要从哪几个方面来回答。一般而言,人们获取新闻的渠道一是通过传统的报纸、电视,二是通过网络。在掌握了回答的几个方面之后,我们来学习一些有用的表达与素材。

◎ 表达与素材

1. The old, traditional way of getting news is through news channels or newspapers. This is how a lot of old people still get their news.

2. However, these days more people are getting their news from the Internet, including from news websites and social media. It's more convenient to get news from the Internet, and there are constant updates.

◎ 表达与素材解读

作为一种传统的新闻传播方式,新闻频道或报纸仍旧受到老年人的青睐,但更多的人则是通过互联网来获得新闻,因为更方便,而且能实时更新。如果需要讨论在网上看新闻的好处与坏处,考生可以参考前面"TECHNOLOGY(科技)"中学过的表达与素材。

以上这些表达和素材同样适用于其他题目,比如在回答"Where do people get news?"时,考生就可以使用以上表达与素材来回答。

◎ 表达积累

为了方便记忆和学习,我们将有用的表达罗列在以下表格中,考生可以尝试用这些表达的组合来回答之前罗列的相关题目。

传统渠道	The old, traditional way of getting news is through news channels or newspapers.	传统的获取新闻的方式是通过新闻频道或报纸。
	This is how a lot of old people still get their news.	现在很多老人仍然是这样获得消息的。
互联网	from news websites and social media	来自新闻网站和社交媒体
	It's more convenient to get news from the Internet, and there are constant updates.	从互联网上获取新闻更方便,而且会不断更新。

3. Movies & Films（电影）

◎ 话题解读

看电影是一种很流行的休闲活动，Part 3 关于这个话题通常会问"中国最受欢迎的电影类型"及"人们通常在哪里看电影"。以下这些口语题目与电影有关，请先通读题目，然后思考回答这些问题时该怎样组织信息和语言。

◎ 题目

What kinds of films are popular in China?

Are action films popular in your country?

Are foreign movies popular in China?

Are films a waste of money?

Is it important for a country to have its own movies?

Do fewer people watch movies in cinemas these days than in the past?

What's the difference between watching a performance live and watching it on TV?

◎ 答题思路分析

这里以"What kinds of films are popular in China?"为例，看看有哪些有用的英文句子可以用来回答这个问题。在学习英文句子之前，请先思考这个问题要从哪几个方面来回答。考生可以任意列举一些电影的种类，比如功夫片、战争片、喜剧片等。如果觉得说不清楚电影的分类，则可以回答"无论哪种类型都很受欢迎，因为看电影是一件非常放松的休闲方式"。在掌握了回答的几个方面之后，我们来学习一些有用的表达与素材。

◎ 表达与素材

1. Popular movies in China include action movies, war movies, and comedy movies. The most popular is probably action movies, like *The Avengers* or *Wolf Warrior*, which have made a lot of money.

2. Watching movies is a good way to relax and take your mind off school or work. You can also learn about a country's culture and social issues through movies, which is why countries should have their own movies.

3. Many people still watch movies at movie theatres because it's a unique experience. The screen is bigger and the special effects and sound effects are better. However, watching things on TV is usually more convenient and comfortable.

◎ 表达与素材解读

在中国受欢迎的电影类型包括"action movies"（动作片）、"war movies"（战争片）、"comedy movies"（喜剧片）等，其中最受欢迎的可能是动作片。为什么电影是受欢迎的休闲娱乐方式呢？因为它可以让人们得到放松，把注意力从学校或工作上转移开，还可以让人们了解一个国家的文化和社会问题。此外，去电影院看电影是一种独特的体验，因为电影院的屏幕更大，特效和音效也更好。当然，在家看电影也有好处，比如更方便、更舒适。

以上这些表达和素材同样适用于其他题目，比如在回答"Do fewer people watch movies in cinemas these days than in the past?"时，考生可以使用以上表达与素材中的第 3 点来回答。

◎ 表达积累

为了方便记忆和学习，我们将有用的表达罗列在以下表格中，考生可以尝试用这些表达的组合来回答之前罗列的相关题目。

受欢迎的电影类型	action movies, war movies, and comedy movies	动作片、战争片和喜剧片
去电影院看电影的优势	a good way to relax	是一种好的放松方式
	take your mind off school or work	把你的注意力从学习或工作上转移开
	learn about a country's culture and social issues through movies	通过电影了解一个国家的文化和社会问题
	a unique experience	一次独特的体验
	The screen is bigger and the special effects and sound effects are better.	屏幕更大，特效和音效也更好。
电影与电视相比有何劣势	Watching things on TV is usually more convenient and comfortable.	在电视上看东西通常更方便、更舒适。

4. Magazines（杂志）

◎ 话题解读

虽然现在杂志已经不那么流行了，但它仍然有自己忠实的读者群体，也有其存在的意义。Part 3 关于这个话题通常会问"人们喜欢看哪种类型的杂志"及"为什么有些人喜欢看杂志"。以下这些口语题目与杂志有关，请先通读题目，然后思考回答这些问题时该怎样组织信息和语言。

◎ 题目

What kinds of magazines are the most popular?

Do men like to read fashion magazines?

Do people read magazines for fun or for learning?

Do you like to read news magazines?

◎ 答题思路分析

这里以"What kinds of magazines are the most popular?"为例，看看有哪些有用的英文句子可以用来回答这个问题。在学习英文句子之前，请先思考这个问题要从哪几个方面来回答。一般来说，现在比较流行的杂志往往和时尚、商业及新闻有关。这类杂志的目标受众非常明确。在掌握了回答的几个方面之后，我们来学习一些有用的表达与素材。

◎ 表达与素材

1. Popular kinds of magazines are fashion magazines, business magazines, and news

magazines.

2. People read magazines for entertainment or learning because magazine articles are usually well-written and can present interesting news or information.

3. News magazines can help you stay informed about what is happening around the world. Also, the articles in news magazines are usually well-researched and offer in-depth coverage on various topics, which can broaden your knowledge and perspective on different issues.

4. Some men may enjoy reading fashion magazines, but it depends on their personal interests and hobbies. Not all men are interested in fashion, and may prefer other types of magazines such as sports or technology.

◎ 表达与素材解读

时尚、商业和新闻类的杂志是目前最受欢迎的三类杂志。人们喜欢阅读这些杂志的原因有杂志文章写得好，可以提供有趣、有深度的信息或评论等。以新闻类杂志为例，这类杂志可以让人们了解世界发生了什么，还可以拓宽人们的视野。此外，对于杂志的偏好因人而异。

以上这些表达和素材同样适用于其他题目，比如在回答"Do people read magazines for fun or for learning?"这个题目时，考生可以使用以上罗列的部分表达与素材。

◎ 表达积累

为了方便记忆和学习，我们将有用的表达罗列在以下表格中，考生可以尝试用这些表达的组合来回答之前罗列的相关题目。

受欢迎的杂志类型	fashion magazines, business magazines, and news magazines		时尚杂志、商业杂志和新闻杂志
受欢迎的原因	read magazines for entertainment or learning		为了娱乐或学习而阅读杂志
	magazine articles are usually well-written and can present interesting news or information		杂志文章通常写得很好，能提供有趣的新闻或信息
	help you stay informed about what is happening around the world		帮助你了解世界各地正在发生的事情
	the articles in news magazines are usually well-researched and offer in-depth coverage on various topics		新闻杂志上的文章通常是经过充分研究的，对各种主题都有深入的报道
	broaden your knowledge and perspective on different issues		拓宽你在不同问题上的知识和视角

5. Benefits & Harmful effects of advertising（广告的正面与负面影响）

◎ 话题解读

广告是如此普遍，人们每天都会接触到各种各样的广告。广告在人们的生活中发挥着重要的作用，但也可能带来一些负面的影响。Part 3 关于这个话题通常会问"广告的正面和负面影响"。

以下这些口语题目与广告的正面与负面影响有关，请先通读题目，然后思考回答这些问题时该怎样组织信息和语言。

◎ 题目

In general, what are the pros and cons of advertising?

In what ways do advertisements influence people?

Do you think there's too much advertising in our daily lives?

Do people usually buy stuff after watching advertisements?

How do advertisements influence children?

Should advertising aimed at kids be prohibited?

Are there any inappropriate advertisements?

◎ 答题思路分析

这里以 "In general, what are the pros and cons of advertising?" 为例，看看有哪些有用的英文句子可以用来回答这个问题。在学习英文句子之前，请先思考这个问题要从哪几个方面来回答。企业通过投放广告来宣传产品，而消费者通过广告来挑选他们需要的产品，这些都是广告带来的好处。但是，有些广告也给人们带来了很多负面影响，比如虚假宣传、过度消费、教坏孩子。在掌握了回答的几个方面之后，我们来学习一些有用的表达与素材。

◎ 表达与素材

Benefits of advertising:

1. Advertisements are good for businesses because it helps promote their products.

2. Advertisements allow people to learn about products that could improve their lives.

Harmful influence of advertising:

1. Advertisements persuade people to buy things that they might not actually need, which wastes their money.

2. Advertisements can cause people to buy things that harm their body, such as junk food or fast food.

3. Advertisements can be bad for children since they are easily influenced. For example, after watching advertisements for expensive toys or junk food, children might ask for these things.

4. Advertisements can make people feel unsatisfied about their body or how they look. Advertisements do this to make people buy their products, but it lowers people's self-esteem.

◎ 表达与素材解读

广告对于企业和消费者都有好处，企业可以宣传自己的产品，消费者可以了解更多能够改善他们生活的产品。但广告带来的负面影响也不少，比如让人们购买很多他们不需要的产品，浪费金钱，让人们买一些对身体有害的东西，引诱孩子买东西，以及制造焦虑等。

以上这些表达和素材同样适用于其他题目，比如在回答 "How do advertisements influence

children?"这个题目时，考生可以使用以上表达与素材中有关广告对于儿童的负面影响的内容。

◎ 表达积累

为了方便记忆和学习，我们将有用的表达罗列在以下表格中，考生可以尝试用这些表达的组合来回答之前罗列的相关题目。

广告的 正面影响	are good for businesses because it helps promote their products	对企业有好处，因为它有助于推广产品
	allow people to learn about products that could improve their live	让人们了解可以改善他们生活的产品
广告的 负面影响	persuade people to buy things that they might not actually need, which wastes their money	说服人们购买他们可能并不需要的东西，这是在浪费他们的钱
	cause people to buy things that harm their body, such as junk food or fast food	导致人们购买对身体有害的东西，如垃圾食品或快餐
	be bad for children since they are easily influenced	对孩子不好，因为他们很容易受影响
	make people feel unsatisfied about their body or how they look	让人们对自己的身体或外表感到不满意（换句话说就是制造各种焦虑）

6. Types of advertising（广告的种类）

◎ 话题解读

广告分为很多种类，根据受众不同，有多种不同的投放形式。Part 3 关于这个话题通常会问"不同种类的广告及其对受众的效果"。以下这些口语题目与广告的种类有关，请先通读题目，然后思考回答这些问题时该怎样组织信息和语言。

◎ 题目

What kinds of advertisements are there in your country?

Can you compare the different kinds of advertising methods?

What are the different forms of advertising that we have in society today?

What do you think is the most effective means of advertising?

What are the advantages of TV advertisements?

◎ 答题思路分析

这里以"Can you compare the different kinds of advertising methods?"为例，看看有哪些有用的英文句子可以用来回答这个问题。在学习英文句子之前，请先思考这个问题要从哪几个方面来回答。人们通常会在哪些场合看到广告呢？看电视时，在节目开始前、节目与节目之间及节目中途都有广告，在浏览网页时也会自动弹出广告，在地铁里、公交车上、马路边、电梯里、商场及包装袋上都有广告，广告无处不在。这些广告各有各的用途，也各有各的优势。在掌握了回答的几个方面之后，我们来学习一些有用的表达与素材。

◎ 表达与素材

There are various kinds of advertisements:

1. Commercials are probably the most effective kind of advertisement. They are hard to avoid because the TV show is put on hold during commercial breaks. Commercial breaks can also be very frequent, and each commercial can last quite long.

2. Online advertisements appear on the side of websites or as popup ads. The advantages of online advertisements are that they're often more related to your interests. For example, if you're on a sports website, there might be sports-related advertisements. However, online advertisements are not as effective as TV advertisements because they can be more easily ignored or closed.

3. Outdoor advertisements can be seen on billboards, walls, and buildings. They also appear on transportation, such as on buses, the metro, and taxis.

◎ 表达与素材解读

第一类广告是"Commercials"（电视上的商业广告），它们通常是最有效的广告，它们很难避免，因为电视节目会在广告播放期间暂停。第二类广告是在线广告，通常在网站的一侧展示或以弹出式广告出现，这类广告的投放非常有针对性，通常与个人爱好有关。这类广告没有电视广告效果好，因为人们可以主动关掉。第三类广告是一些户外广告，比如人们在广告牌、墙壁、建筑物、交通工具上看到的广告，这类广告出现的地方非常固定，人们很容易忽视它们。

以上这些表达和素材同样适用于其他题目，比如在回答"What do you think is the most effective means of advertising？"这个题目时，考生可以说在电视节目之间投放广告最有效。

◎ 表达积累

为了方便记忆和学习，我们将有用的表达罗列在以下表格中，考生可以尝试用这些表达的组合来回答之前罗列的相关题目。

	Commercials are probably the most effective kind of advertisement.	商业广告可能是最有效的广告。
电视上的商业广告	Commercials are hard to avoid because the TV show is put on hold during commercial breaks.	商业广告很难避免，因为电视节目会在广告时间暂停。
	Commercial breaks can also be very frequent, and each commercial can last quite long.	广告间歇也可能非常频繁，而且每次广告都可以持续相当长的时间。
	Online advertisements appear on the side of websites or as popup ads.	在线广告出现在网站的一侧或以弹出式广告出现。
在线广告	are often more related to your interests	往往与你的兴趣更相关
	are not as effective as TV advertisements because they can be more easily ignored or closed	效果不如电视广告，因为它们更容易被忽视或关掉
户外广告	Outdoor advertisements can be seen on billboards, walls, and buildings.	户外广告可以在广告牌、墙壁和建筑物上看到。
	Outdoor advertisements appear on transportation, such as on buses, the metro, and taxis.	户外广告出现在公共汽车、地铁和出租车等交通工具上。

Part 3 补充话题及相关表达与素材

　　雅思口语 Part 3 的题目涉及的范围非常广泛。除了以上常见的话题，还有许多值得考生了解、思考与练习的话题，我们将它们归纳为补充话题。每一个补充话题下面同样包含若干小话题，每个小话题分为话题解读、题目、表达与素材及（表达与素材的）中文翻译。考生依旧可以使用上一节（Part 3 核心话题及相关表达与素材）讲解的学习方法来备考这些题目，本节不再做详细地解读。请考生切记，要灵活搭配及使用这些表达与素材，勿要全盘照抄。

话题 7 FAMOUS PEOPLE & CELEBRITIES（名人）

　　如今的新闻，名人和名人的故事占据了主流媒体的很大一部分。名人有很多仰慕者，人们敬仰他们，渴望成为像他们那样的人。Part 3 关于这个话题通常会问"名人对他人的影响""名人共有的品质"及"成名的好处和坏处"[1]。

1. How people become famous（如何成名）

◎ 话题解读

许多人都想成名，但只有极小一部分人能够实现这个愿望。Part 3 关于这个话题通常会问"成名所需的品质""为什么有的人能成名"。

◎ 题目

How do people become famous?

What types of people become famous in your country?

What qualities do many famous people have in common?

Do you think people are famous as a result of some real talents or because of some other reasons?

Can anyone become a famous artist through hard work?

Why are celebrities popular?

Do you think celebrities need to be good in their field?

Do you think the most popular singer is the best one?

Why are some celebrities able to stay famous for a long time while others cannot?

◎ 表达与素材

People are famous and popular for different reasons:

1. They are really good or skilled at something—for example, singing or playing sports.

---

① 有关名人新闻的问题在"MEDIA & ADVERTISING"（媒体与广告)章节中已有介绍。

For people to become really good at something, they need natural talent, but hard work and dedication is even more important.

2. They look attractive. This can be especially important for actors, singers, and models.

3. They have an entertaining or funny personality. That's why many comedians and variety show hosts become famous.

4. They have done something important—for example, creating a big company or saving many lives.

◎ 中文翻译

人们因为不同的原因出名或受欢迎：

1. 他们真的很擅长或精通某件事情——例如，唱歌或进行体育运动。要想在某件事情上变得擅长，人们需要天赋，但努力和投入更重要。

2. 他们看起来很有魅力，这对演员、歌手和模特来说尤其重要。

3. 他们的个性很有趣，这是许多喜剧演员和综艺节目主持人出名的原因。

4. 他们做了一些重要的事情，例如，创建了一个大公司或拯救了许多生命。

2. Pros and cons of being famous（成名所带来的的好处与坏处）

◎ 话题解读

尽管很多人都想成名，成名带来的好处也很多，但成为名人也有不好的一面。Part 3 关于这个话题通常会问"出名的好处和坏处"。

◎ 题目

What are the advantages and disadvantages of being famous?

What are the advantages and disadvantages of becoming a celebrity?

What are the positive sides of being famous?

What are the advantages and disadvantages of being rich?

◎ 表达与素材

1. The main advantage of being famous is that you have more money, which allows you to live a more luxurious life. You also have more power and influence, which allows you to make the world a better place.

2. The main disadvantage of being famous is that you lack privacy. You can't really go out in public without being bothered by the paparazzi or fans. Famous people also attract fake friends and therefore have trust issues.

◎ 中文翻译

1. 出名的主要好处是你有了更多的钱，这可以让你过上更奢侈的生活。你也拥有更大的权力和影响力，这使得你可以让世界变得更美好。

2. 出名的主要缺点是缺乏隐私。你真的不可能在公共场合不被狗仔队或粉丝打扰。名人也会吸引一些假朋友，因此会产生信任问题。

3. How famous people influence others（名人如何影响他人）

◎ 话题解读

名人经常出现在公共场合，其言行举止可能会对社会或者个人产生影响。Part 3 关于这个话题通常会问"名人如何影响他人"及"他们带来的积极和消极的影响"。

◎ 题目

What influences can famous people have on society?

How do famous people influence ordinary people?

Do you know any popular star who really likes helping other people?

What effects/impacts do famous people have on young people?

What influences do actors or actresses have on young people?

What bad influences can famous people have on young people?

Do you think advertisements aimed at children should be endorsed by famous people?

◎ 表达与素材

1. Famous people influence others through their actions. They have an especially strong influence on young people because young people are easily influenced and lots of them really admire celebrities.

2. Famous people can be a bad influence if they behave poorly—for example, if they lead wasteful lives, lie, cheat, or break the law. However, famous people can also be a good influence if they behave well and actively help society, such as make donations or create charities. Even the life stories of famous people can motivate others, because many famous people overcame challenges and worked hard to become successful.

3. When celebrities endorse or promote something, it can be good or bad for society. It is bad if celebrities endorse a product that's harmful (e.g. junk food) or which people don't need. It is good if celebrities endorse something that helps society, such as charity or environmental protection.

◎ 中文翻译

1. 名人通过他们的行为影响他人。他们对年轻人的影响特别大，因为年轻人很容易受影响，而且很多人都很崇拜名人。

2. 如果名人行为不良——例如，如果他们浪费、撒谎、欺骗或违法——就会产生不良影响。然而，名人也可以产生好的影响，如果他们表现良好，积极帮助社会，例如捐款或创办慈善机构。名人的生活故事也能激励他人，因为许多名人通过克服挑战和努力工作才获得了成功。

3. 当名人代言或宣传某件事时，对社会可能是好事也可能是坏事。如果名人代言的产品是有害的（如垃圾食品）或人们不需要的产品，那就不好了。如果名人支持一些有助于社会的事情，比如慈善或环境保护，那就是件好事。

话题 8 LEISURE（休闲娱乐）

每个人都需要放松，并且各有各的放松和娱乐方式。Part 3 关于休闲娱乐通常会问"最受欢迎的休闲活动"及"有哪些具体的休闲活动"。下面我们将学习如何回答这些问题。

1. Popular leisure activities（流行的休闲娱乐活动）

◎ 话题解读

人不是机器，不可能一直处于学习或工作状态，每个人都需要休息和放松。Part 3 关于这个话题通常会问"普遍流行的休闲活动有哪些"及"年轻人和老年人之间的偏好差异"。

◎ 题目

What leisure activities are popular in China?

What do Chinese people like to do when they have days off?

What kinds of group activities do Chinese people like to participate in?

What leisure activities do young people like?

How do old people spend their free time?

What are the differences between young and old people when choosing places to hang out?

What's the difference between the things people did in their free time in the past and the things they do nowadays?

Do people nowadays have more ways to relax than in the past?

◎ 表达与素材

Popular leisure activities for young people:

1. Home activities: Young people enjoy using computers, cellphones, and the internet. Many young people also like looking at social media, playing games, and watching online videos.

2. Physical activities: Young people have stronger bodies, so they tend to play more intense sports like basketball, badminton, running, or even skiing.

3. Social activities: Young people like going to the movie theatre, eating or hanging out with friends/family, shopping, singing karaoke, or travelling.

Popular leisure activities for old people:

1. Home activities: Old people are not as comfortable with modern technology, so at home, they prefer to read or watch TV.

2. Physical activities: Old people can't do intense sports, but many of them are still very active. They like taking walks in the park, and some even like dancing.

3. Social activities: Old people like visiting neighbours, eating with friends or family, or travelling.

◎ 中文翻译

年轻人喜爱的休闲活动：

1. 家庭活动：年轻人喜欢使用电脑、手机和互联网。许多年轻人也喜欢浏览社交媒体，玩游戏，看在线视频。

2. 体育活动：年轻人身体更强壮，所以他们倾向于进行更激烈的运动，如篮球、羽毛球、跑步，甚至是滑雪。

3. 社会活动：年轻人喜欢去看电影，和朋友或家人一起吃饭或出去玩、购物、唱歌或旅行。

老年人喜爱的休闲活动：

1. 家庭活动：老年人不太适应现代科技，所以在家里，他们更喜欢阅读或看电视。

2. 体育活动：老年人不能进行剧烈运动，但他们中的许多人仍然很活跃，他们喜欢在公园散步，有些人甚至喜欢跳舞。

3. 社会活动：老年人喜欢拜访邻居，与朋友或家人吃饭或旅游。

2. Watching TV（看电视）

◎ 话题解读

看电视是最普遍的放松方式之一。Part 3 关于这个话题通常会问"人们喜欢看的电视节目类型"及"年轻人和老年人之间的偏好差异"。

◎ 题目

Do people in China like to watch TV?

Do young people like to watch TV nowadays?

What kinds of TV programmes are popular in your country?

What kinds of TV programmes do young people like?

What's the difference between the programs that young people enjoy watching and the programs that old people enjoy watching?

Why do people enjoy watching reality shows?

Do people like comedy?

◎ 表达与素材

1. People of all ages like to watch variety shows, comedy shows, and music shows. Many people also like to watch reality shows, especially ones that involve a singing or talent competition. Romance shows and historical dramas—including Chinese fantasy shows—are also very popular.

2. Many young people like to watch cartoons/anime, sports, action shows, or foreign TV shows.

3. Many old people like to watch news and informational programs.

◎ 中文翻译

1. 各个年龄段的人都喜欢看综艺节目、喜剧节目和音乐节目。许多人也喜欢看真人秀节目，尤其是那些涉及歌唱或才艺比赛的节目。言情剧和历史剧——包括中国的玄幻剧——也很受欢迎。

2. 许多年轻人喜欢看卡通动画、体育节目、动作片或外国电视节目。

3. 许多老年人喜欢看新闻和信息类的节目。

3. Watching sports competitions（观看体育比赛）

◎ 话题解读

体育赛事一直是人们关注的焦点，尤其是一些国际性的比赛，比如世界杯、奥运会等。Part 3 关于这个话题通常会问"人们为什么观看体育比赛"及"人们喜欢观看的体育运动类型"。

◎ 题目

Why do some people like to watch live sports contests?

What types of sport contests do Chinese people like to watch?

Why do old people like to watch sports on TV?

Why do some people not like watching sports games?

◎ 表达与素材

1. Many people like watching sports because the games can be very exciting, especially when the top teams or players are competing against each other. It's also fun to cheer for a team or player that you like.

2. Chinese people enjoy watching sports such as basketball, ping pong, badminton, or soccer. People in general also like to watch teams or athletes from their city or country. For example, during the Olympics, lots of Chinese people tune in to watch Chinese athletes. It makes them feel proud when the athletes perform well.

◎ 中文翻译

1. 许多人喜欢看体育比赛，因为比赛非常激动人心，特别是当顶级团队或运动员互相竞争的时候。为你喜欢的团队或运动员加油也很有趣。

2. 中国人喜欢观看篮球、乒乓球、羽毛球或足球等运动。人们一般喜欢观看来自自己城市或国家的团队或运动员。例如，在奥运会期间，许多中国人收看中国运动员的比赛。当运动员表现出色时，他们会感到自豪。

4. Games & Toys（游戏与玩具）

◎ 话题解读

现在的孩子接触电子产品的机会很多，家长难免有些担心。Part 3 关于这个话题通常会问"儿童玩游戏的好处和坏处"。

◎ 题目

How do Chinese people feel about children playing games?

Do parents in your country encourage children to play games?

Is it important to play some games?

Do leisure activities have to be educational?

What do you think of people spending too much time playing computer games?

What are the effects of playing with electronic products?

◎ 表达与素材

Pros of playing games:

1. Playing games is a good way for children to have fun and relax, which is important for their mental health.

2. Playing games help children spend their energy, which promotes better eating and sleeping habits.

3. Games can be educational. They teach children problem-solving skills and can boost their creativity.

Cons of playing games:

1. Playing mobile and computer games too much is bad for children's eyes.

2. Children can become addicted to games, taking away their time for studying or sleeping.

3. It can reduce children's contact with other people, which is bad for their social development.

◎ 中文翻译

玩游戏的好处：

1. 玩游戏是孩子们娱乐和放松的好方法，这对他们的心理健康很重要。

2. 玩游戏帮助孩子们消耗精力，从而养成更好的饮食和睡眠习惯。

3. 游戏可以具有教育意义。它们教给孩子解决问题的技能，并能提高他们的创造力。

玩游戏的坏处：

1. 过度玩手机和电脑游戏对孩子的眼睛有害。

2. 孩子们会对游戏上瘾，占用了他们学习或睡觉的时间。

3. 这会减少孩子与他人的接触，不利于他们的社会发展。

5. Holidays（假期）

◎ 话题解读

假期让人们从繁忙的工作和学习中抽身出来，得到休息和放松。Part 3 关于这个话题通常会问"为什么假期对人们有好处"及"人们在假期会做什么"。

◎ 题目

Do people in your country like to have holidays?

Do you think we should have more public holidays?

Do you prefer short holidays or long holidays?

What do people usually do during long holidays?

What kinds of activities do people like to do for the holidays?

Why do some people prefer to stay at home during the holidays?

◎ 表达与素材

1. Holidays allow people to relax, have fun, and spend time with their family. For busy people, holidays are the only time they can really take a break.

2. There are many different ways to spend a holiday, and it really depends on the person. For short holidays, you can relax at home by playing games, watching TV, reading, or taking naps. For longer holidays, you can travel to other cities, the countryside, or even to other countries. Longer holidays also provide you a chance to visit friends and family members who live far away.

◎ 中文翻译

1. 假期让人们得到放松、获得乐趣以及有时间与家人在一起。对于忙碌的人们来说，假期是他们唯一可以真正休息的时间。

2. 有许多不同的方式来度过假期，这真的取决于个人。对于短暂的假期，你可以在家里玩游戏、看电视、看书或睡觉来放松。对于较长的假期，你可以去其他城市、农村，甚至去其他国家旅游。较长的假期也让你有机会拜访住得很远的朋友和家人。

话题 9 TRAVELLING ABROAD AND TOURISM
（出国游与旅游业）

旅行是最受欢迎的休闲活动之一，因为它能让人们探索世界、获得乐趣。Part 3 关于这个话题通常会问"旅游的好处"及"热门旅游景点"。有时还会问"旅行的一些缺点"（比如在国外旅行时可能会遇到的问题）及"旅游如何影响环境"。下面我们将学习如何回答这些问题。

1. Travelling & living abroad（海外旅行或生活）

◎ 话题解读

随着世界的联系越来越紧密，越来越多的人选择出国度假，甚至在国外长期居住。Part 3 关于这个话题通常会问"出国旅游或生活在国外的好处和坏处"。

◎ 题目

Why do many people like to travel abroad?

How do people benefit from international travel?

Would you like to travel around the world in the future?

Will you live in a foreign country in the future?

Is it good for young people to have the experience of living in other countries?

What do you think is the best way to learn about a foreign culture?

Which is more helpful for learning about a country: reading literature about this country or travelling to this country?

What kinds of problems do people have when they travel or live in a foreign country?

◎ 表达与素材

Advantages of travelling & living abroad:

1. Travelling and living abroad is fresh and exciting because you're going to a new place and experiencing new things. Experiencing something in person is quite different from just reading or watching videos about it.

2. You get to learn more about the world, which helps you expand your horizons. It makes you a more knowledgeable and wiser person.

Disadvantages of travelling & living abroad:

1. If you're not familiar with the country's language and culture, living abroad can be difficult and uncomfortable.

2. You'll be far from family and friends, which might make you lonely and homesick.

3. You might experience discrimination.

◎ 中文翻译

出国旅行和生活的优点：

1. 在国外旅行和生活是新鲜和令人兴奋的，因为你要去到一个新的地方，体验新的事物。亲身体验某件事与仅仅通过阅读或观看有关它的视频了解它是完全不同的。

2. 你可以更多地了解这个世界，这有助于扩展你的视野。这会让你成为一个更有知识、更有智慧的人。

出国旅行和生活的缺点：

1. 如果你不熟悉这个国家的语言和文化，在国外生活可能是困难和不舒服的。

2. 你将远离家人和朋友，这可能使你孤独和想家。

3. 你可能会受到歧视。

2. Popular tourist attractions（著名的旅游景点）

◎ 话题解读

对于假期旅行，大多数人都喜欢去那些受欢迎的旅游景点。Part 3 关于这个话题通常会问"你们国家的热门旅游景点"及"去热门旅游景点的缺点"。

◎ 题目

What are some popular attractions that people like to visit in your country?

What's the most popular tourist attraction in China?

Where do Chinese people like to travel to?

What's the most important factor for a tourist attraction?

What are the disadvantages when there are too many tourists in one site?

What are the advantages of visiting lesser-known places?

◎ 表达与素材

1. Many people like visiting attractions that are important to history. For example, lots of Chinese tourists have visited the Great Wall of China, the Forbidden City and the Tiananmen building, as well as other ancient temples and buildings.

2. Places with lots of natural scenery are also very popular, like lakes or mountains.

3. However, popular tourist sites can be very crowded during holidays. When visiting lesser-known places, you don't have to deal with big crowds, and you don't have to spend as much money for hotels and airplane tickets.

◎ 中文翻译

1. 许多人喜欢参观对历史有重要意义的景点。例如，许多中国游客参观了中国的长城、紫禁城和天安门城楼，以及其他古代的寺庙和建筑。

2. 自然风光丰富的地方也很受欢迎，比如湖泊或山脉。

3. 然而，热门旅游景点在节日期间可能会非常拥挤。当你游览不太出名的地方时，你不必面对拥挤的人群，也不必在酒店和机票上花那么多钱。

3. River & Seaside tourism（河边或海边的旅行）

◎ 话题解读

河流、海滩和海洋通常是比较受欢迎的旅游目的地。Part 3 关于这个话题通常会问"去这些地方游玩的好处和坏处"。

◎ 题目

What are the advantages and disadvantages of vacations to the seaside?

What do you think are the advantages and disadvantages of travelling on the ocean?

Why do people like spending time on the sea?

Which river do people like?

What is the importance of rivers or lakes?

◎ 表达与素材

Things you can do when visiting a river, lake, or seaside:

1. You can row a boat or go on a ship. These are fun and unique experiences.

2. You can enjoy beautiful views of the river or sea.

3. You can go swimming, which is a healthy and relaxing way to exercise.

Disadvantages of seaside tourism:

The main disadvantage of seaside tourism is that it can be very crowded, especially during good weather. Also, tourists may damage the environment by polluting it. For example, tourists create a lot of trash, and they often litter or don't recycle trash properly.

◎ 中文翻译

游览河流、湖泊或海边时可以做的事情：

1. 你可以划船或坐船。这些都是有趣而独特的体验。

2. 你可以欣赏到美丽的江海景色。

3. 你可以去游泳，这是一种健康和放松的锻炼方式。

海滨旅游的缺点：

海滨旅游的主要缺点是非常拥挤，尤其是在天气好的时候。此外，游客可能会污染环境。例如，游客制造了很多垃圾，他们经常乱扔垃圾或不正确地回收垃圾。

4. Tourism & The environment（旅游业与环保）

◎ 话题解读

旅游业并不总是带来好处，也会带来一系列的问题，特别是游客如织的地方。Part 3 关于这个话题通常会问"旅游业对当地环境和历史景点的影响"。

◎ 题目

What effects does tourism have on our environment?

Do you think having many tourists is a positive thing for historical attractions?

What can we do to stop visitors from damaging historical places?

◎ 表达与素材

1. Tourists often damage the environment by polluting it. For example, tourists create a lot of trash, and they often litter or don't recycle trash properly.

2. Tourists sometimes commit vandalism, such as spray painting, making graffiti, or breaking things.

◎ 中文翻译

1. 游客经常污染环境，进而破坏环境。例如，游客制造了很多垃圾，他们经常乱扔垃圾或不正确地回收垃圾。

2. 游客有时会破坏公物，如乱喷涂料、涂鸦或打碎东西。

5. Souvenirs（旅游纪念品）

◎ 话题解读

外出旅行时，许多人都会给自己或家人、朋友购买纪念品。Part 3 关于这个话题通常会问"纪念品是如何让买家和卖家都受益的"。

◎ 题目

Why do people buy souvenirs?

What souvenirs do people buy from tourist attractions?

Is it reasonable for local people to sell souvenirs to make money from tourism?

Is it good that local people sell things to tourists?

◎ 表达与素材

1. Souvenirs help tourists remember their travel experiences. When they look at the souvenir, it brings them back to the place and makes them happy. Some people also buy souvenirs for their friends because it's a nice thing to do, and they appreciate that you were thinking of them.

2. Popular souvenirs include local handicrafts (like necklaces, rings, and bracelets), key chains, clothes (such as "I love Beijing" t-shirts), postcards, coffee mugs, and food.

3. Selling souvenirs is a good way for locals to make money. In fact, locals in many places depend a lot on tourist spending.

◎ 中文翻译

1. 纪念品帮助游客记住他们的旅行经历。当他们看到纪念品时，它会把他们带回那个地方，让他们感到快乐。有些人还会给朋友买纪念品，因为这是一件很好的事情，他们很感激你能想着他们。

2. 受欢迎的纪念品包括当地的手工艺品（如项链、戒指和手镯）、钥匙链、衣服（如写着"我爱北京"的 T 恤）、明信片、咖啡杯和食物。

3. 卖纪念品是当地人赚钱的好方法。事实上，许多地方的当地人在很大程度上依赖游客的消费。

📢 话题 10 WEATHER & SEASONS（天气与四季）

天气在很多方面影响着人们，从人们每天的活动到人们的穿着。下面我们将学习如何回答 Part 3 中有关天气的各种问题。

1. How weather affects people's leisure activities（天气如何影响人们的休闲 活动）

◎ 话题解读

休闲活动可以分为室外活动和室内活动。Part 3 关于这个话题通常会问"天气对人们的休闲活动的影响"。

◎ 题目

Does weather have any impact on people's daily activities?

What kinds of activities will be influenced by season?

What types of weather are suitable for outdoor activities?

If the weather is bad, what would people do indoors?

Why do people do different kinds of sports in different weather?

Do you like to go outside when winter comes?

◎ 表达与素材

1. When it's hot and sunny, people like to go swimming at pools or beaches.

2. During winter, some people like to go skiing or ice skating.

3. During hot, cold, or rainy days, some people prefer to do indoor activities. For example, they might read, watch TV, or play video games.

4. When the weather is mild (like during spring and fall), people tend to enjoy outdoor activities more. They might take walks, ride their bikes, or go hiking.

◎ 中文翻译

1. 当天气炎热和阳光明媚的时候，人们喜欢去游泳池或海滩游泳。

2. 在冬天，有些人喜欢去滑雪或滑冰。

3. 在热天、冷天或者雨天，有些人喜欢做室内活动。例如，他们可能会阅读、看电视或玩电子游戏。

4. 当天气温和时（如春秋季节），人们倾向于更多地享受户外活动。他们可能会散步、骑自行车或徒步旅行。

2. How weather affects people's dressing/clothes（天气如何影响人们的穿着）

◎ 话题解读

随着季节和天气的变化，人们的衣着也在变化。Part 3 关于这个话题通常会问"天气对衣服的影响"。

◎ 题目

What are the impacts of weather on dressing?

What do people wear in different weather?

What kinds of clothes do people wear in summer?

◎ 表达与素材

1. During summer, it's better to wear looser clothes, like shorts or t-shirts, because it helps you stay cooler. You can also wear flip flops or sandals for your feet.

2. During winter, it's better to wear lots of layers of clothes when you go outside, like a jacket and maybe even a scarf.

◎ 中文翻译

1. 在夏天，最好穿宽松的衣服，如短裤或 T 恤，因为它能帮助你保持凉爽。脚上也可以穿人字拖或凉鞋。

2. 冬天外出时最好多穿几层衣服，比如夹克，甚至围巾。

3. Good vs. Bad weather（好天气与坏天气）

◎ 话题解读

一年有四个季节，每个季节的天气各不相同。Part 3 关于这个话题通常会问"人们（包括你）对天气的偏好"。

◎ 题目

What kind of weather do Chinese people like?

Would you prefer working in a cold place or hot place?

What is your least favourite season?

Do you think weather has an influence on people's mood?

◎ 表达与素材

1. Most people prefer mild weather, like the kind of weather during spring or fall.

2. Most people don't really enjoy hot or cold weather, like during summer or winter, because it feels uncomfortable to go outside or do outdoor activities.

◎ 中文翻译

1. 大多数人都喜欢温和的天气，比如春天或秋天那种天气。

2. 大多数人都不喜欢炎热或寒冷的天气，比如夏天或冬天，因为他们不适合出行或者做户外运动。

话题 11 SPORTS & EXERCISE（体育与锻炼）

运动对人们的健康非常重要，现在热爱运动的人也越来越多。Part 3 关于这个话题通常会问"受欢迎的体育活动是什么""运动如何使人们受益"，以及"我们如何鼓励更多人参加运动"。下面我们将学习如何回答这些问题。

1. Popular sports & physical activities（受欢迎的体育运动）

◎ 话题解读

体育运动有很多种，有些是比较受欢迎的。Part 3 关于这个话题通常会问"哪些运动和体育活动比较受欢迎的"及"不同类型的运动之间的区别"。

◎ 题目

What kinds of exercises do Chinese people like?

What kinds of sports are popular in your country?

What sports involve teamwork?

Do you think group sports are more useful than individual sports?

What's the difference between indoor sports and outdoor sports?

What are the advantages and disadvantages of playing outdoor sports?

Why do people do different kinds of sports in different weather?

What else can people do to stay healthy besides sports?

What do people in your country do to maintain their health?

◎ 表达与素材

1. Some of the most popular sports in China are team sports like basketball, soccer, and badminton. Team sports can teach people—especially children—better communication and social skills.

2. Outdoor sports are great for when the weather is nice outside—for example, when it's not too hot, too cold, or raining. Running and cycling are some of the most popular outdoor sports. They allow you to enjoy sunlight and nature.

3. Popular non-sport exercises include taking walks and hiking. Exercises like tai chi and dancing are also pretty popular, especially with old people.

◎ 中文翻译

1. 在中国最受欢迎的一些运动是团队运动，如篮球、足球和羽毛球。团队运动可以教给人们——尤其是孩子——更好的沟通和社交技能。

2. 户外运动适合在天气好的时候进行，比如不太热、不太冷、也不下雨的时候。跑步和骑自行车都是最受欢迎的户外运动。它们能让你享受阳光和自然。

3. 非竞技类的流行运动包括散步和徒步旅行。像太极和舞蹈这样的运动也很受欢迎，尤其是在老年人中。

2. Swimming & Water sports（游泳与水上运动）

◎ 话题解读

游泳这样的水上运动很受人们的欢迎，尤其是在夏天，它不仅是一项娱乐活动，也是一项非常重要的技能。Part 3 关于这个话题通常会问"游泳的好处"及"其他种类的水上活动和运动"。

◎ 题目

Do you think it is important to learn swim?

Do you think children should learn how to swim?

Do you think the government should invest money in developing facilities for water sports?

Do people in your country go swimming in their free time?

Are there any other water sports besides swimming?

What kinds of water sports are popular in your country?

What are popular water activities in China?

Why do some people like water sports?

Why do some people like to play near water?

◎ 表达与素材

1. Everyone should learn swimming because it can save you from drowning one day. It also allows you to rescue other people from drowning.

2. Swimming is a great way to get some exercise and also cool down during hot summers. Swimming is not very intense and it's a low-impact sport, which means that it's good for both young and old people. Swimming is also a pretty relaxing activity that puts you in a better mood.

3. Popular water sports aside from swimming include surfing and scuba diving.

◎ 中文翻译

1. 每个人都应该学习游泳，因为有一天它可以把你从溺水中拯救出来。它也可以让你去拯救其他溺水的人。

2. 游泳是一种很好的锻炼方式，在炎热的夏天也可以降温。游泳不是很剧烈，而是一项低强度的运动，这意味着它对年轻人和老年人都有好处。游泳也是一项非常放松的活动，能让你心情更好。

3. 除了游泳，流行的水上运动还包括冲浪和潜水。

3. Benefits of playing sports（运动的好处）

◎ 话题解读

尽管人们可能没有很多时间去做运动，但肯定认可运动对身体有好处。Part 3 关于这个话题通常会问"运动对孩子和普通人有什么好处"。

◎ 题目

What are the benefits of doing sports?

Do you think physical education is necessary?

Should a city have a lot of sports facilities?

Should children spend more time playing sports?

What are the advantages of children joining sports groups?

How do you think physical classes affect children's development?

◎ 表达与素材

Physical benefits of playing sports:

1. Helps you keep fit and stay in shape.

2. Good for your heart. Gives you a good cardiovascular workout.

3. Helps you build muscle, strength, and endurance.

Mental benefits of playing sports:

1. Helps you relieve stress.

2. Helps you clear your mind.

3. Helps you concentrate better afterwards on your work/studies.

◎ 中文翻译

运动对身体的好处：

1. 帮助你保持健康和体形。

2. 对你的心脏有好处。让你的心血管得到很好的锻炼。

3. 帮助你锻炼肌肉、力量和耐力。

运动对精神有益：

1. 帮助你缓解压力。

2. 帮助你理清思绪。

3. 帮助你之后更好地专注于你的工作 / 学习。

4. How to encourage people to do sports or exercise（怎样鼓励人们去运动）

◎ 话题解读

尽管人们都知道运动对健康有益，但许多人仍然不经常运动或者缺乏锻炼。Part 3 关于这个话题通常会问"政府、家长和学校可以做些什么来鼓励其他人多锻炼或多做运动"。

◎ 题目

What can the government do to encourage people to do sports?

What can the government do to improve people's health?

What can parents do to make their children like sports?

What activities can school organize to keep children fit?

◎ 表达与素材

1. To encourage people to exercise, the government could build more public sports facilities, such as gyms, basketball courts, swimming pools, and running tracks.

2. The government could also build more parks where people can take walks, run, ride bicycles, or do other kinds of exercise.

3. Schools and parents should teach children about the importance of exercising. They could help children build a habit of exercising by having them do sports regularly.

◎ 中文翻译

1. 为了鼓励人们锻炼，政府可以建造更多的公共体育设施，如健身房、篮球场、游泳池和跑道。

2. 政府还可以建造更多的公园，人们可以在那里散步、跑步、骑自行车或做其他运动。

3. 学校和家长应该教导孩子们锻炼的重要性。他们可以通过让孩子们经常做运动来帮助他们养成锻炼的习惯。

🔊 话题 12 SHOPPING（购物）

许多人喜欢购物，购物能让人感到愉悦。Part 3 关于这个话题通常会问"人们喜欢去哪里购物""在这些地方购物的优点和缺点"，以及"人们的购物习惯"。下面我们将学习如何回答这些问题。

1. Big shops and malls vs. Small shops and street markets（购物中心与街边小店）

◎ 话题解读

人们会根据自己的需求到各种各样的地方购物，包括购物中心、街市或小商店。Part 3 关于这个话题通常会问"你在什么地方购物和在不同地点购物的独特优势"。

◎ 题目

What kinds of places are popular for shopping in China?

Where do you like to go shopping?

What kinds of markets are there in China?

What are the differences between shopping in street markets and big shopping malls?

Why do some people prefer street markets over shopping malls?

Do you like shopping in big malls?

Do you think small markets will disappear in the future?

Do you like big shops or small shops?

Why do some people like to visit small shops?

◎ 表达与素材

Advantages of small shops and street markets:

1. Small shops and street markets usually have cheaper products, allowing you to save money, which is why some older people prefer shopping at these places.

2. Small shops and street markets can sell unique products or traditional products (including food, jewellery, and clothes) that can't be bought in other places. That's why tourists or people looking to buy souvenirs might go to these places.

Advantages of big shops and shopping malls:

1. Aside from shopping, there are more things to do at big shops or shopping malls. For example, there are restaurants, coffee shops, gyms, and movie theatres. It's why shopping

malls are a great place for friends to hang out.

2. Big shops and shopping malls sell more prestigious and sometimes higher-quality products. That's why people who want to buy luxury items often shop at these places.

◎ 中文翻译

小商店和街市的优势：

1. 小商店和街市通常有更便宜的产品，可以让你省钱，这就是一些老年人喜欢在这些地方购物的原因。

2. 小商店和街市可以出售在其他地方买不到的独特产品或传统产品（包括食品、珠宝和衣服）。这就是游客或想买纪念品的人可能会去这些地方的原因。

大商店和购物中心的优势：

1. 除了购物，在大商店或购物中心有更多的事情可以做。例如，这里有餐馆、咖啡店、健身房和电影院。这就是购物中心是朋友们闲逛的好地方的原因。

2. 大商店和购物中心售卖更有品牌声望、有时质量更高的产品。这就是想买奢侈品的人经常在这些地方购物的原因。

2. Shopping habits（购物习惯）

◎ 话题解读

每个人都有自己的购物偏好，这其中包含一些共性和个性。Part 3 关于这个话题通常会问"人们常见的购物习惯"，包括"多久购物一次""喜欢买什么样的东西"以及"为什么买这些东西"。

◎ 题目

Do people in your country like to go shopping?

How often do people in your country go shopping?

How often do people in your country buy clothes?

Do you often buy more than you expected?

Why do people buy things that are not necessary?

What kinds of expensive things do people like to buy?

Why do some people like to buy expensive goods?

Why do some people like to buy expensive furniture?

Why do people like or dislike buying clothing?

Why do many people apply for credit cards nowadays?

◎ 表达与素材

1. People in my country like to go shopping a lot, and many of them buy things every week. It's partly because online shopping and credit cards have made it easier to buy things.

2. People like to buy things such as clothes, food, and shoes. Some people also buy expensive products, like fashion items and electronics (such as cell phones).

3. Some people buy expensive things they don't need because they want to appear rich. In other words, they do it to show off to and impress other people, or to keep up with their friends and family who own expensive things.

◎ 中文翻译

1. 我们国家的人很喜欢购物，很多人每周都买东西。部分原因是网上购物和信用卡让购物变得更容易。

2. 人们喜欢买衣服、食物和鞋子之类的东西。有些人还会购买昂贵的产品，如时尚单品和电子产品（如手机）。

3. 有些人会买他们并不需要的昂贵的东西，因为他们想显得富有。换句话说，他们这样做是为了向别人炫耀，给别人留下深刻印象，或者是为了追赶拥有昂贵物品的朋友和家人。

话题 13 FOOD & DIET（饮食）

饮食是人们日常生活中必不可少的一部分。人们每天都要做关于吃的决定，比如是在家里吃还是在外面吃、吃什么等。下面我们将学习如何回答这些问题。

1. Eating at home vs. Eating at a restaurant（在家吃饭和在餐馆吃饭）

◎话题解读

人们通常都是在家吃饭的，但偶尔也会去餐馆吃饭。Part 3 关于这个话题通常会问"在家吃饭和在餐馆吃饭的好处"。

◎ 题目

What are advantages and disadvantages of eating at a restaurant?

What's the difference between eating at home and eating at a restaurant?

Do people these days go to restaurants more than people before?

Is it expensive to eat out in your country?

Is there any difference between home-cooked food and food in restaurants?

Do you think people should eat every meal with their family?

◎ 表达与素材

Benefits of eating at home:

1. Cooking is usually much cheaper than eating at a restaurant, so it helps you save a lot of money over time.

2. Cooking is healthier for you. Many restaurants put lots of oil, salt, and sugar in their food.

3. Eating at home brings the family together. It gives them time to talk about their day.

Benefits of eating at a restaurant:

1. It's more convenient than cooking and saves you time. You don't have to cook, wash dishes, or shop for groceries.

2. Restaurant food often tastes better and there's a greater variety of cuisines, such as Western food, Chinese food, and Korean food.

3. You can meet up with friends at restaurants.

◎ 中文翻译

在家吃饭的好处：

1. 自己做饭通常比在餐馆吃饭便宜得多，所以久而久之，它会帮你节省很多钱。

2. 自己做饭更健康。许多餐馆在食物中放了很多油、盐和糖。

3. 在家里吃饭使家人聚在一起。这给了他们时间来谈论他们的一天中的事情。

在餐馆吃饭的好处：

1. 这比自己做饭更方便，而且节约时间。你不必做饭、洗碗或购买食品杂货。

2. 餐馆的食物通常味道更好，菜系也更丰富，如西餐、中餐和韩餐。

3. 你可以和朋友在餐馆见面。

2. Foreign food（外国食物）

◎ 话题解读

每天吃同样的食物会腻，这就是人们有时会尝试外国食物的原因。Part 3 关于这个话题通常会问"人们对外国食物的一般态度"及"什么样的外国食物是受欢迎的"。

◎ 题目

What kinds of foreign food are popular in your country?

What food is popular throughout the world?

What's the difference between Chinese food and western food?

Are there many western fast food restaurants in China?

Why is fast food so popular?

Do you think young people are more open to new food compared with old people?

Why do some people eat the same things all the time?

◎ 表达与素材

1. Popular foreign foods are Western food, Japanese food, and Korean food. Western food includes Italian food such as spaghetti, as well as fast food like pizza, fried chicken, and hamburgers.

2. Fast food is popular because it tastes good—it has lots of fat, salt, and sugar—and also because it isn't too expensive.

3. Younger people tend to be more open to eating foreign food because they're more open-minded and curious. Older people tend to eat the same food all the time because of habit and

because that's what they're familiar with. However, even older people enjoy eating fast food sometimes, such as KFC.

◎ 中文翻译

1. 受欢迎的外国食物有西餐、日餐和韩餐。西餐包括意大利菜，如意大利面，以及快餐，如披萨、炸鸡和汉堡包。

2. 快餐很受欢迎，因为它味道好——它含有大量的脂肪、盐和糖——也因为它不太贵。

3. 年轻人往往更容易接受外国食物，因为他们更开放、更好奇。老年人总是一直吃同样的食物，因为这是他们的习惯且也是他们熟悉的食物。然而，即使是老年人，有时也喜欢吃快餐，如肯德基。

3. Chinese food for holidays（中国传统节日吃的食物）

◎ 话题解读

食物是大多数庆祝活动的重要组成部分。Part 3 关于这个话题通常会问"中国人在特殊节日里吃的各种食物"。

◎ 题目

What kinds of special food do Chinese people like to eat in a special festival?

What do people in your country like to eat during public holidays?

What do people in your country like to eat on special occasions?

What are some traditional foods in China?

◎ 表达与素材

1. What Chinese people eat during public holidays depends on the holiday as well as the area. For example, in some places people eat hotpot during the Spring Festival eve, while in other places people eat dumplings. Both hotpot and dumplings are popular traditional Chinese foods.

2. Other foods for public holidays include mooncakes for the Mid-Autumn Festival, zongzi for the Dragon Boat Festival, and tangyuan for the Lantern Festival.

◎ 中文翻译

1. 中国人在假期吃什么取决于节日和地区。例如，在一些地方，人们在春节前夕吃火锅，而在另一些地方，人们吃饺子。火锅和饺子都是受欢迎的传统中国食物。

2. 其他节假日的食物包括中秋节的月饼，端午节的粽子，元宵节的汤圆。

4. Coffee & Cafés（咖啡与咖啡厅）

◎ 话题解读

近年来，咖啡的消费量显著增加。Part 3 关于这个话题通常会问"人们喝咖啡和去咖啡馆的喜好和习惯"。

◎ 题目

Do Chinese people like to drink coffee?

Do old people like to drink coffee?

What kinds of people like to go to a café?

Why do people go to coffeehouses?

Why do many young people like studying in a café instead of at home?

What are the differences between cafés and restaurants?

◎ 表达与素材

1. People of all ages like to drink coffee, but younger people tend to drink more coffee. People drink coffee for the energy boost, which helps them concentrate better on studying or work.

2. People go to coffeehouses and cafés not just to drink coffee or tea, but also because it's nice and peaceful there. They can relax, study, or chat with friends there.

◎ 中文翻译

1. 各个年龄段的人都喜欢喝咖啡，但年轻人往往喝得更多。人们喝咖啡是为了补充能量，这有助于他们更好地集中精力学习或工作。

2. 人们去咖啡馆不仅是为了喝咖啡或茶，还因为那里环境很好、很安静。他们可以在那里放松、学习或和朋友聊天。

话题 14 READING（阅读）

每年的 4 月 23 日为"世界读书日"，希望借此推动更多的人去阅读和写作。Part 3 关于这个话题通常会问"人们的阅读习惯和偏好"，以及"阅读带来的好处"。下面我们来学习如何回答这些问题[①]。

1. What people like to read（人们喜欢阅读什么样的书籍）

◎话题解读

书有很多类别，有些书籍适合某一类人，有些书籍则适合大部分人。Part 3 关于这个话题通常会问"人们喜欢阅读的书籍类型"及"不同群体的阅读偏好"。

◎ 题目

What kinds of books do Chinese people like reading?

What are the types of books that young people like to read?

---

① 关于普通书籍和电子书的问题在"TECHNOLOGY"（科技）中已有涉及，请查阅相关章节。

What kind of stories do children like?

What kind of books do children read?

Do boys and girls like the same kinds of books?

What's the difference between men and women in their reading habits?

Do people with different reading levels buy the same kinds of reading materials?

◎ 表达与素材

1. Young adults and children tend to read more fiction books—for example, fantasy, science fiction, mystery, and romance novels.

2. Older people tend to read more nonfiction books, such as books about history or financial management.

3. Women tend to read more books than men do, and they tend to prefer romance and mystery books over nonfiction books. But of course, individual preferences can vary widely.

◎ 中文翻译

1. 年轻人和儿童倾向于阅读更多的虚构类书籍，例如奇幻小说、科幻小说、推理小说和言情小说。

2. 老年人倾向于阅读更多非虚构类书籍，如历史或财务管理类书籍。

3. 女性往往比男性阅读更多的书，而且她们往往更喜欢言情和推理书，而不是非虚构类的书籍。当然，个人的喜好也会有很大的不同。

2. How often people read（人们阅读的频率）

◎ 话题解读

阅读一直是一种流行的休闲活动，但由于更多娱乐活动的出现，使得热爱读书的人越来越少。Part 3 关于这个话题通常会问"不同年龄的人阅读的频率"。

◎ 题目

How often do you read?

Do Chinese people like to read?

Why are people less interested in reading books nowadays?

Which group reads more, young people or old people?

What's the difference between the reading habits of old people and young people?

◎ 表达与素材

1. Chinese people like to read, but not as much as they did in the past. Old people tend to read more often than young people because of habit and because they're less familiar with technology.

2. Young people read less because they're busy with school or work. When they're free,

many young people prefer doing other leisure activities, such as playing games, watching videos, or browsing social media.

◎ 中文翻译

1. 中国人喜欢阅读，但不像过去那么喜欢了。由于习惯和对科技的不熟悉，老年人往往比年轻人阅读更多。

2. 年轻人读得少是因为他们忙于学业或工作。当他们空闲的时候，许多年轻人更喜欢做其他的休闲活动，比如玩游戏、看视频或浏览社交媒体。

3. Benefits of reading（阅读的好处）

◎ 话题解读

阅读不仅是一项令人愉快的活动，它还以许多独特的方式使读者受益。Part 3 关于这个话题通常会问"阅读对人们有什么好处"及"阅读与看视频等其他事情相比有什么不同"。

◎ 题目

Do you think reading benefits us or not?

What benefits do young people get from reading?

What do you think is more important: reading or writing?

Do you prefer books or movies?

What is the more effective way of learning history: reading books or watching videos?

Do you think it's important for parents to read bedtime stories to their children?

◎ 表达与素材

1. Reading improves your vocabulary, reading skills, and imagination.

2. Reading helps you build knowledge and learn more about the world, especially if you read about history or other countries.

3. Reading helps reduce stress and allows you to relax.

4. When parents read bedtime stories, it allows them to spend time with their children, bringing them closer to each other. Children can also learn new words.

◎ 中文翻译

1. 阅读可以提高你的词汇量、阅读技巧和想象力。

2. 阅读帮助你积累知识，更多地了解世界，特别是当你阅读有关历史或其他国家的书籍时。

3. 阅读有助于减轻压力，让你放松。

4. 当父母在睡前读故事时，他们就有了和孩子在一起的时间，拉近了他们之间的距离。孩子也可以学习新单词。

话题 15 CITY LIFE（城市生活）

城市的生活与小城镇和乡村的生活截然不同。关于这个话题，Part 3 提问的方向比较多，包括生活在城市的利与弊、在哪里可以找到安静的地方、公园和花园的作用，以及城市中的各种设施。下面我们将学习如何回答这些问题。

1. Living in the countryside vs. Living in a city（住在乡村与住在都市）

◎ 话题解读

有的人喜欢城市生活，觉得城市生活丰富多彩；有的人则喜欢乡村生活，觉得乡村生活安静舒心。Part 3 关于这个话题通常会问"农村和城市生活的差异"。

◎ 题目

What's the difference between living in the countryside and living in the city?

What are the advantages of living in the countryside?

What are the disadvantages of living in cities?

What are the advantages of living in cities?

Why do many people move from small towns to big cities?

What's the difference between facilities in the countryside and ones in the cities?

Do old people prefer to live in the countryside or in the city?

Do young people enjoy living in the countryside?

◎ 表达与素材

Advantages of living in the countryside:

1. The countryside is quieter and more peaceful. It has a slower pace of life, which some people prefer.

2. There's less pollution and better air.

3. It's closer to nature and wildlife. You can go hiking easily, which benefits your mental and physical health.

4. The cost of living is lower, so it's more affordable than living in the city.

5. You become part of a smaller community. People in small communities usually are friendlier to each other and feel more like a family.

Advantages of living in a city:

1. There are more job opportunities, so it's better for people's career development.

2. It's more convenient. For example, public transport makes it easy to travel around the city. Also, there are shops and facilities everywhere, including supermarkets, libraries, restaurants, and hospitals. The best of these (e.g. the best hospitals), can only be found in cities.

3. It can be more exciting to live in a city. There's a greater variety of leisure activities you can do (e.g. visiting art museums or shopping malls).

◎ 中文翻译

生活在乡村的好处：

1. 乡村更安静、更祥和。它的生活节奏较慢，这是一些人喜欢的。

2. 污染更少，空气更好。

3. 这里更接近自然和野生动物。你可以轻松地去徒步旅行，这对你的身心健康都有好处。

4. 生活成本较低，所以比住在城市更实惠。

5. 你会成为一个更小的社区的一部分。小社区的人们通常彼此更友好，感觉更像一家人。

生活在城市的好处：

1. 有更多的工作机会，所以更有利于人们的职业发展。

2. 这里更方便。例如，公共交通使在城市中走动变得很容易。此外，这里到处都是商店和设施，包括超市、图书馆、餐馆和医院。这其中最好的（例如最好的医院）只能在城市里找到。

3. 住在城市可能更令人兴奋。你可以有更多种类的休闲活动（例如参观艺术博物馆或购物中心）。

2. Quiet places & Dealing with noise in cities（安静的地方与应对都市里的喧闹）

◎ 话题解读

城市可能会很嘈杂，但也有一些安静的地方可以让人们找到平静。Part 3 关于这个话题通常会问"你在哪里可以找到安静的地方"及"人们对安静的地方的偏好"。

◎ 题目

Is it hard to find quiet places in cities?

Do you think cities are much noisier than before?

Do you know other quiet places?

Why is it quieter in the countryside?

Compared to young people, do old people prefer to live in quiet places?

Why do people go to quiet places?

Why do some people not like quiet places?

◎ 表达与素材

1. It can be hard to find quiet places in cities compared to the countryside. In cities, there's more construction work, vehicles, and people. These all contribute to noise pollution.

2. However, there are still some quiet places in cities, like libraries, cafés, and museums.

3. For peace and quiet, you can also escape to the countryside. The countryside is quieter than cities because it's closer to nature and there's less human activity.

◎ 中文翻译

1. 与乡村相比，在城市很难找到安静的地方。在城市里，有更多的建筑工程、车辆和人。这些都造成了噪音污染。

2. 然而，城市中仍然有一些安静的地方，如图书馆、咖啡馆和博物馆。

3. 想要平静和安静，你也可以逃到乡村去。乡村比城市更安静，因为它更接近自然，人类活动更少。

3. Parks & Gardens（公园与花园）

◎ 话题解读

公园和花园是城市的重要组成部分，它们为市民提供了许多好处。Part 3 关于这个话题通常会问"公园和花园的好处"及"人们在那里做什么"。

◎ 题目

What are the benefits of parks and gardens?

What's the importance of building gardens?

Should parks be built in big cities?

Are there enough parks/gardens in your city?

What kinds of facilities should a park provide?

Do you think parks should be free of charge?

What kinds of things do Chinese people like to do in parks?

Do young people go to the park very often?

Where do people in a community usually have social gatherings?

What else can people do to stay healthy besides sports?

◎ 表达与素材

1. Parks and gardens are good places for people to exercise because they can take walks there. Every day, lots of old people take walks in parks, and some of them even dance there. People also walk their pets or ride bikes at parks.

2. Visiting parks and gardens is relaxing and good for your mental health. It gives you a connection to nature, allowing you to take a break from grey roads and buildings.

3. Parks are a good place for social gatherings. You can meet your friends or neighbours there. You can even have picnics with your friends or family at parks.

◎ 中文翻译

1. 公园和花园是人们锻炼的好地方，因为他们可以在那里散步。每天，许多老人在公园散步，有些人甚至在那里跳舞。人们也会在公园里遛宠物或骑自行车。

2. 游览公园和花园令人感到放松，对你的心理健康有好处。这让你与自然有了联系，让你从灰色的道路和建筑中得到休息。

3. 公园是社交聚会的好地方。你可以在那里与你的朋友或邻居见面。你甚至可以和你的朋友或家人在公园野餐。

4. Public facilities（公共设施）

◎ 话题解读

一座城市通常有许多设施，这些设施发挥着不同的功能。Part 3 关于这个话题通常会问"公众经常使用的各种设施"。

◎ 题目

What public facilities does your city have?

What facilities do young people and old people like in your country?

What kinds of leisure facilities are popular in your country?

Should a city have a lot of sports facilities?

What are the differences between old facilities and new facilities?

◎ 表达与素材

1. Leisure or sports facilities include museums, libraries, parks, gardens, playgrounds, gyms, and swimming pools.

2. Some other public facilities are hospitals, restaurants, subway stations, train stations, and airports.

◎ 中文翻译

1. 休闲或运动设施包括博物馆、图书馆、公园、花园、操场、健身房和游泳池。

2. 其他一些公共设施有医院、餐馆、地铁站、火车站和机场。

话题 16 BUILDINGS（建筑）

城市和乡镇都有很多建筑。Part 3 关于这个话题通常会询问不同类型的建筑，包括公寓、老式住宅和历史建筑。下面我们将学习如何回答这些问题。

1. Apartments vs. older-style homes（公寓与老式建筑）

◎ 话题解读

人们居住的建筑主要有两种类型，一种是现代公寓，另一种是老式住宅。Part 3 关于这个话题通常会问"公寓与老式住宅之间的区别"及"人们对它们的偏好"。

◎ 题目

How is modern home design (both inside & outside appearance) in your country different than that of the past?

How are modern homes different than older homes?

In your country, what type of homes do most people live in?

Why do most Chinese people live in apartments rather than houses?

Do people prefer to live in modern homes or older-style homes (e.g. from 50 years ago)?

◎ 表达与素材

1. Most people in cities prefer to live in apartments. Apartments allow you to live closer to the city centre, where it's more convenient. Also, there just aren't many houses in cities these days because of the lack of space.

2. However, some people still live in older-style homes, especially people in villages or rural areas. Homes offer more privacy than apartments because you don't need to share any walls with neighbours. Many houses also have yards, while apartments can only have balconies. A final difference between houses and apartments is that houses are on the ground level instead of being high up.

◎ 中文翻译

1. 大多数城市人喜欢住在公寓里。公寓让你住得离市中心更近，那里更方便。此外，由于空间不足，现在城市里的房子也不多。

2. 然而，有些人仍然住在老式的房子里 [①]，特别是在农村地区的人。老房子比公寓提供更多的隐私，因为你不需要与邻居共用任何墙壁。许多房子也有院子，而公寓只能有阳台。老房子和公寓的最后一个区别是，老房子是在地面上的，而不是在高处（即老房子更接地气）。

2. Old, historical buildings（古老的历史建筑）

◎ 话题解读

老建筑不仅存在于农村，也存在于城市，通常作为历史建筑存在。Part 3 关于这个话题通常会问"古老的历史建筑的重要性"及"如何保护它们"。

◎ 题目

How do people in China feel about old buildings?

Do old people and young people in China have the same attitudes towards old buildings?

Why do people visit historical buildings?

What aspects of culture do old buildings reflect?

How do old buildings affect the appearance of a place?

Is it important to preserve old buildings?

Is it necessary to protect historical buildings?

How can we protect old buildings?

Should old buildings be rebuilt?

---

① 因国情不同，这里的老式房子专指乡下的独栋老屋。

◎ 表达与素材

1. Old, historical buildings should be protected because they preserve our culture and the past. These buildings can attract many visitors and teach them about the history and culture of a place.

2. They improve the looks of a city, adding some variety. For example, many European cities look fascinating because they have lots of old, historical buildings.

3. Because old and historical buildings are important, we should renovate or rebuild the parts that are damaged. We can also pass laws to prevent them from being removed or vandalized, and give strict punishments to those who break the laws.

◎ 中文翻译

1. 古老的历史建筑应该得到保护，因为它们保存了我们的文化和过去。这些建筑可以吸引很多游客，让他们了解一个地方的历史和文化。

2. 它们改善了城市的外观，增加了一些多样性。例如，许多欧洲城市看起来很有趣，因为它们有很多古老的历史建筑。

3. 因为老建筑和历史建筑很重要，所以我们应该翻新或重建那些受损的部分。我们也可以通过法律来防止它们被拆除或破坏，并对那些违反法律的人给予严厉的惩罚。

话题 17 TRANSPORTATION（交通）

交通伴随着人们的日常生活，人们从一个地方到另一个地方，无论是去学校、办公室还是去其他城市，都会涉及交通。Part 3 关于交通的话题通常询问不同类型的交通工具（包括自行车、公共交通和私家车）的优缺点。下面我们将学习如何回答这些问题。

1. Bikes（自行车）

◎ 话题解读

骑自行车是一项儿童和成人都很喜欢的活动，它有许多好处。Part 3 关于这个话题通常会问"骑自行车的好处"及"骑自行车和自己开车有什么不同"。

◎ 题目

Compared with cars, what are the advantages of riding bikes?

What are the differences between bicycles and private cars?

Why do some people prefer riding bicycles?

Do people in your country often ride bikes?

Do you think children should learn cycling?

◎ 表达与素材

1. Riding bikes is a good way to get some exercise in your daily life.

2. Riding bikes is a convenient way to travel to nearby places.

3. Unlike cars, bikes don't pollute the environment.

4. Adults and children can both ride bikes, but only adults can drive cars.

◎ 中文翻译

1. 在日常生活中，骑自行车是锻炼身体的好方法。

2. 骑自行车是去附近的一种方便的交通方式。

3. 与汽车不同，自行车不会污染环境。

4. 成年人和儿童都可以骑自行车，但只有成年人才能开车。

2. Public transport（公共交通）

◎ 话题解读

公共交通在许多城市越来越发达，是使用最广泛的交通方式之一。Part 3 关于这个话题通常会问"公共交通的好处和坏处"。

◎ 题目

Should governments encourage people to use public transportation?

Do you prefer public or private transportation?

What are the advantages of trains and buses?

Do you think people need to change their way of transportation to protect the environment?

How can the problem of traffic congestion be solved?

What kinds of rules on public transportation should we have?

What are uncivilized manners on public transportation?

What do you think needs to be improved in public transport?

◎ 表达与素材

Benefits of public transport:

1. Public transport (which includes buses, the metro, and trains) is cheaper than private transportation, allowing you to save money.

2. Public transport is sometimes the fastest and most convenient way to travel to some places.

3. Public transport helps relieve a city's traffic problems.

4. Compared to cars, public transport is better for the environment. Public transport doesn't produce as much greenhouse gases. This helps us fight climate change.

Downsides of public transport:

1. Public transport cannot reach certain places. It can also be slower than driving a car,

especially if the transportation system in the place is not well-developed, like in rural areas.

2. Public transport is often not as comfortable as driving a car. For example, there may be no seats left or it can be very crowded.

3. People can be rude or noisy on public transport. They might talk loudly on their phones or play music loudly. They might bump into you, or stand too close to you.

◎ 中文翻译

公共交通的好处：

1. 公共交通工具（包括公共汽车、地铁和火车）比私人交通工具便宜，可以让你省钱。

2. 公共交通有时是去一些地方旅行最快、最方便的方式。

3. 公共交通有助于缓解城市的交通问题。

4. 与汽车相比，公共交通更有利于环境。公共交通不会产生那么多的温室气体。这有助于我们应对气候变化。

公共交通的缺点：

1. 公共交通不能到达某些地方。它也可能比开车慢，尤其是在交通系统不发达的地方，如农村地区。

2. 公共交通往往不如开车舒服。例如，可能没有座位或者可能非常拥挤。

3. 人们在公共交通工具上可能会变得粗鲁或吵闹。他们可能会大声打电话或大声播放音乐。他们可能会撞到你，或者站得离你太近。

3. Cars（汽车）

◎ 话题解读

虽然公共交通已经很发达了，但仍旧有很多人会选择自己开车。Part 3 关于这个话题通常会问"开车的好处和坏处有哪些"。

◎ 题目

What are the advantages and disadvantages of private transport?

Why do some people prefer driving cars instead of taking public transport?

Why do people like to have private cars?

What are the downsides of having a car?

What are the problems caused by the increasing number of cars?

Is it fair to limit the use of private cars?

◎ 表达与素材

Benefits of cars:

1. Sometimes, you can save time by driving. Cars are able to reach certain places that public transport cannot.

2. Cars can be more comfortable than taking public transport or riding a bike. Cars have more comfortable seats, you can play music, and there's a greater sense of freedom because you can drive anywhere. There's also more privacy and you are less affected by bad weather.

Downsides of cars:

1. It can be expensive to buy a car, and you have to pay for gas and parking. By contrast, public transport is much cheaper.

2. Cars are bad for the environment because they produce a lot of greenhouse gases, which contributes to air pollution and global warming.

3. Car accidents are pretty common, which makes driving less safe than taking public transport.

4. Having more cars causes more traffic jams.

◎ 中文翻译

汽车的好处：

1. 有时，开车可以节省时间。汽车可以到达公共交通不能到达的某些地方。

2. 汽车会比乘坐公共交通工具或骑自行车更舒适。汽车有更舒适的座位，你可以播放音乐，还有更大的自由感，因为你可以开车去任何地方。开车有更多的隐私，也不太会受到恶劣天气的影响。

汽车的缺点：

1. 买一辆车可能很贵，你还得支付油钱和停车费。相比之下，公共交通要便宜得多。

2. 汽车对环境有害，因为它们产生大量的温室气体，导致空气污染和全球变暖。

3. 车祸相当常见，这使得开车比乘坐公共交通工具更不安全。

4. 拥有更多的汽车会导致更多的交通堵塞。

 话题 18 ENVIRONMENTAL PROTECTION（环境保护）

◎ 话题解读

环境保护在现代社会是一个非常重要的问题，人类活动、气候变化都给环境造成了威胁。Part 3 关于这个话题通常会问"阻止气候变化的重要性"及"如何保护环境"，有时也可能会问其他环保问题，如"如何回收利用和进行垃圾分类"。

◎ 题目

Is it important to teach students environmental protection at school?

How you feel about the climate in recent years?

What are the possible results if the temperature continues going up?

What can we do to stop the greenhouse effect?

How can we protect the environment?

Why don't some people care about the environment?

Do you think there is more pollution or less pollution nowadays than in the past? How about in the future?

Do people in your country care about waste classification?

◎ 表达与素材

1. We should teach people about climate change so that they become more aware of environmental problems, especially climate change. Climate change is getting worse because people continue to burn fossil fuels and cut down forests, and farm livestock for meat. If climate change is not stopped soon, many places in the world will become unsuitable for human life.

2. There are different actions we can take to protect the environment. For example, people should be encouraged or forced to recycle their trash using waste classification, and if possible also take public transport or ride bicycles instead of driving cars.

◎ 中文翻译

1. 我们应该教给人们有关气候变化的知识，使他们更加意识到环境问题，特别是气候变化。由于人们继续燃烧化石燃料和砍伐森林，气候变化正在变得更糟。如果气候变化不尽快停止，世界上许多地方将变得不适合人类生活。

2. 我们可以采取不同的行动来保护环境。例如，应该鼓励或强迫人们利用垃圾分类回收垃圾，如果可能的话，乘坐公共交通工具或骑自行车而不是开车。

Part 3 特殊话题及相关表达与素材

Part 3 口语话题中有一部分题目与国人的偏好、年龄、性别有关，这一类题目比较特别，一方面因为不同的人、不同的年龄、不同的性别，很多问题的回答会不同；另一方面无论什么地方的人，什么年龄或性别，有些回答是一样的。因此，针对这类题目，考生需要提前准备一些固定的表达和素材，以不变应万变。关于这些话题，我们将着重讲解素材准备和回答结构。

 话题 19 CHINESE PEOPLE'S HABITS & PREFERENCES
（中国人的习惯与偏好）

◎ 话题解读

Part 3 通常会问考生所在国家的人们的习惯和喜好。例如，如果在 Part 2 被问到参观过的历史建筑，Part 3 有可能会问中国人是否喜欢参观历史建筑。

当被问到关于本国人的问题时，通常最简单的回答是正反面都涉及。考生可以使用在"答题要素"章节提到的"比较与对立观点型"的回答结构。请看以下例子：

Question: Do Chinese people enjoy…?

Answer: Well, it depends on the person. In my experience, some Chinese people… <u>However</u>, other Chinese people…

让我们看看这个策略的实际应用。

Question: Do Chinese people like social activities?

Response: Well, it really depends on the person. In my experience, some Chinese people really enjoy social activities like parties or hanging out with friends. But other Chinese people prefer to stay home and relax, read, or do other things by themselves.

Question: Do Chinese people like to drink coffee?

Response: Yeah, I think that lots of Chinese people like to drink coffee, but it also depends on the person. In my experience, younger Chinese people like drinking coffee because, you know, it gives them an energy boost. However, older Chinese people like my grandparents don't really drink coffee. They prefer tea.

Question: Do Chinese people like to watch comedies?

Response: I think it depends on the person. Some Chinese people do like to watch comedy shows, probably because it's makes them laugh and helps them relieve stress. But other Chinese people prefer watching more serious things, like dramas or action movies.

请使用以上方法回答下列题目：

Do Chinese people like to hold parties?

Do Chinese people like to visit historical buildings?

Do Chinese people like to borrow things from others?

What kind of weather do Chinese people like?

Do you think Chinese people like visiting other people's homes?

How do Chinese people make friends?

Do people like crowded places in China?

What kind of arts do Chinese people like?

Are most Chinese people talkative?

When do people usually sleep in China?

Is it difficult for Chinese people to express their feelings?

Do people in your country like to grow plants at home?

话题 20 OLD PEOPLE'S HABITS AND PREFERENCES
（长辈的习惯与偏好）

◎ 话题解读

雅思口语的话题涵盖了广泛的人群，当然也包括老人。无论何时遇到关于老人的问题，一个很好的策略就是用自己的祖父母作为例子。这能让考生不必为要说什么而绞尽脑汁，也能让考生延长答题时间。雅思口语考试考查的是说得好不好，而不是想法有多好或回答是否准确。

让我们来看看这个策略的实际应用。

Question: Do old people grow plants?

Reponse: Some of them do. My grandma grows plants on the balcony of our apartment. She also likes to visit the flower market to buy plants, and she takes pretty good care of them. So yeah, I think compared to young people, old people are more likely to grow plants.

Question: What do old people like to listen to?

Response: In my experience, they like to listen to classical Chinese music, like from Chinese operas. They definitely are not big fans of modern music. For example, my grandparents never listen to any rap or pop music.

Question: Do old people prefer living in the countryside or in the city?

Response: Well, I think it depends. Some old people might prefer the countryside, but others—like my grandparents—prefer living in the city because it allows them to be closer to their children and grandchildren. Also, living in the city is more convenient for a lot of things.

请使用以上方法回答下列题目：

What do old people in your country do to stay healthy?

Do old people prefer letters or emails?

How do old people spend their money?

Do old people like to drink coffee?

What do old people usually do in their daily life?

What can old people teach young people?

Do old people choose the same types of transportation as young people do?

Do old people share the same interests as young people?

What's the difference between the dressing style of young people and that of old people?

What's the difference between the reading habits of old people and young people?

Compared with old people, do you think that young people are more open to new kinds of food?

Who prefers travelling abroad more: young people or old people?

What's the difference between the programmes that young people enjoy watching and the programmes that old people enjoy watching?

话题 21 DIFFERENCES BETWEEN MEN AND WOMEN
（性别差异）

由于生理结构不同，男女之间存在许多差异，无论是在习惯和喜好方面，还是在思维方式方面。下面我们将学习如何回答 Part 3 中有关性别差异的问题。

1. Men and women's habits and preferences（男性与女性的爱好与偏好）

◎ 话题解读

Part 3 中有些问题是关于男性和女性的习惯或偏好的差异的，例如"女性和男性在买东西方面有什么不同"。一个简单的回答这些问题的方法就是以自己的父母为例。此外，考生还可以使用"答题要素"部分中学过的"比较与对立观点型"结构，对比两者的差异。

让我们来看看这个策略的实际应用。

Question: Are there any differences in men and women's preferences for clothes?

Response: Well, it really depends, but... like my mom and grandmother prefer clothes that have brighter colours and nice designs on them, like flowers. By contrast, my dad usually wears clothes that are plain and have one colour. He doesn't care about clothes as much, and doesn't shop for clothes that often, unlike my mom.

Question: Do men and women like different leisure activities?

Response: Well, it really depends on the person, but for example, my dad likes to watch TV a lot and sometimes he plays golf, while my mom prefers to read or go shopping. So yeah, in my experience, they do prefer different activities.

Question: What's the difference between men and women's preference for cars?

Response: Well, the women I know, like my mom and my grandmother, they don't really care about cars. On the other hand, my dad is quite interested in cars and likes expensive cars. So yeah, I can't speak for most men and women, but at least the ones that I know, are like that.

Question: What's the difference between males and females in terms of expressing their feelings?

Response: Well, it depends, but the women I know, like my mom and grandmother, are pretty good at expressing their feelings. If they're angry at you or worried about you, they'll let you know. On the other hand, men like my dad can be quite poor at expressing their feelings. Sometimes, they even hide it.

请使用以上方法回答下列题目：

What's the difference between women and men in buying things?

What do men like to talk about? How about women?

What's the difference between men and women in their reading habits?

What's the difference between men and women in being polite?

Who smiles more, men or women?

Do men and women have different reasons for giving gifts?

Do you think women are more likely than men to talk about other people?

Are men better at decision-making in a family?

Are men more likely than women to do extreme sports?

2. Gender equality（性别平等）

◎ 话题解读

性别平等体现在方方面面。关于这个话题，Part 3 通常会问"为什么要有性别平等"及"如今各地、各行业是否做到了性别平等"。回答这类题目时，考生可以使用任何一种答题结构，核心观点可以包括以下几点：

1. 区别对待男性和女性是不公平的，性别平等是一项基本人权。

2. 性别平等带来更快乐、更健康和更稳定的环境。生活在性别不平等的社会中的女性更不幸福。

3. 虽然现在性别越来越平等，但我们还有很长的路要走。例如，我们仍然需要更多的女性政治家、商界领袖和警察。男性也应该在家庭和育儿方面承担更多的责任。

让我们来看看这个策略的实际应用。

Question: Do you think both men and women can be police officers?

Response: Yes, both men and women can be police officers. It is unfair to discriminate against someone based on their gender when it comes to job opportunities. Gender equality is a basic human right, and everyone should have the opportunity to pursue a career they want regardless of their gender.

Question: Do women have more responsibility for taking care of children?

Response: No, women do not have more responsibility for taking care of children. Parenting responsibilities should be shared equally between both parents. Gender equality results in a happier, healthier, and more stable environment for both parents and children. Women who live in societies without gender equality are unhappier because they have to bear the burden of child-rearing and household responsibilities alone.

Question: Do you think there is equality in the workplace for men and women nowadays?

Response: Well, there has been progress towards gender equality in the workplace, but there is still a long way to go. For example, many companies and organizations have implemented policies to promote gender equality, like equal pay. However, there are still significant differences in areas such as promotion opportunities, leadership positions, and work-life balance. So, while we are moving in the right direction, there is still much work to be done to achieve true gender equality in the workplace.

Question: Do you think the fact that more men than women are leaders will change in the future?

Response: Yes, I think that there will be more female leaders in the future. As society becomes more aware of the importance of gender equality, we will see more women in leadership positions. More and more people understand that it is unfair to discriminate against someone based on their gender, and there is a growing movement to promote equal opportunities for women in leadership positions.

Question: Do you think it's women's privilege to be late in your country?

Response: No, women don't have the privilege to be late in my country. Everyone is expected to be on time. It's an important aspect of being professional and having respect for other people's time. It is unfair to assume that women are allowed to be late because of their gender, and it goes against the principle of gender equality, which states that everyone should be treated the same, regardless of their gender.

请使用以上方法回答下列题目：

Do you think that women should be able to do the same sorts of jobs that men do?

Should more women be encouraged to work in male-dominated fields such as science and technology?

Are there more male or female managers and executives? Why do you think this is?